THE LIFE OF MILAREPA

THE LIFE OF MILAREPA

translated by
LOBSANG P. LHALUNGPA

SHAMBHALA
Boulder & London 1984

Shambhala Publications, Inc.
Boulder, Colorado 80306-0271

9 8 7 6 5 4 3 2 1
First Shambhala edition

Distributed in the United States by Random House
and in Canada by Random House of Canada Ltd.

Printed in the United States of America

Library of Congress Cataloging in Publication Data

Gtsa n-smyon He-ru-ka, 1452-1507.
The life of Milarepa.
Translation of: Mi-la-ras-pa'i rnam thar.
Reprint. Previously published: London;
Granada Pub., 1979.
Includes bibliographical references.
1. Mi-la-ras-pa, 1040-1123. 2. Lamas—China—Tibet—
Biography. I. Lhalungpa, Lobsang Phuntshok, 1926-
II. Title.
BQ7950.M557G813 1984 294.3′923′0924 [B] 84-5467
ISBN 0-87773-281-7 (pbk.)
ISBN 0-394-72696-0 (Random House: pbk.)

Contents

Introduction
by Lobsang P. Lhalungpa

I recall the childhood experience of listening to Milarepa's life in the form of folktales from the south of Tibet, the home province of Marpa. Deep admiration rose up in me at his will to give his whole life for the sake of his mother and at his undying determination later to save the sinking ship of his own destiny, the ship that subsequently carried innumerable people to safety across the sea of Samsara.

To the people of Tibet and to fellow Buddhists in the Asian highlands and the Himalayas, Mila, although he lived in the twelfth century, is not a myth but still a vital figure – the embodiment of supreme excellence as well as the father of awakened masters. Never, in the thirteen centuries of Buddhist history in Tibet, has there been such a man, who not only inspired an intellectual elite and spiritual luminaries, but also captured the imagination of the common people.

To those of us who read his life and songs as the true account of liberation, and who have also received the secret transmission of higher teachings to which he contributed so much, Milarepa has great significance in our lives. The experience of illumination is being quietly repeated in an almost unbroken order in the tradition up to the present, even extending to many parts of the modern world.

Throughout pre-Communist Tibet Milarepa was held in universal veneration. It was so in the past and is still so among the thousands of refugees in the settlements of northern India, Bhutan, and Sikkim. Figures of Milarepa, in the form of icon and painting, were worshipped in temples and private homes. Wandering storytellers sang the life of Milarepa, illustrating their stories with painted scrolls. Both the narrative and the songs were simple, full of folk idioms, homely metaphors, and humorous expressions. Repas – the 'cotton-clad ones' – sang the songs of Milarepa as they wandered through villages across the country. Folk operas depicting the main events of his life were acted. Milarepa's delicate, gentle features and pale complexion in the tankas and paintings contrasted strangely with his extraordinary physical tenacity and loyalty to the Truth.

In some important aspects the autobiography of Milarepa resembles the life of the Buddha, whose twelve major events correspond to the twelve chapters of Milarepa's life. Both teachers resorted to dramatic acts of renunciation and to asceticism of an extreme kind as supports for their quest, though for different reasons and under contrasting circumstances. The Buddha's purpose was to seek a new, practical way of eliminating the miseries of humanity and their karmic causes. Milarepa's, at least initially, was to save himself from fear of the natural consequences of his crimes.

Besides being 'the greatest of (Buddhist) saints,' Milarepa fills a central place in the history of Buddhism in Tibet. Until the ninth century A.D., the hold of the Buddhist religion over the sorcery of earlier religions was precarious. With Milarepa the swing began toward the realization of inner power through meditation. The Kagyupa, the Order of Oral Transmission, has faithfully maintained this meditational tradition up to the present time. The Nyingmapa, the Ancient Mystic Order, also emphasizes the practice of meditation.

On the other hand, there were teachers who considered an intellectual foundation in Buddhist training to be indispensable. One such was the great Sakya Pandita, one of the founders of the Sakyapa, the White Earth Order. And three hundred years after Milarepa the incomparable Tsongkhapa gave Tibetan Buddhism new intellectual depth and dynamism when he elevated Buddhist studies to unprecedented profoundity through the revival of monastic discipline and moral purity. This movement, which came to be known as Gelukpa, the Order of Excellence, is the one to which the Dalai Lama belongs.

The Life, on the whole, is genuine autobiography, a ritual drama recounting significant events in Mila's apprenticeship rather than his comments on them. The unfolding story shows profound knowledge of human psychology but there is no analysis of Milarepa's feelings, no explanation of the paradoxes in, for example, Marpa's behavior toward his pupil, which is allowed to speak for itself until Marpa provides a brief summation, such as conventionally appears in the final pages of a detective story.

The teaching in *The Life* is very condensed. Discourses are few and are given mostly in homely, unsophisticated verse. Milarepa's disciples are mentioned for the first time in a short chapter near the end of the book, where after the Master has provided a catalogue of the caves in which he meditated, his biographer makes the promising statement 'I will now enlarge a little on the Master's life.' But what follows is merely a list of the principal disciples' names, with details of where the Master met them. Thus the dramatic character and style of *The Life*, as a celebration of spiritual endeavor rather than a description of it, is preserved.

In its first three chapters the story deals with the ugliest realities of life, showing how easily human beings fall victim to selfishness, greed and vanity and even resort to deceit and the meanest acts of cruelty. Milarepa's paternal uncle and aunt made a pledge to his dying father to act as the trustees of his wealth until Milarepa had reached his maturity. No sooner was the father dead than the uncle and aunt seized the property, denied ever having made the pledge and began treating Milarepa's family with the grossest cruelty and injustice. The uncle and aunt exemplify human stupidity, selfishness and greed. Their prosperity and power resulting from ill-gotten wealth are in sharp contrast to the poverty and misery brought to Milarepa and his family.

The mastermind directing vengeance against these usurpers is Milarepa's mother, who in no way conceals her desire to see them destroyed. The negative power of her will, and the resourcefulness and shrewdness she possessed help to fulfill her plan. In the youthful Mila she finds a very devoted son and a ready instrument. Out of deep love for his mother and the bitterest resentment against the uncle and aunt, he strives single-mindedly toward his mission to destroy the relatives 'down to the ninth generation.' The lamas, masters of sorcery, sympathize with him and, after he has shown them his extraordinary determination and need, they teach him the secret magic of destruction and guide him in his practice until he is able to accomplish all that his mother had wished – and more. At a wedding feast for the uncle's eldest son, Milarepa's art brings down the home of the uncle and aunt, killing all the wedding guests. Soon after, the mother sends word to her son that the people of the village seek to take their own vengeance against this slaughter. She demands that he now cause fierce hailstorms to destroy all their crops.

'This is the way I accumulated black deeds out of vengeance against my enemies' – so ends the First Part of *The Life*. The destruction of Milarepa's enemies has been carried out in a manner they themselves had indicated in a moment of injured pride, when they challenged the widow to 'wage war against us if you are many and cast a spell upon us if you are few.'

The moral consequences of his crimes dawn on Milarepa with heart-splitting agony and a consuming fear of the karmic consequences he must face in all his future lives – to be whirled round and round into further acts of destruction, inevitably ending in the annihilation of his possibilities of escape. The evident lack of any civil system of social justice seems to point up the certainty that Milarepa will not and cannot escape the karmic consequences of his moral offenses. With the same unbending determination that characterized his quest for the secrets of black magic, he now begins the search for the path of enlightenment and liberation.

Throughout *The Life*, the teaching about the law of karma is presented by Milarepa to his pupils in just this way, as an idea which the seeker must begin with and which has meaning at many different levels of the path. For Milarepa it represents his first awakening to the sense of a deeper order in life, a call from another level. This call to what in the text is termed 'religion' appears together with a tremendous shock of recognition. All along one has been obeying the wrong voice, and this is seen and felt. The second phase of Milarepa's life begins:

> I was filled with remorse for the evil I had done by magic and by hailstorms. My longing for the teaching so obsessed me that I forgot to eat. If I went out, I wanted to stay in. If I stayed in, I wanted to go out. At night sleep escaped me. I asked myself unceasingly and passionately by what means I might practice the true teaching.

Milarepa's drastic renunciation is in sharp contrast with the inward renunciation Lama Marpa had chosen. To both Marpa and Mila as to all Buddhists the sensory pleasures and cares of samsara are no doubt devoid of true benefit. In the case of those who are powerfully self-centered, renunciation of a normal external life may be like a shock treatment, a drastic means toward breaking loose from the grip of self-clinging and thereby leading on to higher awareness, new insights and ultimately into the reality behind appearances.

Life and the seeking of the Dharma, whether through renunciation of comforts or through any other means, are incompatible, so long as a *personal* liberation is desired. Even asceticism, as such, is utterly hollow and liable to be taken for a means to a personal goal. Milarepa's renunciation aimed at gaining personal liberation and did not come up to the true spirit of Dharma until his inbred motive had been completely changed into the highest aspirations for emancipation on a universal scale according to the way of Boddhisattva.

Young Mila finally met Marpa at his country home. The events that constitute his relationship with Marpa are well known to every student of the Buddhist tradition. In all of world literature there is no more dramatic portrayal of the kind of learning that a Master provides for his pupil. No matter what else the reader may or may not take from this book, the account of 'the ordeal of the towers' will remain with him for the rest of his life.

A foreknowledge of what lay ahead for Milarepa, not merely in unequalled achievement but in more practical terms of the obstacles that were in store for him, came to Marpa through his reading of the omens. This knowledge accounts for his initial behavior and many of his unexplained acts. To set in motion auspicious events charged with pure thoughts and acts of pity, it was expressly necessary to create a circumstantial conscious force so as to steer the wheel of Karma, that is like a floating boat. Both the secular and the sacred traditions of Tibetans stress the turning away from the waves of samsara. Marpa guided Mila's journey of destiny along the course marked out by his karma. From the beginning to the end of their direct relationship, each time an event did not augur well Marpa would improvise an additional phase, whose significance only he knew and did not explain till the end. For example, Marpa took the empty copper pot his new disciple offered him into his shrine room and after making it ring through the house quickly filled it with melted butter to make an offering of light. The empty container signified Mila's scanty fare during retreats in the mountains; the ringing signified his future fame spreading everywhere; the filling with butter, fulfillment of his aspirations.

Marpa was absolutely clear in his mind that this big-hearted little man whose mind was completely shamed and shattered could not gain the desired transformation by any normal training. Thus, as the condition for receiving the Dharma, Mila was required to fulfill a series of bitterly demanding and dispiriting tasks. In enforcing the great ordeals, Marpa used shifting tactics and seemingly deceitful ways.

Milarepa struggles under the ordeals out of a need for himself. The son, whose mother declared 'he has no willpower,' proves himself to be a disciple of extraordinary patience and tenacity. It is only when he is brought to the brink of suicide that the ordeals are hastily ended and, much against the plan, Marpa grants Milarepa the teaching. When the ordeals are over, his 'great sins have been erased' and his personal need has been mysteriously transformed and is felt now 'for all sentient beings.'

Marpa is pictured for us (and we have no reason to doubt the historical accuracy of this) as big, corpulent, fierce-looking, a personage of importance – physically the exact opposite of Milarepa. Acclaimed as the King of Translators, Marpa had used his wealth for such purposes as journeying to India, where he received the teachings of esoteric Buddhism from his own Master, Naropa, and brought back to Tibet many of the most important tantric scriptures. In Tibet, Marpa successfully revived the non-monastic form of training which was begun in the seventh century by Tibet's emperor Songtsen Gampo and his learned minister Thonmi Sambhota, and which was furthered in the eighth century by a host of lay Tibetans who were disciples of the great Guru Padmasambhava.

Marpa was not only a man of vast erudition but an enlightened teacher and a superb psychologist, who blended harmoniously the role of spiritual guide by private tutorship with a family life style. Milarepa regarded Marpa as a wise father and protector from fear, as well as the supreme guide. As for his wife, Dakmema, her compassion for Mila was humanly noble and circumstantially necessary and she was indeed his friend, mother and spiritual guide. Her biography, if found, might throw more light onto the unknown aspects of Marpa's life and even that of Milarepa.

After he left Marpa, Milarepa's life of asceticism and retreat is in sharp contrast to the external life of Marpa. When Milarepa is asked why he does not follow Marpa's example in externals, he answers that for him to do so would be like a hare trying to follow the steps of a lion. And, late in the text, when one of his disciples asks 'Can we engage in an active life if it proves beneficial to other beings?' Milarepa answers 'If there is no attachment to selfish aims, you can. But that is difficult.'

Milarepa knew he was not Marpa. Similarly, the reader of this story will, in his own way, know he is not Milarepa. Yet Milarepa became, as it is said, 'even greater than his teacher.'

In order to understand what Milarepa created as a field of spiritual work for those who came after him, it is useful to consider some fundamental aspects of the Vajrayana and Mahayana traditions.*

The fulfillment of a seeker's higher aspirations is not so much dependent on accumulating knowledge as on overcoming mental obstacles and gaining insight into the truth in oneself. For this, the guidance of an experienced teacher is a practical necessity. The role of teacher in an esoteric path of self-transformation through meditation and action, such as Vajrayana, is even more important, because it is only after the initiatory empowerment and elucidating instructions and guidance have been given that the disciple can settle himself in the work.

The 'success' of Dharma practice differs markedly from individual to individual. Each responds differently. Even the effectiveness of initiation depends on the presence or absence of appropriate conditions. Sometimes all the inner vision and power of the initiatory master is not enough, for as we say even a strong hook will not catch an object with no hollow ring attached to it. The opposite case is also possible, as illustrated at the end of Milarepa's story. While he himself took a long time and much hazardous labor to reach a state of mind conducive to enlightenment, many of his own disciples achieved the glimpse of illumination instantly on hearing words of wisdom from him!

What is a spiritual master? Selection of one's personal lama is certainly a matter of cardinal importance. In the Tibetan tradition, treatises lay down descriptions and guidelines for the qualities a lama should possess. The modern approach of judging a spiritual teacher from chance personal impressions cannot be a reliable way of examining his qualities. The present generation of lamas is fast approaching its extinction since the occupation of Tibet. Not only

* See my study of Tibetan Buddhism in *The Path of the Buddha*, edited by Kenneth W. Morgan (Ronald Press, New York, 1956), pp. 237–307. Also my recent English translation of *Mahamudra, The Great Seal* by the great Kagyupa Master Dwakpo Tashi Namgyal (1512–1587), to be published shortly. This major doctrinal exposition of the metaphysics and meditation practice of the Kagyüpa order, founded by Milarepa, is directly related to the essence of his teachings.

Western students and seekers of the Dharma, but even Tibetan refugees, no longer have much to choose from.

We may say that a master has perfect knowledge of the doctrine and the methods of practice, and embodies the ideals of the doctrine through his own personal attainment and service to humanity. He must be a compassionate person who combines knowledge of the Dharma with the experience of illumination. The role of a spiritual master or teacher in the life of the seeker is to be a true friend. Only when a master is himself free from inner delusions and is the source of transcendent wisdom can he or she perceive the hidden barriers and potentialities of individuals and respond according to the specific need of each person. Once the psychological obstacles in devotees are overcome through the lama's skillful means, rapid illumination presents itself without the need for heroic effort.

Yet the emphasis on the role of the teacher and the disciple's devotion to him should not be allowed to reduce the pupil to a passive state of helplessness and absolute dependence. Like the doctrine itself, the teacher is a means and not an end. The meaning of the term 'yong-dzin,' a synonym for teacher, suggests that he is one who holds others from falling into an abyss of inner delusion and destructive karma.

We must remember that, before his realization under Marpa, three teachers failed in guiding Milarepa in the path. The first teacher, Rongton Lhaga, failed by giving his pupil teachings that were too advanced for him. The second teacher was Dakmema, Marpa's wife, who gave Milarepa the higher teachings of Mahamudra, also without demanding an adequate preparation. The third was Lama Ngokpa, one of Marpa's own chief disciples, to whom he was sent by Dakmema during the culmination of his ordeals without the approval of Marpa.

The term 'teacher' does not always mean a human being. Milarepa speaks of three types of lamas – first, an 'external lama' who shows the way through linguistic symbols; second, the 'inner lama,' one's own power of understanding the teaching; and, third, the 'inmost lama,' one's own inmost awareness. In the word 'lama,' the syllable 'la' means transcendent wisdom; 'ma' refers to motherly love and compassion. These two aspects are united in Ultimate Awareness. Milarepa looked upon Marpa as the true embodiment of Enlightenment and as the irreplaceable means for the development of his own supreme understanding through which Milarepa realized the 'inmost lama' in himself.

In general, the Vajrayana Buddhist training which Milarepa underwent seeks to respond to the varied psychological factors in different individuals and lead aspirants toward higher consciousness, the complete realization of human excellence and finally supreme illumination. It is thus a process of psychological transformation. In practical terms, the aim is to cultivate goodness consciously in thoughts, words and deeds and to become a 'jewel among humanity.'

Fom the outset, one works to free oneself from all superstitious complexes of superiority or inferiority based on sex, race, color, or creed. A deeper sense of one entire human family and universal fellowship has to be developed as the foundation for a right attitude to human relationships. Only then is the seeker led toward a process of spiritualization. In order to discover his non-deceptive, or real, identity, each individual is encouraged to free himself from the solid and strong influence of his conditioning. This psychological reorientation, which is the basic aim of all true culture, embraces the totality of factors and forces that go to make up an individual's whole stream of being and his attitude toward life. The inner illusions are so subtle that they are often imperceptible. Without this preparatory development of a sound and sane basic attitude toward the goals of living, the whole spiritual endeavor is susceptible to egoistic self-love, as distinguished from a practical concern for one's permanent freedom. For even where consciousness has achieved an exalted level, its need must be further developed into an effective instrument for the process of universal emancipation of all human beings.

The essence of Mahayana Buddhism can be seen in one single term, 'Bodhichitta,' which we have generally translated as 'Enlightened Mind.' This is at once an enlightening attitude and a state of awareness, each of which is both a means to the goal and the goal itself. Here attitude implies action, a non-egoistic view which a man brings to bear upon both his inner practice and outer life. Through this attitude the discipline of meditation combines inseparably with the practice of outer magnanimity, thus leading to the achievement of enlightened awareness. It is through such an awareness that one may perceive things as they really are and as they appear in non-conflicting diversity, while remaining continuously open to manifest the warmth of compassion. Yet such innate purity simply cannot be perceived or realized without first detecting the causes of illusions and defilement in the human psyche. Thus the process of transformation of consciousness takes the form of purification traditionally spoken of as the elimination of illusions and accumulation of virtues.

The training of Milarepa may serve as a worthy illustration of some aspects of this Buddhist education, centering around the way of discovering for one's self the unknown secret of the truth. As in any great human endeavor, no real achievement is possible until one meets the challenges the training throws before oneself with openness, humility and determination. An acute awareness must repeatedly be brought to bear on reappraisal of what really is the foundation of lasting happiness for oneself and also for all others. In working toward an aim such as this, one is bound to awaken to one's own inadequacies, thereby bringing life's challenges into focus.

It was the stark realization of his own inadequacies that brought Milarepa to Lama Marpa. After completing the heart-melting ordeals which Marpa imposed on him, Milarepa soon encountered another series of ordeals, namely, the rigors of training. He began the training by accepting the Triple Refuge as fundamental in the path of liberation: the Buddha, the Dharma, and the Sangha. The Buddha, the Enlightened One, is the supreme guide; Dharma, the sacred Doctrine (or Law), is the means to gaining one's own enlightenment; and the Sangha, the assembly of Awakened Adepts, maintains the tradition and supports the search of all who come to the path.

For the ordinary devotee, the master of Dharma is expected to play the role of the Triple Refuge. But in the Vajrayana tradition, practically speaking, it takes another form: the initiatory lama represents the source of spiritual influence, the yidam the source of understanding and the dakinis the source of the ever unfolding support which comes to the seeker's aid.

The true meaning of going to the Triple Refuge for protection can be realized only if the seeker is meaningfully committed, not so much to formal acts of veneration as to a relentless striving toward realizing within his own nature the qualities represented by the Triple Refuge. Buddha said 'O mendicant monks, you alone are the Refuge unto yourselves. Who else can be such a Refuge?'

In fact, man is his own refuge or protector as soon as he wakes up from life's illusions and finds a way to discover what is called the Buddha nature in him. This is the most original nature of human awareness or consciousness, which is indistinguishable from the essence of enlightenment. A seeker need not wait to realize it until some future time. He is only required to resolve and act here and now, for he can and will realize it in this very life! But the sense of self, of ego or I, is not the same thing as consciousness; it is a form that consciousness takes under certain conditions which in man are connected with the senses and the complex organization of forces and substances that make up the human body.

In meditation man seeks to establish a relationship between the sense of self and consciousness, which is its root and foundation. Discovery of the Buddha nature is the beginning and the end of the work of meditation. Between the beginning and the end, however, there lie many levels. The relationship between consciousness, thought, emotion, and the stupendous complexity and potentiality of the human body in all its functions is a subject about which a great deal must be understood before a person can be accurately guided along the path of self-transformation. We modern people have special difficulties here because we have abandoned the mythic language of earlier traditions, a language that resonated with the deeper mental structures of human beings according to their hereditary conditioning. Our own language is scientific, that is to say, based on sensory experience and abstract generalizations – the latter being a function of the mind, which is relatively the same in all human beings, unconditioned by innate forces of feeling and instinct and therefore unresponsive to the truth and power which these innate forces embody. Thus, words like 'awareness' and 'consciousness,' which are connected to a complex set of instructions in the Buddhist tradition as well as to a vast array of elements within the human organism, are not readily understandable to us on the basis of everyday experience and speculation. The tremendous simplicity of Milarepa's path of meditation and enlightened attitude has its full counterpart in the vast complexity of what in the Buddhist tradition is called 'relative reality' – meaning the world of appearances within appearances, even the most superficial of which requires an exceptionally clear mind to see rightly.

The reader of *The Life* must therefore resist the tendency to associate the word 'meditation' with some physical posture or attitude of mind known to him. To think of meditation as the struggle to be aware of oneself is more to the point, but even that can take one only so far in grasping the nature of the discipline that Milarepa created. One may take note of an openness that this text itself can arouse when it is read with attention that is born of need. Is this sensitivity related to awareness? The question is, what actually took place to bring it about? Facing one's complete lack of certainty and resisting the impulse to speculate or go to one's thought associations for an answer, the reader may realize that what Milarepa means by 'meditation' is a movement within oneself that is both more accessible and far more subtle and comprehensive than is usually imagined. In fact, it cannot be imagined.

'Any ordinary man can persevere as I have done,' Milarepa tells his disciples. These disciples are disciples – they are not the reader, or even loyal followers contemporary with Milarepa. It is not possible for any book, however great, to communicate the entire atmosphere of a tradition, including the thousand and one impulses that the teacher sets in motion by interacting with individuals who in their turn may succeed or fail in the outer expression of their understanding. It is easy to accept intellectually that a tradition is a world, but not so easy to feel what this means, especially when the very core and heart of a tradition, in this case the practice of meditation, is presented with such intuitive force.

A tradition is a world. In that world, the essence of the tradition, the single movement that created it from the beginning and that continues to maintain it in the lives of all who follow it, permeates and suffuses all the forms and details of life and perhaps may never be spoken of explicitly. But when it is spoken of explicitly, and in a language that seems familiar (such as the language of psychology), it is a mistake to appropriate it as one's own without asking why all these other forms are also part of the tradition.

In *The Life of Milarepa* we are actually witness to the creation of a spiritual world, an approach to the whole of life. Everything in *The Life* has a meaning from this point of view. But what that meaning is often lies between the lines. For example, when Milarepa reminds himself not to go down to the village for sustenance and when groups of hunters then raid his cave, are we not being offered an illustration of a new attitude to the problems of life – to money, success, crime, power? Is it not that an uncompromising reorientation of the mind brings with it an unforced joy that is the greatest natural object of attraction to man? The responses of the robbers and hunters who sense the holiness of the strange, emaciated 'bag of bones' they encounter in the cave reflects the possible contact with Mind of every impulse and desire within human nature. And what is the basic teaching in Milarepa's conversations with his sister Peta about sex, marriage and shame? That the only real happiness and self-respect possible for man lies in the purification that results from awareness. As simple and elusive as meditation is, so too is the encompassing vision through which one may enter every aspect of life as a seeker. Certainly, the warmth of feeling that the text engenders in the reader should be sufficient to counter any suggestion that asceticism and self-denial are being held as rigid ideals. Another kind of discipline is communicated, in which the pure energy of all life situations can be collected without violence, blind faith or unnecessary enthusiasm.

Meditation, considered as the foundational act of spiritual effort in the Vajrayana tradition as transmitted by Milarepa, may also be considered in terms of the possible development within man of a link between the Buddha-nature and the ordinary deluded mind. The great idea behind this notion of a relationship between the highest and the lowest in human nature, which (we are told) only the greatest masters have realized, is expressed in the Vajrayana as the essential identity of nirvana and samsara: nirvana is the understanding of samsara!

Concerning the role of the human body in the establishment of this link, there are sufficient hints in the text to let the reader know that he must leave behind all conventional notions about the 'evils of the flesh' as well as modern fantasies about the sacralization of sensuous indulgence. Emerging from his first intensive period of solitary meditation, Milarepa relates to Marpa, 'I have understood that this material body, made of flesh and blood along with mental consciousness, is gathered together by the twelve chains of cause and effect – one of which is volition – originating from ignorance. This body is the blessed vessel for those fortunate beings who wish for freedom, but it also leads sinners into the lower realms. I understand that in this body lies the vital choice between enormous profit and loss, relating to eternal happiness or misery on the border between good and evil ...'

It is obvious that, as Milarepa pursues his spiritual search, some transformation is taking place in his body of a nature that is at the same time miraculous and in accordance with higher law. Yet at no point is the reader ever led to think of this material transformation as anything but a result of the work of meditation. It is never presented as anything to be striven after directly, even though it seems that what we are dealing with here is the process of creation within the human organism of a spiritualized body that provides extraordinary energy and support to the basic work of meditation. In other words, the link between the sacred and profane natures of man is established within the body itself, which then, in a great Bodhisattva, becomes the stepping stone to further levels of consciousness and compassion.

One might say of Milarepa that he uncompromisingly separated awareness from the manifold possible results of awareness and never allowed those who sought him out to confuse those two. In this connection, one may recall the dictum of Jesus, 'Seek ye first the kingdom of heaven.'

Samsara, the wheel of birth and death, the eternally recurrent round of suffering and desire, is rooted in delusion and ignorance. Man perceives the apparent as the real, takes lies and fantasy for truth. From this two effects ensue. On the one hand, the natural unfolding of conditioned relativity is denied; man simply does not see or participate actively in the life and the world around him which, while not the absolutely real, is not merely a creation of his own subjectivity. In addition, by attributing the quality of substantiality to the world he 'sees' and to himself, the 'seer,' – by taking both his own being and the 'object' of his subjective experience to be fixed entities, he endows them with a unique character of 'eternity,' which rules out any possibility of self-transformation. But these delusions are precisely what he may study. To understand them means to gain insight into the foundation of nirvana, that is, the character of one's original primal awareness.

The monk's study begins from the effort to listen with an open attention to spoken discourses on the teaching, followed by reading appropriate sacred texts in a way that allows him to take in at least something of the diverse levels of meaning contained in them. Even such knowledge, however, acquired in a way that is far more serious than is customary, will by itself fall apart like a house of cards at the first gentle breeze of criticism or life difficulty. Far more is needed, even to begin. A penetrating discernment needs to be developed through firmness of concentration and a more subtle, rational investigation. Equipped with the requisite knowledge and a sharpened critical mind, one proceeds with an exhaustive examination of the whole teaching – sparing nothing, not even the words of the Buddha – until one senses and begins to feel a deep underlying coherence and harmony in what may hitherto have seemed contradictory thrusts in the doctrine, the psychological strategies, and various practical applications.

The Buddhist tradition strongly emphasizes that mere study and inquiry without the corresponding practice and experience inevitably inflate delusion and conceit, leading to spiritual ruination for oneself and even contributing to social decadence. The plights of both the sorcerer-lama and the dialectician called Geshe Tsakpūhwa referred to in *The Life* clearly demonstrate this. The same is true for those who indulge overtly or covertly in other forms of self-gratification with the ostensible purpose of leading a spiritual life.

Direct observation in an acquiescent state exposes the fantasy of conceptual designations of reality. Therefore, whatever intellectual conclusions the pupil arrives at need to be reassessed and transformed through direct experience and self-observation. This demands the first real initiative that a human being, who is otherwise the pawn of all the forces and conditionings of the inner and outer world, can exercise. But precisely because it is really the first act of freedom in an otherwise totally conditioned human life, it is extraordinarily fragile. Consultation with the master and with appropriate texts is bound to help at this stage. The student must be able to follow directly both his psychological fantasies and habitual imagery and also the innate immensity of his true nature. Only then can he directly realize the truth as being non-dual, simple, calm, pure and lucid, and beyond the scope of definition and thought-process. A persistent consolidation and deepening of this realization will in due course complete the process of complete transformation known as the 'five stages.' This is what Milarepa had achieved.

In Hinayana Buddhism, ordinary Enlightenment is identified with nirvana, which means 'rising beyond miseries.' Nirvana is thus a subjective state of freedom attained through active elimination of inbred defilements such as ignorance, lust and hatred, which are recognized as being the sole cause of human miseries. According to the Vehicle of Hearers (Shravakas) and of self-emancipated ones (Pratyeka-Buddhas), nirvana is liberation from the bondage of self-delusion and the cycle of life.

In most forms of the Mahayana tradition, however, and all the more in the Vajrayana, it is not possible to develop a spiritual psychology without the necessary cosmological teachings. Confrontation with the infinitely greater objective scale of reality and truth is persistently offered even to the most advanced devotee. The Mahayana tradition, therefore, is quite clear about the distinction between the state of nirvana, as just described, and the state of Abi-buddhi, or the Supreme Wisdom. Granted that there is much in common between these two exalted states of being, the Bodhisattva Path considers that at a certain point emphasis solely on achieving personal liberation actually hinders the full development of man's spiritual potentialities and brings to a halt the movement toward what we are translating in this text as Complete Enlightenment.

Complete Enlightenment may be spoken of in a great many ways. In *Milarepa* it is presented in terms of the Buddhist doctrine of Trikaya, the Three Levels of Enlightenment: Dharmakaya, Sambhogakaya and Nirmanakaya.

The term Dharmakaya, literally 'The Body of All Things,' refers to the ultimate state of Enlightenment and to the ultimate unity of samsara and nirvana. Obviously, few human beings are able to awake fully to this wondrous treasure of the Ultimate Truth. It is depicted as unfolding, radiating, expressing itself throughout all levels of cosmic reality, including both the material world and the realms of subtle reality. In its latter manifestation it is Sambhogakaya; in the former, as an earthly incarnation of the Supreme Reality, it is Nirmanakaya – Buddha present as a human body.

In the idea of Dharmakaya one finds an expression of the Mahayana equation of consciousness (in its highest sense) and reality. Analytically speaking, Dharmakaya is essentially comprised of Transcendent Awareness and its inmost nature of emptiness. Its innate character of total simplicity and purity of awareness is what is ordinarily regarded as nirvana, the state in which the stains of delusion and distortion have been wiped out. Here it is not only a 'subjective' state (as in Hinayana Buddhism) but an ontological reality – *the* ontological reality. Being unconditioned, it is described as unborn, non-localized and indissoluble. Its character is such that it transcends discursive thought and can be neither designated nor discriminated against.

Sambhogakaya may be understood as the highest and subtlest manifestation of Dharmakaya or Enlightenment in the realm of relative reality, and it is thus Compassion on the metaphysical and cosmic level. It is the essence of Awareness to manifest itself for the sake of all beings – both subjectively and objectively; both in an individual realized human being and in the deepest nature of reality. In the idea of Dharmakaya, we have seen how Mahayana Buddhism understands Enlightenment as the essence of both the human mind and the entire universe; in the idea of Sambhogakaya, Compassion is added to Enlightenment on the cosmic and meta-cosmic level – or, to put it in another but equivalent way, in the subtlest, innermost levels of the mind.

The Sambhogakaya Buddha, the meta-cosmic Buddha, the subtle body of the Buddha – these three phrases may give the reader some hint of what is being spoken of here. The waves of Sambhogakaya's powerful compassion unceasingly permeate all the worlds containing all levels of beings so as to help hasten the process of their liberation by destroying the root of harmful karma. The immense diversity of Sambhogakaya's manifestation is exemplified by symbolic forms such as the yidams and the Five Victorious Buddhas. Awakened minds are said to be capable of perceiving Sambhogakaya and receiving direct guidance from it. And even ordinary human beings who are aware of the true nature of Sambhogakaya can grasp its messages.

However, since Sambhogakaya is imperceptible to sentient beings at their ordinary level of consciousness, Sambhogakaya responds to their needs through its earthly manifestations called Nirmanakaya incarnations. Nirmanakaya is the Buddha as literally understood – a human being born in a specific time and place, or a great saint, a Bodhisattva, an incarnation of the highest reality. (The concept of the reincarnated lama has its roots in this aspect of the Trikaya doctrine.) But in a more fundamental sense, Nirmanakaya is any manifestation whose source is on the level of fully enlightened Mind sent to and perceptible by beings caught in the illusions and sufferings of samsara.

The secret teachings of the Vajrayana speak of 'three levels of Trikaya' – the human existential life, the transformative process, and the final realization. In the Vajrayana all these levels of awareness are to be realized and unified in man's ordinary life, 'in one life,' as it is said. The Sanskrit term 'vajra' refers to the inseparable wholeness of cosmic awareness and reality (the adamantine scepter); 'yana' is the way or vehicle, a term which ordinarily would denote a transposition from one level to another, but which here implies the instantaneous transformation of the human mind into a conscious state of supreme vision and boundless compassion.

In the esoteric teachings, the Trikaya is not limited to the cosmic dimension alone, but is also understood to exist, at least potentially, within the individual himself. In this sense, Dharmakaya is man's deepest, most inner awareness which is hidden beneath the stains of distortions and defilements; Sambhogakaya is the 'nucleus' of supremely subtle energies which emanate from this inmost awareness and which ordinarily lie dormant within the psychophysical complex of the human mind.

But even the ordinary human mind at its everyday level represents the Trikaya structure. For example, the innate emptiness or non-substantiality of mind is Dharmakaya; the innate clarity and purity are Sambhogakaya, which becomes Nirmanakaya when it manifests and unfolds without obstruction in the thoughts and imagination of the individual.

This doctrine of Trikaya and Buddhist cosmology may help to dispel some of the confusion about the nature of the yidams, dakas, dakinis, guardian deities, the eight armies of gods and demons and other psycho-cosmological symbols that figure prominently in this text.

The masters of the Vajrayana tradition perceived the cosmic and meta-cosmic universe in the following way:

The endlessly vast material universe was characterized as the product of the incessant interplay and interpenetration of energies and matters in the unimaginably infinite realms of space. In the material universe nothing is static. Everything is in a constant, dynamic state of movement and flux. There are ultimately no frontiers to be seen or conceived of in the whole cosmic universe.

Similarly, the mental universe consists of spiritual, psychophysical or biological forces referred to as the six realms of the Wheel of Life. The armies of gods, demons, serpent-gods and so on, and belief in the existence of a spirit hierarchy in general, stems originally from the pre-Buddhist Bon religion of Tibet, which included a hierarchical cosmology corresponding in many respects to the common Buddhist conception of the six spheres of samsara.

In the higher metaphysics of Buddhism, the material and the mental universes are taken to exist only as pure concepts. The basic idea is that all phenomena, whether material or mental, are unreal, being merely the products of constantly shifting, interacting causes and energies. Just as Buddhism teaches that there is no 'self' or 'psyche' corresponding to a definite entity within the individual, so it also teaches that the entire material and mental realm has no independent reality. Through the practice of the teaching, through rational investigation, meditative experience, and the resulting intuitive insight which exposes all notions of duality as false it is seen that all beings – no matter where they exist in the psycho-cosmic hierarchy – are only temporary, causally conditioned aggregates of the streams of energy in the universe. The so-called formless beings or spirits are not exceptions, since they too are said to possess inherent consciousness and energies.

But there is a third category of reality, which we might term 'meta-cosmic,' containing beings that exist and function as counter-cosmic movements in the sense that their action runs counter to the absorption in the wheel of samsara of all beings in the six realms of the mental universe. These beings are the Enlightened Ones at their varying levels of illumination – Bodhisattvas, yidams, dakas, dakinis, and guardian deities.

The yidams are symbolic manifestations and embodiments of Sambhogakaya. Even as dynamic creative energies of Enlightened consciousness, they are still to be understood as symbols in the sense that they exist as a means of transmission and communication at the highest levels of awareness. Evans-Wentz calls them 'tutelary deities.' Communication with them is not given to people automatically, but is the rare result of intensive practice in the discipline of the path. This confirms Buddhism's cardinal principle that liberation and enlightenment are to be earned and are not given. The different forms of yidam associated with the practices of visualization and the transformation of energies are indeed a psychological device in the work of meditation. The yidams symbolize and actually represent the character, qualities, attributes, and powers of Enlightened Beings. As such, they are approached by the practicing initiate as a representation of the highest reality that is in himself and toward which he may strive. They are to be perceived neither as the Supreme Deity nor as supernatural agents. To the practicing initiate, their significance is as a reminder of his own undeveloped potentialities.

The guardian deities are regarded as secondary manifestations of Sambhogakaya. They are often described as emanations of Bodhisattvas.

As for the dakinis, who play such a prominent role in the spiritual imagery of *The Life*, the term means literally 'she who moves through the space.' Among the many interpretations of this term, the one that is perhaps most germane to our text is 'she who enjoys the expanse of Emptiness' – that is, who has attained higher illumination. In a certain sense, the dakinis (and the dakas, their male counterparts) correspond to the yidams in that they are manifestations of the highest state of Enlightenment within both man and the universe. But the sense of their beauty or wrathfulness strongly suggests that an element of emotional relationship is fundamental. As one observer has put it, 'The lama is the Buddha outside oneself; the yidam is the Buddha within oneself; the dakinis are the Buddha as beloved.'

On the trans-cosmic scale of realization, these beings of the third category are entrusted with the task of preserving the vast treasure of the esoteric teachings. On another scale, with the dakas and dakinis, they assist the yogin in fulfilling his highest spiritual aims, and thus symbolize the counter-cosmic movement in the whole of the universe. Here, the Vajrayana surpasses the Mahayana's profound concept of the ultimate unity of samsara and nirvana by positing as inherent in the structure of the universe forces which actually assist man in the work of harmonizing and unifying these two opposite movements within the realm of human consciousness.

The key to achievement lies in one simple and singular act of spontaneous awakening. This is already a state of awareness not distinguishable from the ultimate nature of Enlightenment, yet it is also the rapid path of immediate transformation, and thus gives scope for limitless possibilities of experience and inexhaustible skillful methods. The inward transformation at diverse levels of consciousness ultimately incorporates all the senses and functions of man, including reactions to pleasant or unpleasant circumstances as well as all actions arising from the physical organism – 'body, speech, and mind.' Whatever the method of spiritual practice, one essentially strives toward developing his inborn concern for universal release from suffering, ever extending the scope of love and compassion yet remaining aware of the true nature behind all apparent realities, which sees the hidden unity of all forms and its inherent emptiness. In so doing, one establishes a firm ground of inner experience so that even emotions of despair, fear, lust, and anger may be turned into the most beneficial and ecstatic experiences of Reality.

To an initiate every traditional symbol conveys multiple levels of meanings, as indicated in our textual note (p. 215) dealing with the 'six modes and the four methods' of elucidating the Buddhist tantric doctrine. Such symbols include icons, diagrams, sacred syllables, mandalas, the ritual scepter (dorje), bell, drum, costumes, ornaments, music, dance, and movements. In addition there are natural symbols equally esoteric in terms of their meaning, such as sound, voice, the human body, colors, the natural elements, sun, moon, sky, sea, animals, trees, birds, space and, indeed, the whole cosmic universe.

Merely by realizing the true significance of these symbols one may achieve insight into the reality that lies behind phenomena, thus transforming psychological distortions and fantasies. Through seeing things as no more than symbols or concepts a person does not thereby ignore their relative value and their practical significance in his life and relationships. One must appreciate that Emptiness and the ultimate non-substantiality of all relative realities is what opens up their dynamic possibilities in the evolutionary, counter-cosmic stream of spiritual release.

As in the universe, so also within man himself: karmic process is inherent in everything. Man is therefore conditioned by diverse forces – inwardly through psychological factors and outwardly through physical, environmental, and circumstantial influences. The primal state of original awareness is submerged under the muddy swamp of all these conditions, and the course of human destiny is thereby bound within the cycle of the existential realm. The esoteric path is considered to be the most effective means of breaking this vicious cycle of existential movements, and of effecting the upsurge of spontaneous awakening.

Spiritual practices are thus what we have been speaking of on a cosmic scale as counter movements designed to help man gain control over the inner and outer tendencies which enslave him. When fully harnessed, these tendencies themselves become invaluable instruments for re-activating hidden sources of higher energy within man – the 'nucleus' of subtle elements and the Inner Fire (Tummo). All these diverse forces are harmonized by progressive steps of perfect seeing and the incessant warmth of compassion so that persistent endeavor brings a man ever closer to the goal of final illumination.

Concerning the practice of Inner Fire (Tummo), the reader is referred to our textual note (p. 213). Here it is sufficient to say that the theory and practice pertaining to Tummo involve the deepest concepts of metaphysics and psychology, as well as diverse practices of higher yoga.

The Westerner needs to be aware that many of the Vajrayana teachings are written down in what amounts to a coded language. The key to true understanding lies not only in the secret oral instructions, but in practicing with the humility and persistence exemplified by Milarepa himself.

The practices of higher yoga are grouped under different headings, such as the Six Secret Transmissions of Naropa, Five Steps to Complete Termination according to the Unified Excellence of the Unknown, Six Transformations according to the Transcendent Dimension of Time and so on. Milarepa's critical remarks on mere scholarship and booklearning stem not so much from prejudice against the study of ideas as from insight into the way the sacred pursuit of study may be profaned to satisfy egoistic desires and fulfill selfish aims. Though Milarepa admitted he had never worked toward scholarship, he demonstrated a thorough knowledge in depth of Buddhist metaphysics and doctrines, especially Madhyamika and Mahamudra.

His ability to present complex teachings in simple and lucid style is astonishing. His means of communication – singing the poems or hymns he had composed extempore – was all his own. An inner revolution had transformed the working of his critical mind into spiritual satire. His songs represent diverse approaches within the tradition and often reveal vividly the hidden contradictions in human attitudes and behavior.

Through the years of dedication to meditation and related practices in the mountain solitude, living as he did like a piece of rock, subjecting himself to the severest form of asceticism, Milarepa achieved the highest attainable illumination and the mind power that enabled him to guide and shape the destiny of innumerable human and non-human disciples. Through him, the contemporary movement for reviving Buddhism in Tibet received a tremendous impetus. Like millions of stars, the awakened disciples, lamas and cotton-clad yogins lighted up the country even as Milarepa passed into the all-embracing expanse of Dharmakaya. The subsequent history of the Kagyü tradition with its four major and eight minor orders has been one of magnificent achievement.

The miraculous powers that Milarepa openly demonstrated were the by-product of his absolute dedication to and mastery of meditation and yogic practice, and especially of his achievement of integrating the transparency of awareness with all the subtle energies of the human organism through the activation of Inner Fire. Although with good reason the tradition generally forbids both the acquisition and display of these powers, Milarepa used them as a means to drive home spiritual messages to his followers and foes alike. It is the inexhaustible power of compassion sustained by undeluded discernment and supreme insight that plays a vital role in training devotees and serving humanity. The supra-normal cognition achieved through these qualities enables its possessor to perceive unhindered both the dilemma and the hidden potentialities of other human beings, in a manner demonstrated by Marpa and Milarepa.

Milarepa was thus the true embodiment of the highest that man can aspire to and attain. His own attitude and approach were staggeringly akin to those of the Buddha in meeting the diverse needs of individuals. He was proclaimed as the undisputed master of Buddhist metaphysics and as 'supreme among awakened yogins,' a rare honor conferred by the masters of all schools of Tibetan Buddhism.

Finally, the autobiography is in itself a profound act of compassion. As was said by His Holiness Dudjom Rimpoche, who graciously consented to read this introduction during his visit to the United States in 1976, *The Life of Milarepa* is not an exhortation to external privation in any form, but an example which proves that to obtain liberation in this life unremitting effort is necessary.

The text upon which the present translation is based is a modern Indian print produced by Kalsang Lhundup in Varanasi. Unlike most editions of *The Life*, it was published without the corresponding invocation which customarily appears at the end of the text. This 'Invocation to Milarepa,' in verses written by Nankha Gyaltsen, the

Great Yogin of Lachi, summarizes the main features of both the *Life* and the *Songs*. The three texts traditionally appear together as one set dealing with the life and teachings of Milarepa.

The original xylograph of the autobiography and the collected songs was compiled by Tsan Nyon (1452–1507), writing under the esoteric name of Dürtö Nyulwai Gyenchen. The identity of the compiler as Tsang Nyon has been confirmed beyond reasonable doubt. One may refer to passages in his biography, entitled *The Life of the Saint of Tsang*, edited by Dr E. Gene Smith, in which the eleventh chapter deals exclusively with Tsang Nyon's efforts at compiling the texts and commissioning the woodblocks. The biographer of Tsang Nyon writes (folio 68, p. 137): 'The Revered One (Tsang Nyon) thought that even though many editions of the autobiography and collected songs did exist, I must revive this uncommon version based on the oral tradition ...' Evidence also indicates that the woodblocks were probably executed between the years 1488 and 1495 at Latö Shelpuhk. Incidentally, folio 73, p. 148 refers to the compiler as 'the sovereign yogin, Tsang Nyon, who was the reincarnation of Milarepa.'

Concerning the numerous other editions and versions of this great masterpiece, the reader may refer to Dr Smith's preface to the abovementioned text. One notable version was compiled by the twelve Great Disciples and another by Lhatsun Rinchen Namgyal (1473–1557), who was a disciple of Tsang Nyon. Although I have not seen this latter edition myself, I am reliably informed that it contains additional information about the details of Milarepa's life. I also understand that among the comparatively little-known versions is one compiled by Shijey Repa, a contemporary of the great Bodong Panchen (1377–1451). The life of Situ Chokyi Junnay refers to this version as 'the manuscript preserved at the monastery of Chuwar in Drin.' Lama Deshung Kunga Tenpai Nyima III informs me that he saw the second and perhaps only other copy of this manuscript when it was in the possession of Lama Kaygüpa Rimpoche at Horse Tooth White Rock. This particular version speaks of Milarepa's visits to the Kham and Ü regions of Eastern and Central Tibet after he became an illuminated Master.

There exists a Chinese translation by Garma C. C. Chang and also a Malayan version, but the first known translation was completed in Mongolian in 1618 and published in 1756; there appear to be two other Mongolian translations as well. The French translation, *Le Poète Tibétain Milarepa* by Jacques Bacot, was published in Paris in 1925 and was reissued under the title *Milarepa: Ses méfaits, Ses épreuves, Son illumination* in 1971. The first English version translated from the Tibetan by Kazi Dawa-Samdup of Sikkim and W. Y. Evans-Wentz, was published in 1928 as *Tibet's Great Yogi Milarepa*, a second edition appearing in 1951. A modern adaptation of this version by an English Buddhist monk, Lobsang Jivaka, was published in 1965. The complete life of Milarepa as illustrated in tankas (painted scrolls) with English commentary was produced by Toni Schmid and published in Stockholm in 1952.

I was overjoyed when the Far West Translations team in San Francisco asked me to serve as a consultant in translating the remarkable French translation of Bacot, which in important respects is different from the English version of W. Y. Evans-Wentz. But we soon discovered that far more was needed than merely rendering the Bacot into English. For one thing, Bacot entirely omitted the last chapter (Nirvana), in which the meaning of Milarepa's life and teaching is communicated through an account of the miraculous events surrounding his death. But even apart from this, and some minor errors in Bacot's translation, we found ourselves drawn inescapably and joyously toward the challenge of undertaking an entirely new translation of *The Life* directly from the Tibetan original. Along with the members of the team, I felt the enormous help a new translation could bring to all seekers, if we could succeed in being simple and direct.

Evans-Wentz succeeds in conveying the essence of Milarepa's story, as thousands who have been deeply moved by it over the past half-century can attest; but as Professor John Blofeld, who was kind enough to read through our present translation and who made several important suggestions, has said, 'It is a mistake to give translations of books in Far Eastern languages a biblical flavor . . . Whereas Near and Middle Eastern languages are much more ornate than straightforward English, the opposite is true of somewhat Chinese-type languages such as Thai, Burmese and Tibetan.'

In contrast to the Evans-Wentz, the Bacot translation is concise and direct, and in spite of some inaccuracies and distortions, we remain considerably in debt to it, especially in the earlier chapters. My good friend Marco Pallis, who is quite at home in the Tibetan language, considers the Bacot translation a work of inspiration in its own right. In his book, *Peaks and Lamas*, he aptly characterizes the Tibetan text as 'a model of brevity; the style is vigorous and free from padding and the dialogue is vivid in the extreme.' And of the Bacot version, he writes that it 'keeps almost all the qualities of the original.'

In any case, we do not presume to measure our new translation against the pioneering labors of Evans-Wentz and Bacot. To render a text such as *The Life* in a modern Western language is a task of almost disheartening difficulty: it requires not only the mastery of two languages and a profound knowledge of the Buddhist tradition, but also the ability to reconcile and put into words two views of human experience and psychology which are so fundamentally different as to appear almost contradictory. At the same time, close study of the text has been an ample reward to us for the effort expended, as we hope it will be to others.

Since our translation is intended for the general reader, as well as those familiar with Eastern teachings, we have minimized the use of Sanskrit and Tibetan terms, except for those, such as the word 'karma,' that have become part of the living vocabulary of the West. On the other hand, we were conscious of the risk involved in borrowing Judaeo-Christian terms or Western philosophical and scientific terminology. As for the spelling of the Tibetan names, we have kept the general reader in mind rather than introducing the conventional scholarly system of phonetics and transliteration.

In accord with the aim of this translation, we at one point considered doing without notes altogether, but there are simply too many places in the book where readers unfamiliar with the tradition need additional information. A few of the notes are taken directly from the Bacot and are so indicated with the initials JB.

I wish to thank my friend, Professor David Seyfort Ruegg, for his great kindness in examining the final version and offering extremely helpful suggestions and encouragement.

I am grateful to my friend, James Eban, for making available his Tibetan copy of the autobiography so that I was able to compare it with my own xylographic copy – so old and worn.

Finally, my appreciation is due John Pentland, Dierdre DeGay Fortman, Professor Jacob Needleman, and all the Far West translation team who looked after me with such warmth, hospitality, and care during my numerous extended visits to the city of San Francisco.

THE LIFE OF MILAREPA

The Story of
the Great Master Milarepa
Supremely Powerful Yogi
Showing the Path of Liberation
and All-Knowingness

Prologue

Homage to my Lama

From the beginning, in the celestial space of your Dharmakaya,[1]
unclouded by ignorance,
Your two resplendent manifestations, sun and moon,
Free from the demonic Rahu,[2]
Have been radiating actions of compassion and wisdom
in infinite glory.

Encompassing the whole realm of knowledge,
You have dispelled all the dark ignorance of the Dharma
in sentient beings,
Not only in those on the Path, but in those of every temperament
in the stream of consciousness,
All beings who through the several modes of birth are born into
Time.

You brought peace to all sentient beings, past and present,
Cast upon the path of sensory attachment by the five Skandas[3]
Which result from harmful actions done under the influence
of inner poison,
And you guided them away from that path.

Even more, you led these sentient beings to the Path of Complete
Enlightenment,
To the eight perfect attributes[4] in this life.
You who are endowed with the ten transcendent powers,[5]
You who are renowned as Mila,
Glorious refuge of sentient beings, everywhere in the universe.
I prostrate myself before you.

The ocean of your mind's compassion
Has sent forth waves of unfolding action for the benefit
of sentient beings

And filled my mind, a hollow hoof print, with rivulets of
original awareness
Bearing the gems of faith and all other virtues,
Thereby relieving me from spiritual impoverishment
And the scorching heat of inner defilement.

I am filled with joy,
Like the joy of a hot-blooded man encountering a bejeweled
woman of majestic beauty in a solitary place.
Although he honors the precepts of chastity,
In the face of her radiance he cannot even wish to move a
single step away from her.

When, like an enchanting beauty adorned with jewels of
compassion,
The story of the Master's liberation reached the ears of this
fortunate seeker,
I was filled with joy.
Now I share the feast of this wonderful and glorious story
to bring joy and laughter to all.

In the scented waters of devotion and effort
I wash away the stain of concealment from the jewel of the
Master's story;
And, setting this jewel upon the banner of the Buddha's teaching,
I offer it my veneration.
May my lama and the dakinis[6] bless me.

And so, at the beginning, in the snows of Tibet, the Master was repelled by the painful nature of samsara as though it were a raging fire.

Desiring none of this, not even the celestial happiness of Brahma and Indra, he was deeply moved by the ideal and lotus-like qualities of liberation and Complete Enlightenment.

He possessed such wisdom and compassion, faith and perseverance that without the slightest fear or hesitation he would have sacrificed his life for the sake of the Dharma.

In the middle period, he was guided by the holy lama.

Having tasted the nectar of the Dharma which flowed from the mouth of his lama, he liberated himself in the mountain solitude from the bondage of defilement, and shoots of awakening sprang up within him.

Through his intense determination to renounce worldly aims and by raising the banner of meditation through the supreme example of his unceasing efforts, he was able to evoke in the minds of fortunate disciples a longing for the path of liberation, free from worldly attachment or indolence.

Guided by his yidam[7] and the dakinis, he attained self-perfection in the Dharma by overcoming every obstacle to his practice, and by enhancing his spiritual progress and expanding the experiences of awakening.

His veneration for the masters of the lineage was so perfect that he was entrusted with the secret oral teachings of the Compassionate Masters, inheriting innumerable lines of transmission and possessing the marks of unequaled spiritual blessing.

He engendered in himself such an intense and far-reaching enlightened awareness (Bodhicitta) that by listening to him or even by hearing his name human beings who had no inclination toward the Dharma were moved to tears of faith, causing the hairs on their bodies to vibrate, and bringing about such a transformation of their whole perception that the seed of Enlightenment was sown in them; thus they were protected from fears of samsara and the lower realms.

Having attained a critical stage as awakened supporters[8] on the Vajrayana[9] path, the enlightened consort dakinis[10] helped the Master to realize supreme awareness by arousing blissful joy in his body.

Finally, having completely dissolved the two defilements into the expanse of emptiness and having rid himself of all that was to be eliminated, the Master attained true awareness beyond duality, and perfected all the virtues such as wisdom and compassion, so that he became a Buddha through his own efforts.

Like the topmost jewel of the banner-of-victory, he became the supreme Master, recognized by all religious systems, both Buddhist and non-Buddhist, as the undisputed paradigm of Enlightenment.

He realized rapidly the highest experience of illumination through mastery of the Vajrayana path.

The banner of his renown streams throughout the ten directions, for the dakas and dakinis speak of his greatness everywhere.

The descending bliss flowing through his body down to his very toes, and the ascending bliss reaching up to the crown of his head, brought him to the ultimate bliss of fruition.

Through this process there took place the untangling of the subtle and coarse knots, opening up the three parts of the sympathetic nervous system and the four energy centers. Thus, he fully activated the tsa-uma (median nerve).

Because of this achievement, songs of indestructible truth flowed spontaneously from him in an endless stream, revealing the real meaning of the Sutras with their twelve subject matters, and of the Tantra with its four divisions.[11]

He perceived all things as the Dharmakaya, going beyond the deceptive duality of the mind.

He so mastered the inner science of mental phenomena that he saw the external universe as a sacred book.

His power of wisdom and compassion was so inconceivably great that he was able to awaken animals and thereby guide them toward their liberation.

Having transcended acceptance or rejection of the Eight Worldly Reactions,[12] and being free from the need to please others, he remains a serene and resplendent object of worship by all celestial and human beings.

Through his supreme striving in meditation on the profound path, he has become the incomparable Master venerated even by similarly blessed Bodhisattvas.[13]

With the great lion's roar of non-selfhood which he himself had realized, he, the white lion, soared unbridled over the snowy mountains amidst the endless expanse of space, overpowering the deer of wrong assumptions.

Internally, he achieved the contemplative power to transmute all psychophysical forces so that externally he controlled the adverse forces of the four elements of nature, harnessing them for spiritual benefit.

Because of his supremely transcendent power over mind and subtle energy, he was able to glide across the sky like an eagle, to move, walk, rest, and sit while remaining in the air.

Through the miraculous transfiguration of his body, assuming myriad forms at will, and producing from his body raging flames and torrents of water, he eliminated the false views of the misguided, and led them toward attainment through perfect seeing, contemplation, and right action.

Grounded in the four initiations, his practice of Vajrayana transformation reached ultimate perfection, so that the dakas and dakinis gathered in a swirling cloud in the twenty-four energy centers of his vajra-like body.[14]

He was Heruka,[15] presiding over the assembly of these dakas and dakinis.

With fearless mind and unwavering confidence, he dominated the eight armies of gods and demons,[16] so that they served him in the fulfillment of the four actions.

He was the master craftsman who perceived the essential emptiness and lucidity of all things.

He was the physician who cured the chronic disease of the five inner poisons with the medicine of the five aspects of enlightened awareness.

He was the master of sound, who understood the essential nonduality of sound and emptiness, and who interpreted the meaning of the prophetic signs, good and evil, revealed by the inner and outer sounds of nature.

He clearly perceived all things hidden, both within the human mind and outside it.

He was the master metaphysician who knew by direct perception that all phenomena are devoid of substance.

He was the truly learned Master who understood all external phenomena to be internal phenomena of the mental world, then discovered the mind itself as being lucid awareness, unborn and empty.

Through the power intrinsic to perceiving without obstruction this emptiness and lucidity of all things, he attained inner freedom in the indivisible Trikaya.[17]

He achieved by his miraculous power the ability to visit in one moment all the inconceivably infinite number of Buddha realms.

There the miraculous actions of his enlightenment were spoken of by Buddhas and Bodhisattvas in disseminating the Dharma, and the Master thus fulfilled his role within the Buddha realms.

Appearing in suitable forms before the sentient beings of the six realms, he sowed seeds of illumination by showing them the Path with analogies and discourses which were in accord with the intent of the Buddha, thereby guiding them to the ripening of liberation.

In one life and one body he attained the enlightened state of the Buddha Vajradhara[18] in its Four Aspects of Enlightenment[19] and Five Transcendent Awarenesses.[20]

He is the holiest of the holy, who has liberated countless sentient beings from unbearable sufferings and helped them to reach the City of Great Freedom with the Four Joyful Perfect Manifestations.

Everywhere the name of the glorious Mila Zhepa Dorje was as renowned as the sun and the moon.

Inconceivable and unutterable were the wonderful and astonishing actions which he performed for the benefit of his chief disciples.

All this is a summary of the greatness of Milarepa's story of liberation.

Even the actions he performed for the benefit of the common people are indescribable and beyond our imagination.

Thus, the story of the Master consists of two parts, illustrating his worldly career and his rapid achievement of Supreme Enlightenment.

FIRST PART

Concerning the paternal name, Mila, the origin of his ancestors, and the manner of his birth.

How, in his youth, after his father's death, his nearest relatives rose up in enmity; and how, stripped of all he owned both outside and inside, he knew to its depths the whole reality of suffering. Finally, how, at the urging of his mother, he destroyed his enemies by acts of sorcery.

Such are the first three chapters of this marvelous story.

First Chapter

Birth

The story is heralded by the following preface:

O marvel! While residing at the dwelling cave called Dopapūhk (Stomach Like Cave) in Nyanang, the renowned Master, Mila Zhepa Dorje (Laughing Vajra), a Heruka supreme among all yogins, was surrounded by his great disciples and followers, the awakened yogins[1] and great Bodhisattvas: Retchung Dorje Drakpa (Renowned Vajra), Shiwa Ö Repa (Calm Light), Repa of Ngandzong, Repa of Seban, Khira Repa (The Hunter), Repa of Digom, Repa of Len, Sangye Kyab Repa (Enlightened Protector), Shengom Repa (Hermit of Shen), Dampa Gyakpūhwa (Saint of Gyakpūh), Master Shakyaguna, and others. Also the women devotees: Legse Būm (Hundred Thousand Virtues) and Shen Dormo (Vajra of Shen), together with other lay disciples. Also among the assembly were Tshering Chenga (the Five Immortal Sisters) and other dakinis who achieved subtle bodies. There were still others – gods, men, and women – who had assembled there. The Master was setting in motion the Wheel of Sacred Law in accordance with the teaching of Mahayana.

At that time Retchung was in deep contemplation in his cell. For a whole night he had this dream: In an enchanting country called Ugyen (Abode of the Dakinis) he entered a great city where houses were built and tiled with precious material. The inhabitants of this city were of enchanting beauty, dressed in silk and adorned with ornaments of bone and precious stones. They did not speak, but only smiled joyfully and exchanged glances.

Among them was a woman disciple of the Lama Tepūhwa, named Bharima, whom Retchung had known earlier in Nepal. She was dressed in red robes and seemed to be their leader. She said to Retchung, 'Nephew, you have come! Welcome.' Having said this, she led him to a mansion made of precious stones and filled with a myriad of treasures to delight the senses. She treated him as an honored guest and set before him a great feast of food and drink.

Then she said, 'At this moment, the Buddha Mikyupa, the Immutable, is teaching the Doctrine at Ugyen. Nephew, if you wish to hear him I will ask his permission.'

Longing to hear him, Retchung answered, 'Yes, yes!' And they left together.

At the center of the city, Retchung saw a great high throne of precious materials. Upon this throne sat the Buddha Immutable, resplendent and more sublime than he had visualized Him in meditation. He was teaching the Doctrine in the midst of an ocean of disciples. At this sign, drunk with joy, Retchung thought he would faint. Then Bharima said to him, 'Nephew, stay here for a moment. I will ask the Buddha's permission.'

She went forward and was granted her wish. Led by her, Retchung prostrated himself at the feet of the Buddha. He asked for a blessing and remained before him listening to the teaching.

The Buddha gazed at him for a moment with a smile, and Retchung thought to himself, 'He is thinking of me with compassion.' While listening to the history of the births and lives of the Buddhas and Bodhisattvas, the hairs on Retchung's body vibrated, and he believed.

Finally, the Buddha told the story of Tilopa, Naropa, and Marpa,[2] which was even more astonishing than the preceding ones. And those who listened felt their faith grow.

When he had finished, the Buddha said, 'Tomorrow I shall tell the story of Milarepa, a story still more wonderful than the ones I have just told. Let everyone come to hear it.'

Then some of the disciples said, 'If there are works more wonderful than the ones we have just heard, their miraculousness exceeds all bounds.' Others said, 'The virtues which have just been revealed are the fruit of spiritual merits accumulated during innumerable births and through the elimination of delusion and desire. Milarepa, in one life and in one body, reached an equal perfection.' The first ones then said, 'Well, if we do not ask for such a wonderful teaching for the good of sentient beings, we shall be unworthy disciples. We must try to get it with wholehearted effort and courage.'

Another asked, 'Where is Milarepa now?' Someone answered, 'He is either in the Buddha realm of Ngonga or Ogmin.'[3] Then Retchung thought, 'Actually, the Master is living in Tibet. All these remarks have no other aim than to awaken my ardor, therefore I certainly must ask for the story of the Master for the benefit of all beings.' As Retchung was thinking in this way, Bharima took him by the hand and shook him, saying, 'Nephew, you have understood!'

Retchung awoke as dawn was breaking. He felt his inner perception had never been more lucid or his contemplation firmer. Recollecting the dream, he continued to reflect. 'I have heard the Buddha Immutable teaching among the dakinis of Ugyen. That is indeed marvelous. But it is still more marvelous to have met my venerated Master, Mila. To have heard the Buddha Immutable is a blessing from the venerated Master. It was said that the Master lives in Ngonga or Ogmin.' And Retchung berated himself saying, 'How stupid to think that the Master lives in Tibet! That is placing yourself on his level and already showing disrespect. First of all, since the Master is Buddha in body, speech, and mind, his actions are inconceivably great and profound. And you, ignorant fool, forgot that wherever the Master is, that place is always Ogmin and Ngonga. He who was teaching the Doctrine in my dream and those who listened to him, Bharima and the others, indicated that I should ask the Master for his story. And so I shall ask.'

Feeling extraordinary veneration for the Master, he prayed to him from the depths of his heart and from the very marrow of his bones. While he was absorbed in contemplation for a few moments, in a mixture of torpor and lucidity, he saw five beautiful young girls standing before him wearing the diadem and robes of Ugyen, one white, the others blue, yellow, red, and green. One of them said, 'The story of Milarepa will be told tomorrow, let us go and listen.'

A second said, 'Who will ask for it?' Another answered, 'The great spiritual sons will ask for it.' At the same time, their eyes were smiling at Retchung.

The young girl added, 'Everyone would be happy to hear such a marvelous teaching, so it is fitting that each of us ask for it with prayers.' And another continued, 'It is up to the elder disciples to ask for the story. Our own task is to propagate and protect the teaching.' After these words the girls vanished like a rainbow.

Then Retchung awoke from his trance. The dawning sun rose resplendent in the sky. He thought in his heart, 'I understand the dream as a direction given by the Five Immortal Sisters.'

In an active state of awareness, Retchung prepared his meal. When he was satisfied and cheerful, he went to find the Master and saw him surrounded by monks, disciples, and lay devotees, forming a colorful throng. Retchung prostrated himself and asked the Master about his health. Then, remaining on his knees and joining the palms of his hands, he addressed this prayer to the Master:

'Venerable and precious Master, long ago for the good of sentient beings, the Buddhas of the past told the story of the twelve labors of their lives and other inconceivable works of liberation. In this way the teaching of the Buddha has spread throughout the world. In our day, fortunate seekers have the possibility of being guided on the way to liberation because Tilopa, Naropa, Marpa, and other saints have told their own stories.

'O Precious Master, for the joy of your disciples, for the fortunate ones who will be your disciples in the future, and finally for the sake of guiding other sentient beings on the way to liberation, tell us, O Compassionate Master, the origin of your family, tell us your story and your works.' So he pleaded.

Then, with smiling face, the Master answered, 'Because you ask, Retchung, I shall grant your prayer.

'The name of my clan is Khyungpo, my family name is Josay, and my name is Milarepa. In my youth I committed black deeds. In maturity I practiced innocence. Now, released from both good and evil, I have destroyed the root of karmic action and shall have no reason for action in the future. To say more than this would only cause weeping and laughter. What good would it do to tell you? I am an old man. Leave me in peace.'

So he spoke. Retchung prostrated himself and said this prayer:

'O Precious Master, at first through terrible asceticism and determination, you penetrated the hidden truths. By applying yourself wholly to meditation you have attained awakening to the real nature of things and to the state of emptiness. Free from the bonds of karma, you are beyond future suffering. This is common knowledge to us all. That is why there is an incomparable interest in your descent from Khyungpo, in your family Josay, in the reason you were called Mila, and in why the black deeds you committed at first and the good deeds of your maturity may cause tears and laughter. Thinking with compassion of all sentient beings and not remaining in the depths of equanimity, please tell us the whole of your story. All of you, brothers and sisters of the Path, and lay disciples brought here by your faith, join me in my prayer.'

Having spoken thus, Retchung made several prostrations. And when the foremost disciples, spiritual sons, and faithful followers had prostrated themselves, all voiced the same prayer as Retchung, asking that the Master turn the Wheel of the Law.

Then the Venerable Master spoke as follows:

Since you ask me with such pressing insistence, I will no longer hide my life from you, but will reveal it now. My tribe descends from the great clan of herdsmen in the Northern Center. Its name is Khyungpo. My ancestor was a yogin named Josay, the son of a Nyingmapa[4] lama. Inspired by his yidam, he acquired great powers through mantra.[5] He also visited the holy places of the country and their shrines.

In the north, in Upper Tsang, he was welcomed in the village of Chungpachi. In this region he subdued evil demons. His powers made him very useful, so that his influence and the importance of his work increased. He was named Khyungpo Josay and lived in this region for several years. Whoever fell ill called upon him.

Once there was a terrible demon who could not come near Josay, but whom no one else could withstand. The demon persecuted a family which had little faith in Josay. This family called upon another lama to perform the exorcisms. But the demon only laughed and mocked, continuing to torment them.

At this point a relative who believed in Josay secretly advised the family to send for him. He quoted the proverb 'One even uses dog fat if it cures the wound.' And they sent for Khyungpo Josay.

When he came near the demon, Josay drew himself up proudly and cried out with a loud voice: 'I, Khyungpo Josay, have come. I shall eat the flesh of demons and drink their blood. Just wait!' As he spoke he lunged forward. The demon was panic-stricken and screamed out with terror, 'Papa Mila! Papa Mila!'[6] When Josay approached him, the demon said, 'I have always stayed out of your way, so spare my life.' Josay made him swear never again to hurt anyone and sent him away.

From this moment on, everyone called him Mila to illustrate the power of Josay's virtues, and Josay kept Mila as the family name. Since the demon did no more harm, everyone assumed he had been born into another realm of existence.

After this, Khyungpo Josay took a woman and had a son. This son had two sons and he called the eldest Mila Dhoton Senge (Lion-like Master of Sutras). The latter had a son called Mila Dorje Senge

(Vajra Lion). From this time on, each descendant had only one son.

Mila Vajra Lion was a very clever dice player and was able to win much by it. Now in this region there was a man from a powerful family, a cheat, who was also clever with dice. One day, to test the strength of Mila Vajra Lion, he began by playing a little game to take the measure of his adversary. On this particular day he did what was necessary to win. Displeased, Mila Vajra Lion said to him, 'Tomorrow, I will get even with you.'

'Very well,' said the other.

The cheat raised the stakes, and let himself be beaten three times. Then he said, 'Now, I must get even.' Both having agreed to the stakes, they wagered irrevocably their fields, their houses, and their entire fortunes. They bound themselves by a written contract and played. The cheat won and took possession by placing his family in charge of the fields, the house, and all the goods.

Thereupon the two Milas, father and son, left the region. Arriving in the village of Kya Ngatsa, in Gungthang near Mangyul, they settled down. The father, Mila Lionlike Master of Sutras, was called to the houses of people living there to read the sacred books, offer sacrificial effigies,[7] protect them from hailstorms, and save children from evil spirits. Much in demand, he accumulated many gifts. In the winter, Vajra Lion traveled to do business in the south of Nepal; in the summer, he went among herdsmen of the north. On minor business, he traveled between Mangyul and Gungthang. In this way the father and son amassed great wealth.

At this time, Mila Vajra Lion loved a village girl and married her. They had a son whom they named Mila Banner of Wisdom. When this son was nearly grown up, his grandfather, Mila Lionlike Master of Sutras, died. After he had concluded the funeral ceremonies, Mila Vajra Lion increased his wealth still more through trade, and became richer than before.

In the neighborhood of Tsa,[8] there was a man named Worma who had a field of good earth, triangular in shape. After procuring gold and merchandise from the north and from the south, Mila Vajra Lion bought this field and named it Fertile Triangle.

On the edge of this field, there were the ruins of a house belonging to their neighbor. Mila Vajra Lion bought that also and laid the foundations of a manor house. During the construction of the house, Mila Banner of Wisdom reached his twentieth year.

At Tsa, in the noble family of Nyang, there was a very beautiful girl named White Jewel. She was skillful at housekeeping and as extreme in her love for her friends as in her hatred of her enemies. Mila Banner of Wisdom married her and called her Nyangtsha Kargyen (White Jewel of Nyang).

Thereafter the construction of the manor house was continued. On the third floor they built a courtyard with a granary and a kitchen along one side. This house was the most pleasant in Kya Ngatsa. Since it had four columns and eight beams, it was called Four Columns and Eight Beams. The father and son lived there, joining happiness with a good name.

Some time later, at Chungpachi, after hearing of the fame of the father and son, the son of the first cousin of Mila Vajra Lion, named Yungdrung Gyaltshen (Eternal Banner of Victory), left his part of the country and came to Kya Ngatsa with his wife, children, and sister, Khyung-Tsha Peydon (Glorious Contestant of Khyung).

Mila Banner of Wisdom, having brought many goods from the south, had gone to sell them in the north near Tiger Point and was away for a long time. White Jewel was then pregnant. It was in the middle of autumn in the year of the Water Dragon[9] under the star Victorious of the eighth constellation, on the twenty-fifth day of the moon, that my mother gave birth to me. She sent a message to my father. The letter said: 'Here at the time of harvest, I have given birth to a son. Come quickly to name him and celebrate his name day.' When he delivered the letter, the messenger told him the whole story.

My father was filled with joy. He exclaimed, 'Marvelous! My son already has his name. In my family there has never been more than one son in each generation. This son born to me I shall call Good News, since the news brings joy. Now that I have finished my business, I shall leave.' And he went home. This is how I was given the name Good News, which was celebrated by a joyous name-day festival.

I was raised with love and, hearing only gentle voices, I was happy. So all men said, 'This Good News has been well named.'

When I reached my fourth year, my mother gave birth to a girl who was named Gonkyi (Happy Protectress). Since her nickname was Peta, she was called Peta Gonkyi (Peta Happy Protectress). I remember our silken hair, hers of gold and mine of turquoise, falling on our shoulders.

In this region our words were listened to with respect and we were all-powerful. Therefore the nobles of the region were our allies and the peasants were in our service. Although we had all these privileges, the villagers in their secret meetings used to say, 'These foreigners were immigrants to this region and now they are greater and richer than any of us. The farmhouse and field implements and the jewels of the men and the women are a sight to behold.'

All his wishes fulfilled, Mila Vajra Lion died. His funeral ceremonies were lavishly performed.

Thus spoke Milarepa, and this is the first chapter, which is that of his birth.

Second Chapter

Youth

Then Retchung asked, 'O Master, you are said to have suffered many misfortunes after the death of your father. How did these evils come upon you?' Thus he pleaded, and the Master continued:

When I was about seven years old, my father, Mila Banner of Wisdom, was wasting away with a terrible disease. The doctors and magicians predicted that he would never get well and so abandoned him.

His relatives and friends also knew that he would not live. He himself was certain he would die. My uncle (Eternal Banner of Victory) and aunt (Glorious Contestant of Khyung) and all our relatives, close and distant friends, and prominent neighbors gathered together.

My father agreed to put his family and affairs in the care of a trustee. Then he made a detailed will to insure that his son should later take possession of his patrimony. And he read the will aloud for everyone to hear:

'To sum up clearly, since I shall not recover from my present illness and since my son is still small, here are the arrangements by which I entrust him to all his relatives and friends and especially to his uncle and aunt.

'In the mountains: my animals – yaks, horses, and sheep; in the valley, first of all, the field, Fertile Triangle, and several other parcels of land of which the poor are envious; under the house: cows, goats, and asses; in the loft: implements, gold, silver, copper, and iron, turquoise, fabrics, silk, and a granary. All of this makes up my wealth. In short, I have so much that I need not envy anyone. Take a part of these riches for the expenses which will follow my death. As to the rest, I entrust everything to all of you assembled here until my son will be old enough to take care of his property. I entrust him completely to the care of his uncle and aunt.

'When this child is of an age to assume the family responsibilities let him marry Zessay, to whom he has been betrothed since childhood. Then let them receive all my goods without exception, and let my son take possession of his inheritance.

'During this time let the uncle, aunt, and near relatives be aware of the joys and sorrows of my two children and their mother. Do not lead them into misery. After my death I shall be watching you from the realm of the dead.' Having thus spoken, he died.

Then the funeral rites were performed. All the relatives came to an agreement on the remainder of the possessions, and all, particularly the well-wishers, said, 'White Jewel, take charge of the property yourself. Do what you think is good.' But the uncle and aunt said, 'All here are your friends, but we, your near ones, will be better than friends. We shall do no wrong to the mother and children. In accordance with the will, we shall take charge of the property.'

Without listening to the arguments of my mother's brother or of the family of Zessay, my uncle took the men's goods and my aunt the women's. The rest was divided in half. Then the aunt and uncle said: 'You, mother and children, will take turns to serve us.' We no longer had any control over our possessions. In summer, at the time for work in the fields, we were the servants of the uncle. In winter, while working with wool, we were the servants of the aunt. Our food was fit for dogs, our work for donkeys. For clothes, some strips of rags were thrown over our shoulders and held together with a rope of grass. Working without rest, our limbs became raw and sore. Due to bad food and poor clothing we became pale and emaciated. Our hair, which at one time had fallen in curls of turquoise and gold, became sparse and gray, filled with nits and lice. Those with feeling, who saw or heard of this, shed tears. They spoke bluntly behind the backs of my uncle and aunt. As we were weighed down with misery, my mother said to my aunt, 'You are not the Glorious Contestant of Khyung, but rather Dumo Takdren, Demoness Equal of Tigers.' This name, Demoness Equal of Tigers, remained with my aunt.

In those days there was a well-known proverb: 'When the false master is master, the true master is driven out of the house like a dog.' This proverb aptly described us, mother and children.

In the days when our father, Mila Banner of Wisdom, was there, everyone, strong or weak, watched to see if our faces were smiling or sad. Later, when the uncle and aunt were as rich as kings, it was their faces, smiling or sad, which people regarded. The men said about my mother, 'How true is the proverb: "To a rich husband, an able wife: from soft wool, good cloth." Now that the husband is no longer there, it is as the proverb says. In times past, when her husband was master and held up his head, White Jewel was courageous and wise, as well as a good cook. Now, she is weak and timid.' Even those who had served us mocked us. Thus they acted according to the proverb 'One man's misery is another man's fun.'

The parents of Zessay gave me boots and new clothing, and said, 'Do not think you are poor when riches pass away, since they are said to be ephemeral like the dew in the meadow. In the past your ancestors did not become rich until quite late. For you also the time of abundance will come again.' And speaking in this way, they consoled us.

At last I reached my fifteenth year. There was at this time a field given to my mother as a dowry by her parents, called by the not very beautiful name of Trede Tenchung (Little Fur Carpet), which nevertheless produced an excellent harvest. My mother's brother had cultivated it himself, and had done everything he could to store away its yield.

Thus he had secretly collected a surplus of grain which he sold to buy a great quantity of meat. With white barley, flour was made. With black barley, beer was made for a feast, which he said was to reclaim the patrimony of White Jewel and her children. Then my mother borrowed carpets and put them in my house called Four Columns and Eight Beams.

She first invited my uncle and aunt, then close relatives, intimate friends, and neighbors, and finally those who had knowledge of the will written by my father, Mila Banner of Wisdom. To my uncle and aunt she presented a whole animal; to the others, according to their rank, a quarter of an animal or a third of a quarter. And she gave them beer in porcelain cups.

Then my mother stood up in the middle of the assemblage and said, 'When a son is born he is given a name. When one is summoned to a beer feast this means it is time to talk. I have something to say to all of you gathered here, both uncle and aunt, and the older ones who remember the last words of Mila Banner of Wisdom at the moment of his death.' So she spoke. And my mother's brother read the will. Then my mother continued, 'I do not need to explain to the older people who are here the terms of this will. Until now, the uncle and aunt have taken the trouble to direct us, both mother and children, in all things. Now my son and Zessay are old enough to have their own home. This is why I beg you, restore to us the goods which were entrusted to you, let my son marry Zessay and take possession of his patrimony according to the will.'

Thus she spoke. The uncle and aunt, who almost never concurred, became united in their greed. On our side, I was an only son. On their side, they had many children.

And so my uncle and aunt retorted with one voice, 'You have goods? Where are they? In former times, when Mila Banner of Wisdom was in good health, we loaned him a house, fields, gold, turquoise, dzos,[1] horses, yaks, and sheep. At the time of his death he returned these goods to their owner. Do you possess a single piece of gold? A single ounce of butter? A single garment? A single scrap of silk? We have not even seen the hoof of an animal. Who has written this will? We have had the goodness to nourish you when you were orphaned and destitute, so that you would not die of hunger. The proverb "As soon as they have power, greedy men will even measure out water" is indeed true.'

Having said this, the uncle snuffled, blew his nose, got up quickly, snapped his fingers, shook the panel of his skirt, stamped his foot, and said, 'What is more, even this house belongs to me. So, orphans, get out.' Saying this, he slapped my mother and struck my sister and me with the sleeve of his chuba.[2]

Then my mother cried out, 'Father Mila Banner of Wisdom, see the fate of your family. You said you would watch us from the realm of the dead. Look at us now.' Thus she spoke and, weeping, she fell and rolled on the ground. We children could do nothing for her but weep. My mother's brother, fearing my uncle's many sons, could not fight back. People of the village, who loved us, said they felt sorry for us and there was not one of them who did not weep. The others present sighed deeply.

The uncle and aunt said to me, 'You demand your goods, but you already have a great deal. You prepared a feast for the neighbors and the people of the village without regard for the beer and the meat you squandered. We do not have such wealth. Even if we did, we would not give them to you, miserable orphans. So if you are many, make war on us. If you are few, cast spells.' With these words, they went away. Afterward, their friends also left.

My mother wept without ceasing while her brother, Zessay's parents, and our friends remained to console her, saying, 'Do not cry; tears serve nothing. Ask for something from each one who has come to the feast. Everybody here will give you what you need, even the uncle and aunt may give you something good.'

My mother's brother then said, 'Do as they say and send your son to learn a skill. Then you, mother and daughter, can live with me and work in my fields. It is always good to occupy yourself with something useful. In any case, you must do something so as not to be helpless in front of your uncle and aunt.' My mother replied, 'Dispossessed of all my goods, I have never begged for anything to raise my children. I will not accept from the uncle and aunt a single piece of my own property. Persecuted by the uncle and aunt we will run at the sound of the drum, and run when the smoke rises.[3] We shall put them to shame. After that, I myself will till my field.'

In the region of Tsa, in the village of Mithogekha, there was a master magician of the Nyingmapa Order, very much in demand in the villages, who knew the Cult of the Eight Nagas.[4] My mother sent me to him to learn how to read. At the same time, our relatives, offering us their own goods, gave each of us a few things. The parents of Zessay brought me supplies of oil and firewood and, to console me, they even sent Zessay to where I was learning to read. My maternal uncle fed my mother and sister and thus they did not have to beg or work somewhere else.

Because her brother would not allow her to become destitute, my mother did work at home, one day spinning, the next day weaving. In this way she obtained some money and what was necessary for us, her children. My sister worked for others as much as she could to earn food and clothing. She ran at the sound of the drum and ran when the smoke was rising.

Suffering from hunger, our clothing in tatters and spirits low, we were not happy.

Thus the Master spoke. As he said these words all the listeners were deeply moved and, with grief in their hearts, remained silent for a moment, shedding tears. This is the second chapter, laying bare to the highest degree the reality of sorrow.

Third Chapter

Misdeeds

Then Retchung said, 'Master, you told us that at first you had done evil deeds. How, may I ask, did you commit them?'

'I accumulated sins through casting spells and causing hailstorms.'

'Master, what circumstances led you to cast spells and cause hailstorms?'

Then the Master continued:

While studying at Mithogekha, one day I accompanied my tutor to the lower valley of Tsa, where he was invited to preside at a wedding feast. Drinking much beer, not only what I poured for him but also what all the others poured for him, my tutor became drunk. He sent me ahead with the presents he had received. I also was drunk. Hearing the singers, I too had a desire to sing, and having a good voice, I sang as I went along. The road passed in front of my house and I was still singing when I arrived at the door. In the house my mother was roasting barley[1] and heard me. 'What is this?' she said to herself. 'That sounds like the voice of my son. But how could he be singing while we are so miserable?' And not believing what she heard, she looked outside. As soon as she recognized me she cried out in surprise. Her right hand dropped the tongs; her left hand dropped the whisk; and, leaving the barley to burn, she took a stick in one hand and a handful of ashes in the other. She ran down the big steps, leaped over the little ones, and was outside. She threw the ashes in my face, struck me several times on the head, and shouted, 'Father Mila Banner of Wisdom, is this the son that you have begotten? He is not worthy of you. Look at our fate, mother and son!' And with this she fainted.

At this moment my sister came running up and said, 'Elder brother, what are you doing? What has happened to mother?' And her weeping brought me to my senses. Then I too shed many tears. We rubbed our mother's hands and called her name. After a moment she came to herself and got up. Then, fixing her tear-filled eyes on me, she said, 'Since we are the most unfortunate people on earth, is it proper to sing? When I think of it, I, your old mother, am consumed by despair and can only cry.' Then, lamenting loudly, all three of us began to weep. I said to her, 'Mother, you are right. Do not be so distressed. I will do whatever you wish.'

'I wish you were dressed in the mantle of a man and mounted on a horse, so that your stirrups would rip the necks of our detested enemies. That is not possible. But you could do them harm by guileful means. I would that, having thoroughly learned magic together with the destructive spell, you first destroy your uncle and aunt, then the villagers and the neighbors who have treated us so cruelly. I want you to curse them and their descendants down to the ninth generation. Now, see if you can do it.'

I replied, 'Mother, I will try. Prepare provisions and a gift for the lama.'

So that I might learn magic, my mother sold half the field, called Little Fur Carpet. With the money she bought a turquoise called Great Sparkling Star, a white horse, well-loved in that area, named Senge Submey (Unbridled Lion), two bundles of dye, and two packs of raw sugar, which were soon used up. Thus she finished the preparations for my departure.

First I went to stay a few days in a caravanserai called Lhundup in Gungthang.[2] Five amiable young men arrived saying they came from Ngari Döl and were going to the region of Ü and Tsang to study religion and magic. I proposed that they let me join them since I also was going to learn magic. They agreed. I brought them to my mother's house in Gungthang and treated them as guests for several days.

My mother secretly told them, 'This son of mine has no willpower. So you, his companions, should exhort him and spur him on to become deeply skilled in magic. When that time comes I shall offer you hospitality and generous rewards.' Then, loading the two sacks of dye onto the horse, and carrying the turquoise on my person, we went on our way. My mother accompanied us for some distance.

While my companions were drinking a cup of farewell wine, my mother offered them much advice. Hardly able to separate herself from me, her only son, she held my hand tightly and took me aside. With her face bathed in tears and her voice choking with sobs, she said to me, 'Above all, remember our misfortune and let the signs of your magic be manifested in our village. Then come back. The magic of your companions and ours is not the same. Their magic is that of well-loved children, who want it only for pleasure. Ours is that of people who have suffered tragedy. That is why an unyielding will is needed. If you return without having shown signs of your magic in our village, I, your old mother, will kill myself before your eyes.'

This I promised, and so we parted. I assured my mother of my love. I looked back continuously, and shed many tears. And my mother, who loved me dearly, watched us with tears in her eyes until we disappeared from view. In the ardor of my tender feelings, I asked myself if I should return to my mother for a moment. I had the feeling that I would never see her again. Finally, when we were out of sight, she went back to her village, weeping.

Some days later, it was rumored that the son of White Jewel had gone away to learn magic.

We took the road to Ü and Tsang and arrived at Yakde in the valley of Tsangrong. There I sold my horse and the dye to a very rich man. In payment I received gold, which I carried on my person.

After crossing the Tsang Po, we turned toward Ü. In a place named Tūhnlok Rakha (Sheepfold of Tūhn) we met many venerable monks. I asked them if they knew of a master in the Ü region who was skilled in magic, spells, and hailstorms. One of the monks answered, 'At Kyorpo, in Yarlung, lives a lama named Yungton Trögyel (Terrifying Conqueror) of Nyag. He has great power in charms, spells, and terrible incantations.' This monk was his disciple. So we set out to find Lama Yungton and arrived at Kyorpo in Yarlung.

When we presented ourselves before the lama, my companions offered him only insignificant gifts, but I gave him everything, gold and turquoise. And I said, 'I further offer you my body, speech, and mind. My neighbors and certain people in my village cannot bear the happiness of others. Have compassion and grant me the most powerful spell that can be cast upon my village. Meanwhile, mercifully grant me food and clothing.' The lama smiled and answered, 'I shall think about what you have told me.' But he did not teach us the real secrets of magic.

About a year passed, and all he had given us were a few incantations to make heaven and earth clash, and a smattering of various formulas and useful practices. All my companions were getting ready to leave. The lama gave each of them a well-sewn garment of broadcloth from Lhasa. But I was not satisfied. These practices were not powerful enough to produce any effect in my village. Thinking that my mother would kill herself if I returned without my spells having been effective, I resolved not to go. Seeing that I was not preparing to leave, my companions asked me, 'Good News, are you not leaving?' I answered, 'I have not yet learned enough magic.' They replied, 'These formulas are supremely magical if only we can strive to master them. The lama himself said that he had no others. We no longer have any doubts about it. Just go and see if the lama will give you others!' After thanking the lama and bidding him goodbye, they left. I too donned the clothing given by the lama and accompanied them for half a day on their journey. After we had wished each other good health, they set out for their homeland.

On the way back to the lama I filled the front of my garment with horse and donkey manure, cow dung, and dog droppings for the lama's field. Digging a hole in his fertile and life-giving field, I buried them there. The lama, who was on the terrace of his house, saw me and said to some of his disciples, 'Of the many disciples who have come to me, none is more loving than Good News, and there will never be another like him. The proof is that this morning he did not say farewell and now he has come back. When he came here for the first time, he told me that the people of his village and his neighbors could not endure the happiness of others. He asked me for magic and offered me his body, speech, and mind. Such persistence! If the story he told is true, it would be a pity not to give him the secrets of black magic.'

One of the monks repeated these words to me. I said to myself joyfully, 'At last it is settled, I will get the real secrets of magic.' And so I went to the lama. He said to me, 'Good News, why did you not go home?' Then I returned the garment the lama had given me. I put my head down at his feet and told him, 'Precious lama, there are three of us, my mother, my sister, and myself. My uncle and aunt, a few neighbors, and some villagers have become our enemies. Through treatment we did not deserve, they reduced us to misery. I did not have the strength to defend myself. That is why my mother sent me to learn magic. If I return home without a single sign of magic having resulted from my efforts, my mother will kill herself before my eyes. It is to keep her from destroying herself that I have not left. That is why I am asking you for the real secrets of magic.'

Having said this, I wept. The lama asked, 'In what way have the people of your village harmed you?' Sobbing, I told how my father, Mila Banner of Wisdom, had died and how, after his death, the uncle and aunt had crushed us with misery. Then tears fell one by one from the lama's eyes. He said, 'If what you say is true, it is a sad case. The magic that I practice will do. But we must not hurry. For this same magic I have been offered fortunes in gold and turquoise from Ngari Korsum in the west; vast quantities of tea, silk, and clothing from the three mountain regions of Kham in the east; horses, yaks, and sheep by the hundreds and thousands from Jyayul, Dakpo, and Kongpo in the south. But you alone have given me your body, speech, and mind. I am going to verify what you have told me right away.'

Living with the lama at that time was a monk who was swifter than a horse and stronger than an elephant. The lama sent him to my village to verify my story. The monk quickly returned[3] and said, 'Precious lama, Good News has told the truth. He needs to be taught much magic.'

The lama said to me, 'If I had taught you such magic right away, I fear that you, with your stubbornness, would have made me regret it. But now, since you are sincere, you must go to another master for further instruction. I have an incantation from the cult of the Maroon-faced Dza,[4] whose powerful mantra Hūm[5] causes death, while the mantra Paht[6] causes unconsciousness.

'In the region called Nub Khulung in the Tsangrong lives a lama named Yönten Gyatso (Ocean of Virtues) of Khulung, who is a great doctor and magician. I gave him my secret formula. And in return he taught me how to call down hailstorms with the tip of one finger. After he had taught me this, we became friends and associates. Now those who come to me to learn magic, I must send to him. Those who go to him to learn how to cause hailstorms, he must send to me. Go with my son and find him.'

The elder son of the lama was called Darma Ouangchuk (Powerful Youth). In addition to provisions for the journey, the lama gave us a length of broadcloth and serge from Lhasa, a few small gifts, and a letter. Having arrived at Nub Khulung, we met the young lama of Nub. We offered him some pieces of wool and serge as well as the gifts and the letter from the lama. I carefully told him all the circumstances of the story and earnestly begged him to teach me magic. The lama answered, 'My friend is a loyal friend and true to his word. I shall teach you all sorts of magic. For this purpose construct a cell on the ridge of this mountain which will put you beyond human reach.'

We built a house above ground, which was made of solid beams laid side by side. We surrounded it with a continuous enclosure of stone blocks as big as yaks, without leaving any openings, so that no one else could see a door to the house or discover a means of attacking it. Then the lama gave us the magic incantation.

After we had performed the spell, seven days passed. Then the lama came and said, 'Formerly seven days were enough, and that should still suffice.' I replied, 'As my magic must work at a distance, I ask to continue for seven more days.' The lama answered, 'Very well, continue.' And so I did.

On the evening of the fourteenth day, the lama returned and said, 'Tonight there will be a sign around the mandala[7] that magic has taken place.' And that same evening the loyal deities, guardians of the Order, brought us what we had asked for: the heads and the bleeding hearts of thirty-five people. They said, 'For several days you have repeatedly been invoking us. Here is what you wanted.' And they piled the heads all around the mandala. The next morning the lama returned and said, 'Of those to be destroyed, two people remain. Should they be destroyed or spared?' Full of joy, I said, 'I beg you to let them live so they may know my vengeance and my justice.'

Thus it was that the uncle and aunt were unharmed.

We offered the loyal guardian deities a sacrifice of thanksgiving and we left our retreat. Today, our cell can still be seen at Khulung.

Meanwhile I wondered how the spell had manifested itself in my village of Kya-Ngatsa.

There had been a wedding feast for my uncle's eldest son. My uncle's sons and daughters-in-law arrived first with the men who hated us, thirty-five in all.

The other guests, who were friendly toward us, were talking on the way to the house, saying, 'When the false master becomes master, the true master is thrown to the dogs, just as the proverb says and as these pitiless people prove. If the magic of Good News has not yet taken effect against them, the power of the guardian deities of the Dharma will make itself felt.' Together they walked toward the house.

The uncle and aunt had gone out to discuss the meal to be served and the speech to be given. At this moment a former servant of ours who was now with my uncle had gone to draw water. She did not see the many horses tied up in the stable, but instead she saw scorpions, spiders, snakes, toads, and tadpoles. She saw a scorpion as big as a yak which grasped the pillars between its claws and tore them out. At this sight, the servant fled, terrified. Hardly was she outside when the stallions in the stable began mounting the mares and the mares began kicking the stallions. All the rearing, kicking horses struck against the pillars of the house, which then collapsed. Under the debris of the fallen house, my uncle's sons, his daughters-in-law, and the other guests, thirty-five in all, lay dead. The inside of the house was filled with corpses buried in a cloud of dust.

My sister Peta, seeing everyone weeping, ran quickly to get our mother. 'Mother! Mother! Uncle's house has collapsed and many people are dead. Come and see.'

My mother gave a cry of joy, and got up and went to look. She saw my uncle's house reduced to a cloud of dust and heard the shrieks of the villagers. As happy as she was astonished, she fastened a scrap of cloth to a long stick and, waving it in the air, cried in a loud voice, 'Glory to you, gods, lamas, and the Triple Refuge![8] Well, villagers and neighbors, does Mila Banner of Wisdom have a son? I, White Jewel, am clothed in rags and eat bad food. Do you see that it was to nourish my son? In the past the uncle and aunt said to us, "Mother and children, if you are many, then make war on us; if you are few, cast spells." So this is how we, few in number, have obtained more by magic than, had we been many, we would have obtained by war. Think of the people who were upstairs in the house, think of the treasures which were in their midst and think of the livestock in the stable. I have lived long enough to see and revel in this spectacle brought about by my son. Imagine what my happiness will be from today onward!'

Even those who were in their houses heard my mother's cry of vengeance. Some of them said, 'She is right.' Others said, 'She may be right, but her vengeance is too brutal.'

Hearing by what power these people had been killed, the villagers gathered together and said, 'Not satisfied with provoking this disaster, she now rejoices in it. It is going too far. Torture her and then rip the living heart from her breast.' The elders said, 'What is the use of killing her? What has happened to us is really her son's doing. You must first of all find her son and kill him. Afterward it will be easier to kill the mother.' Speaking thus, they came to an agreement.

The uncle heard this remark and said, 'Now that my sons and daughters are dead, I am not afraid to die.' And he set out to kill my mother. But the villagers stopped him, saying, 'It is because you did not keep your word in the past that this misfortune has befallen us. If you kill the mother before killing the son, we will oppose you.' They did not give my uncle a chance to act. Then the villagers conspired to kill me.

My maternal uncle went to my mother and said, 'After your words and conduct yesterday, the neighbors are ready to kill you and your son. Why did you shout out your vengeance? Was it not enough that the spell worked?' And he rebuked her strongly. My mother replied, 'Ill-fortune has not fallen on you. I understand what you are saying, but after the way they stole my goods it is difficult to keep silent.' And without saying another word, she wept. Her brother continued, 'It is true. You are right. But assassins may come, so lock yourself in.' Having spoken, he went away. And my mother, locking herself in, began to plan and scheme.

Meanwhile my uncle's servant, who had formerly been in my service, heard the people plotting together. Because of her attachment to my family she could not tolerate this and went secretly to tell my mother what had been decided by the council, advising her to look out for her son's life. My mother thought to herself, 'This decision, for the moment, clouds my joy.' She sold the remaining half of the field, Little Fur Carpet, for seven ounces of gold. As there was no man from the neighborhood that she could send to me, and as no courier had arrived from elsewhere, my mother thought of coming herself to bring provisions and give me advice.

At this particular moment a yogin from Ü province, who was returning from a pilgrimage to Nepal, came to the door begging, and my mother asked him his story. As he was suitable to be a messenger, she said to him, 'Stay here a few days. I have a son who is in Ü and Tsang and I have to send him some news. Be good enough to take it to him.'

In the meantime my mother offered him abundant hospitality. Then having lit a butter lamp, she invoked help. 'If my wish is granted, may my son's lama and the protecting deities cause the lamp to burn a long time. If it is not to be granted, let the lamp die quickly.' The lamp lasted a day and a night. My mother, believing that her wish would be fulfilled, said to the pilgrim, 'Yogin, to journey across the country, clothing and boots are of great importance.' And she gave him leather and thread to mend his boots. She herself patched his worn cloak. Without telling the yogin, she sewed seven ounces of gold inside the lining of his cloak, over which she placed a square piece of black cloth. She embroidered this piece with stars of coarse white thread representing the constellation of the Pleiades in such a way that it could not be seen from the outside. Then she paid the yogin well, entrusted him with a sealed letter in secret writing, and dismissed him.

Afterward, my mother thought, 'As I do not know what the neighbors have decided to do, I must adopt a menacing air.' She then told Peta, 'Announce to everybody that this yogin has brought a letter from your brother.'

Here is the letter which my mother wrote as though it came from me:

'Doubtless my mother and sister are in good health and have seen signs of the magic that has taken place. If certain neighbors persist in their hatred of you, send me their names and the names of their families. By means of spells, it will be as easy for me to kill them as to throw a pinch of food[9] into the air. Thus I will destroy them to the ninth generation. Mother and sister, if the people of the village are still hostile to you, come and join me here. I will destroy every trace of this village. Although I am in seclusion, I have wealth and provisions beyond measure. Do not worry about me.'

Having written this, my mother folded the letter. She showed it first to her brother and his friends. Then she left it with her brother so that everyone would see it. As a result, they all changed their minds and gave up the idea of killing us. They took back the field, Fertile Triangle, from my uncle and gave it to my mother.

*

Meanwhile, the yogin came looking for me. Learning that I was in Nub Khulung, he sought me out. He gave me the letter and I stepped aside to read it.

'I hope, Good News, that you are in good health. Your old mother's wish to have a son is realized and the lineage of your father, Mila Banner of Wisdom, has been assured. Signs of your magic have appeared in the village and thirty-five people have been killed in the house that collapsed. As a result of this, the local people have ill-will toward us both, mother and daughter, so that is why you must make hail fall as high as the ninth course of bricks.[10] Then the last wishes of your old mother will be realized. The people of the neighborhood say they will seek you out and that, after having killed you, they will kill me. For both our sakes, mother and son, let us guard our lives with the greatest care. If your provisions are exhausted, look in the region facing north where, against a black cloud, the constellation of the Pleiades will appear. Beneath it are the seven houses of your cousins. There you will find all the provisions you could wish for. Take them. If you do not understand, ask no one else but this yogin who lives in that region.'

I did not understand the meaning of this letter. I missed my homeland and my mother. As I was in great need of provisions, being ignorant of the region and knowing no relatives there, I shed many tears. I asked the yogin, 'Since you know the country, where do my cousins live?' The yogin answered, 'In the central plain of Ngari.'

'Do you not know any other regions? Which is yours?'

'I know many other regions, but I do not know any others where your cousins live. I am from Ü province.'

'Now then, stay here a moment, I will be right back.'

I went to show the letter to the lama and asked him for the explanation. The lama scanned the letter and said to me, 'Good News, your mother is full of hatred. Even after the death of so many people she now wants you to send hailstorms. Who are your cousins in the north?' I answered, 'I have never heard of them. It is the letter that mentions them. I asked the yogin but he does not know.'

The wife of the lama, who was marked with the sign of the great dakinis, read the letter aloud and said to me, 'Send for the yogin.'

When the yogin came, the lama's wife made a big fire and gave him some excellent beer. Then, removing the cloak from the yogin's back, she put it on herself and said, 'This is a nice cloak for traveling from place to place.' Having spoken, she walked up and down. Then she went up to the terrace of the house. There she removed the gold from the cloak, resewed the piece as before, and returning, placed the cloak on the yogin's back.

After having served the yogin the evening meal, she led him to his room and said, 'Go and tell Good News to come before the lama.' I arrived and she gave me the seven ounces of gold. I asked, 'Where did this gold come from?' The lama's wife answered, 'It was in the yogin's cloak. Good News, you have a prudent mother. The region facing north *where the sun does not shine* means the cloak of the yogin that the sun does not penetrate. The *black hanging cloud* means the square of black cloth which is patched on it. *The constellation of the Pleiades* which will appear means the stars sewn with white thread. And underneath, *the seven houses of your cousins* means the seven ounces of gold. *If you do not understand, since the yogin lives in that region, ask no one else.* That means, If you do not understand, since the gold is in the yogin's cloak, do not look elsewhere.'

Thus spoke the lama's wife. And the lama said, 'You women! They say that you are full of guile. And it is very true.' And he laughed.

After that I gave a tenth of an ounce of gold to the yogin and he was satisfied. To the mistress of the house I offered seven-tenths of an ounce. Then I offered the lama three ounces of gold and said to him, 'You see that my old mother is also asking for a hailstorm. Please find it in your heart to teach me.'

The lama answered, 'If you want hailstorms, go and find Yungton Trögyel (Terrifying Conqueror) of Nyag.' And he gave me a letter and some gifts.

I left for the village of Kyorpo in the Yarlung. When I arrived before the lama, I laid at his feet three ounces of gold, the letter, and the gifts. I told him why I wished to send hailstorms. He asked me, 'Have you succeeded in making magic?'

I answered, 'I have been completely successful, and through magic thirty-five people have been killed. Now, in addition, this letter asks for hailstorms. Please find it in your heart to teach me.'

'Very well, so be it,' said the lama. And he gave me the secret formula. I went to perform the rites in my old cell.

Beginning with the seventh day, a cloud invaded the magic cell. Lightning flashed, thunder rumbled, and the voice of the Maroon-faced Dza was heard. This led me to believe that I could call forth hail with my fingertip.

Every now and then the lama asked me, 'So as to know when to send the hail, how high is the harvest now, in your village?'

And I replied, 'It is hardly sprouting.'

And some time later, 'It is hardly high enough to hide the wood-pigeons.'

The lama said, 'And now where is it?'

I replied, 'The wheat is just beginning to bend.'

'Then it is time to send the hailstorm,' said the lama.

He gave me as a companion the messenger who had already been to my village. Disguised as wandering monks, we set out.

In the country, the old people could not remember such a good year. They had made a harvesting law, forbidding anyone to harvest when he pleased. When we arrived, the harvest was to be reaped the following day and the day after. I established myself in the high country.

After I had repeated the incantations, a little cloud hardly as big as a sparrow drifted by. I was disappointed. I invoked the guardian deities by name. My pleas were based on the terrible treatment I had received from the villagers. I threw off my cloak and began to cry. Then, inconceivably huge black clouds suddenly gathered in the sky. They swept down in a single mass and in an instant the hailstones burst upon the harvest and covered the whole valley up to a height of three courses of brick. Deep gorges were cut into the mountains. Seeing the loss of the harvest, the villagers wept.

Suddenly there was a great wind mixed with rain. As my companion and I were cold, we went into a cave whose entrance faced north. There we made a fire of tamarisk and there we stayed.

Some men of the village were hunting for sacrificial meat for the harvest thanksgiving. And they said, 'This Good News has sent us a misfortune that no other could have sent. He has already slain so many men! Now, through his art, we no longer see anything of our magnificent harvest. If he fell into our hands we would tear out his still beating heart. And each of us would eat a piece of his flesh and drink a drop of his blood.'

They spoke thus because the wound in their hearts was incurable. As they talked in this way, coming back down the mountain, they happened to pass in front of the cave. An old man said, 'Silence! Silence! Speak softly! Smoke is coming out of the cave. Who can that be?'

'It is surely Good News. He has not seen us. If we men of the village do not kill him soon, he will surely succeed in destroying the whole region.' So saying they turned back.

My companion said to me, 'Leave ahead of me. I will pretend that I am you. I will tell them when leaving that this is my revenge. We will meet again four days' journey to the west at the caravanserai of Dingri.'

As he was conscious of his strength, he remained alone and without fear. At this moment, I longed to see my mother one more time, but, frightened of my enemies, I fled quickly and ran to Nyanang. Having been bitten in the leg by a dog, I could not arrive on time at the meeting place.

My companion, even though he was surrounded by the villagers, broke through their circle and escaped. The more they gained on him, the faster he ran but when they were outdistanced he slackened his pace. They were shooting at him with their weapons, and he returned blow for blow by hurling large stones.

He shouted at them, 'I will lay a curse on whoever ventures against me. How many men have I not already killed for revenge? And now what about your beautiful harvest which has disappeared? Is this not also my revenge? That being so, if you are not good to my mother and my sister, I will lay a curse on your whole region from the top of the valley to the bottom. Those who are not killed will see their line destroyed to the ninth generation. If death and desolation do not strike this country, it will not be my fault. Wait and see! Wait and see!'

Speaking thus, he moved away. And in fear they began to accuse one another, 'It was all your fault, it was all your fault.'

Quarreling among themselves, they turned back.

My companion reached Dingri ahead of me. He asked the keeper of the caravanserai if someone resembling a yogin had arrived. The keeper answered, 'He has not come. But all you so-called yogins are very fond of drinking. In the next village there is a beer banquet. Go there. If you have no cup, I can lend you one.' And he loaned him a wooden cup as deep and gray as the face of Yama, Lord of Death.

Having taken the cup with him, my companion went into the banquet hall and, since I was there at the end of the row of guests, he came and sat down beside me. He said to me, 'Why were you not at the meeting place yesterday?'

'Yesterday I went to beg. A dog bit my leg and I could not walk very fast. But there is nothing to worry about.'

Setting out again from the banquet, we arrived at Kyorpo in Yarlung.

The lama said to us, 'Well, you two, you have done good work!'

'No one has been here before us. Who told you of it?'

The lama answered, 'Guardian deities have come, their faces beaming like the full moon. I have thanked them.'

And speaking thus, the lama showed great joy.

This is the way I accumulated black deeds out of vengeance against my enemies.

Thus spoke the Master. This is the third chapter, that of the destruction of enemies. Such was the work of Milarepa in the world.

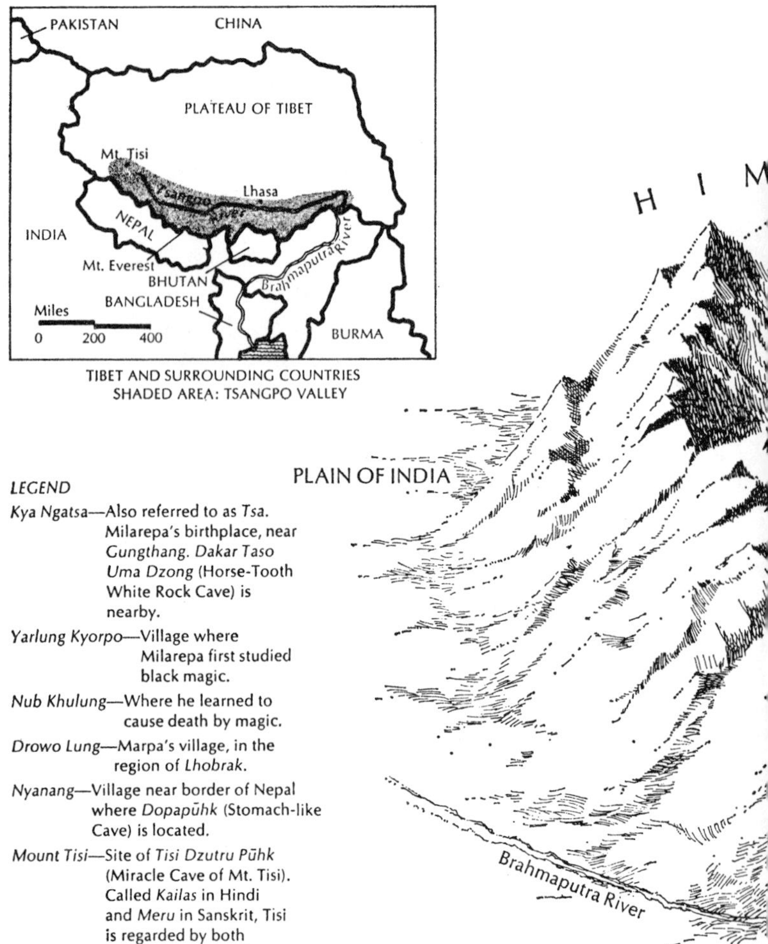

TIBET AND SURROUNDING COUNTRIES
SHADED AREA: TSANGPO VALLEY

LEGEND

Kya Ngatsa—Also referred to as *Tsa.* Milarepa's birthplace, near *Gungthang. Dakar Taso Uma Dzong* (Horse-Tooth White Rock Cave) is nearby.

Yarlung Kyorpo—Village where Milarepa first studied black magic.

Nub Khulung—Where he learned to cause death by magic.

Drowo Lung—Marpa's village, in the region of *Lhobrak.*

Nyanang—Village near border of Nepal where *Dopapūhk* (Stomach-like Cave) is located.

Mount Tisi—Site of *Tisi Dzutru Pūhk* (Miracle Cave of Mt. Tisi). Called *Kailas* in Hindi and *Meru* in Sanskrit, Tisi is regarded by both Buddhists and Hindus as the center of the world.

Lachi Gangra—Region near Mount Everest. *Kyungi Gonga* (Great Cave of the Conquered Demon) is in this area.

Langda—Village where Milarepa was seen flying.

Dingri—District where many of Milarepa's caves are located.

Drin—Where Milarepa accepted the poisoned drink.

Chuwar—Where Milarepa died. *Chuwar* is in the village of *Drin.*

(Note—The Tsangpo River becomes the Brahmaputra River in East India.)

VALLEY OF THE TSANGPO RIVER
IN
SOUTHERN TIBET

SECOND PART

The second part, consisting of nine chapters, shows how Milarepa worked his way toward the supreme peace of nirvana.

First Chapter: Disgust and remorse will make him search for a truly perfected lama.

Second Chapter: When he has found him and submits to his discipline, he will undergo such incredible ordeals that he will be entirely cleansed of the impurity of evil deeds and mental defilements.

Third Chapter: Then, having gained the lama's affection, he will obtain from him the teaching and the methods leading to Enlightenment.

Fourth Chapter: Meditating in the very presence of the lama, he will experience the dawn of awakening.

Fifth Chapter: After he perfects the practice of these teachings, he seeks out the secret instructions as commanded in a dream. He then leaves the lama.

Sixth Chapter: Meeting new evidence of the vanity of the world, he vows to devote himself to meditation.

Seventh Chapter: In order to carry out the instructions of the lama, he abandons all attachment to worldly life and devotes himself wholly to meditation and intense asceticism in mountain solitude.

Eighth Chapter: By thus meditating, his experience of awakening will lead to perfection. As a result of his achievement he will bring benefit to the teaching and to all sentient beings.

Ninth Chapter: Having completed all the activities of an Enlightened Being, he will dissolve his body into All-Encompassing Space in order to arouse a spiritual impulse in all human beings.

First Chapter

The Seeking of the Dharma

Then Retchung asked, 'O lama, you spoke of having done white deeds, and no deeds are worthier than those devoted to the Dharma. How, Master, did you first encounter the teaching?' And the Venerable One continued thus:

I was filled with remorse for the evil I had done by magic and by hailstorms. My longing for the teaching so obsessed me that I forgot to eat. If I went out, I wanted to stay in. If I stayed in, I wanted to go out. At night sleep escaped me. I dared not confess my sadness to the lama or my longing for liberation. While I remained in the lama's service, I asked myself unceasingly and passionately by what means I might practice the true teaching.

At that time, the lama continuously received provisions and other necessities from a wealthy landowner. This landowner was stricken by a terrible illness. The lama was the first to be called to look after him, and three days later he returned, silent and downcast. I asked him, 'O Master, why this silence and this sad face?'

The lama replied, 'All composite things are impermanent. Yesterday my very kind benefactor died. That is why the cycle of birth and death troubles my heart. But above all I am old. And from the white teeth of my youth to the white hairs of my old age, I have done harm to many beings by evil spells, magic, and hailstorms. You also, though young, have accumulated crimes of magic and hailstorms. These crimes, too, will be on my head.'

I asked, 'Have you not in some way helped these victims to reach higher realms and attain liberation?'

The lama replied, 'All sentient beings have the Buddha-nature within them. I know theoretically how to lead them to higher realms and liberation, but when conditions arise which test my actual attainment, I only remember words and ideas. I have no confidence in my ability to help beings. But now I am going to practice the Dharma to be able to meet any circumstances that arise.

Either you must take over the guidance of my disciples so that I can devote myself to the practice leading to the higher realms and liberation, or you must practice the Dharma yourself and help us all achieve the higher realms and liberation. Meanwhile I shall support you with all the provisions you need.'

Thus my wish was fulfilled and I answered that I would practice the Dharma myself.

'Well then,' said the lama, 'since you are young, since your ardor and your faith are so great, practice the purest of all Dharma.'

And he gave me a yak with a load of woolen cloth from Yarlung.

Then he said to me, 'In the village called Nar in the Tsangrong, there is a lama called Rongton Lhaga (Joy of Gods). His knowledge of the teaching of Dzogchen (Great Perfection) has led him to the goal. Go there and have this teaching explained to you and purify yourself.'

Following the lama's instructions, I went to Nar in the Tsangrong and made inquiries.

The lama's wife and some monks who were there said to me, 'This is the mother monastery. The Lama Rongton Lhaga is not here at the moment. He is at the son monastery on the mountain of Upper Nyang.'

'Very well,' I said, 'I am a messenger sent by the Lama Yungton Trögyel. Help me find your lama.'

I told them my whole story. The lama's wife asked a monk to guide me to the lama, and I met him at Rinang in the Upper Nyang. I offered him my yak and the woolen cloth as gifts.

After paying my respects, I said, 'The one who comes to you is a great sinner. Grant me the teaching in this life which will deliver me from the cycle of existence.'

The lama replied, 'This Teaching of the Great Perfection[1] leads one to triumph at the root, to triumph at the summit, and to triumph in the fruits of achievement. To meditate on it by day is to be Buddha in one day. To meditate on it by night is to be Buddha in one night. For those fortunate ones with favorable karma who merely chance to hear it, without even meditating on it, this joyous teaching is a sure means of liberation. That is why I wish to give it to you.'

And the lama gave me initiation and instruction.

Then I thought, 'In the past, I attained great results with spells in fourteen days. Seven days were enough for the hailstorms. But here is a way to attain enlightenment that is even easier than sending hailstorms and death through magic. If I meditate on it by night I will be purified in one night, if I meditate on it by day I will be purified in one day. Through this meeting, I, too, have become one of these fortunate Bodhisattvas who, having heard the teaching, do not even have to meditate on it.' Triumphant, and thinking in this way, without meditating, I spent the time sleeping. So I put religion on one side and the human condition on the other, and at the end of a few days the lama said to me, 'When you first paid your respects to me, you told me you came as a great sinner. That is quite true. Proud of my teaching, I have spoken to you too soon. I am not able to guide you to liberation. Go to the monastery of Drowo Lung (Valley of the Birches) in the southern province of Lhobrak. There lives the renowned Marpa, personal disciple of the Great Master Naropa of India, saint of the new esoteric order and king of translators, who has no equal in the three realms. You and he have had karmic links in the past. That is why you should go to him.'

Hardly had I heard the name of Marpa the Translator than I was filled with ineffable happiness. In my joy every hair on my body vibrated. I sobbed with fervent adoration. Locking my whole mind in a single thought, I set out with provisions and a book. Without being distracted by any other thoughts, I ceaselessly repeated to myself, 'When? When will I see the lama face to face?'

The night before my arrival at Drowo Lung, Marpa saw the Great Master Naropa in a dream. The latter blessed him. He gave him a slightly tarnished, five-pronged vajra [scepter] made of lapis lazuli. At the same time he gave him a golden vase filled with nectar and told him, 'With the water in this vase wash the dirt from the vajra, then mount it on top of the banner-of-victory.[2] This will please the Buddhas of the past and make all sentient beings happy, thus fulfilling both your aim and that of others.'

Then Naropa vanished. Following the instructions of his Master, Marpa washed the vajra with water from the vase, and mounted it on top of the banner-of-victory. Then the brilliance of this vajra lit up the whole universe. Immediately the six classes of beings,[3] struck with wonder by its light, were freed from sorrow and filled with happiness. They prostrated themselves and paid reverence to the Venerable Marpa and his banner-of-victory, which had been consecrated by the Buddhas of the past.

Somewhat surprised by this dream, Marpa awoke. He was filled with joy and love. At this moment his wife came to serve him a hot morning drink and said, 'O Lama, last night I had a dream. Two women who said they came from Ugyen in the north were carrying a crystal stupa.[4] This stupa had some impurities on its surface. And the women said, "Naropa commands the lama to consecrate this stupa and to place it on the summit of a mountain." And you yourself cried out, "Although the consecration of this stupa has already been accomplished by Master Naropa, I must obey his command." And you washed the stupa with the lustral water in the vase and performed the consecration. Afterward you placed it on the mountaintop, where it radiated a multitude of lights as dazzling as the sun and moon and where it projected numerous replicas of itself upon the mountaintops. And the two women watched over these stupas. Such was my dream. What is its meaning?'

Marpa thought to himself, 'These dreams are very much in accord,' and his heart was filled with extreme joy, but to his wife he only said, 'I do not know the meaning since dreams have no source. Now I am going to plow the field near the road. Prepare what I need.'

His wife replied, 'But that is a work for laborers. If you, a great lama, do this work everyone will ridicule us. Therefore, I beg of you, do not go.'

The lama paid no attention to her. 'Bring me plenty of beer,' he said. And he picked up a full jar, adding, 'I will drink this beer. Bring more for a guest.'

He took another full jar, and departed. When he reached the field he buried it in the earth and covered it with his hat. Then, while plowing the field, he watched the road. And having drunk his beer, he waited.

In the meantime, I was on my way. Starting from the lower part of the Lhobrak (Southern Cliffs), I began asking all passers-by where great Marpa the Translator lived. But no one knew him. As I reached the pass from where one could see the monastery of Drowo Lung, I put the same question to a man who was passing.

He replied, 'There is certainly a man called Marpa. But there is no one called great Marpa the Translator.'

'Then where is Drowo Lung?'

He pointed it out and I asked him again, 'Who lives in Drowo Lung?'

'The man called Marpa lives there.'

'And he has no other name?'

'Some call him Lama Marpa.'

'Then that must be where the lama lives. And this pass, what is it called?'

'It is called Chola Gang (the Ridge of Religion).'

I continued on my way, still inquiring. There were many shepherds and I questioned them. The old ones answered that they did not know. Among them was a child with a pleasant face, well-oiled hair, and good clothes. He spoke well and said, 'Do you speak of my father? If so, he bought gold with all our wealth and went to India with it. He brought back many books studded with precious stones. Usually he does not work, but today he is plowing his field.'

I thought to myself, 'From what the child says it seems to be the lama, but would a great translator be plowing his field?' And I continued on my way.

At the side of the road, a tall and corpulent monk, with large eyes and awesome look, was plowing a field. I had scarcely seen him when I was filled with unutterable joy and inconceivable bliss. Stunned for a moment by this vision, I remained motionless. Then I said, 'Master, I have heard that the learned Marpa the Translator, personal disciple of the glorious Naropa, dwells in this region. Where is his house?' For a long time he looked at me from head to foot. Then he said, 'Who are you?'

I replied, 'I am a great sinner and I come from the Upper Tsang. Marpa is so renowned that I have come to beg for his teaching.'

'Very well, I shall arrange for you to meet Marpa. Meanwhile, plow the field.'

He took from the ground the jar of beer which he had hidden under his hat and gave it to me. This beer was refreshing and very good.

'Work hard,' he added, and went away.

Having drunk all the beer that remained, I worked with a will. Some time later the young child, who had spoken to me from the midst of the flocks, came to fetch me.

Much to my joy, he said, 'Come to the house and serve the lama.'

As he was impatient to introduce me to the lama, I said to him,

'I am anxious to finish this work.' So I plowed the part which remained to be done. As this field had been the occasion of my meeting with the lama I called it Tūhngken (Field of Opportunity). In summer the footpath runs along the edge of the field, but it goes straight across it in winter.

I joined the child and went into the house. The same monk whom I had met a short time before was seated with a pillow at his back on two square cushions that were covered with a rug. He had wiped his face but his eyebrows, his nostrils, his moustache, and his beard were still covered with dust and he was eating his meal.

I thought, 'This is the same monk as before. Where can the lama be?' Then the lama said, 'It is true that you do not know me. I am Marpa. Prostrate yourself!'

So I bowed down at his feet. 'Lama Rimpoche,[5] I am a great sinner from Nyima Latö.[6] I offer you my body, speech, and mind. I ask for food, clothing, and the teaching. Please teach me the way which leads to Enlightenment in this lifetime.'

The lama replied, 'I don't want to hear your ravings about being a great sinner. I have not made you commit any sins. What sins have you committed?'

Then I confessed fully the story of my crimes. The lama said to me, 'So, you have done all that. In any case, it is good that you offer your body, speech, and mind. But I will not give you food and clothing as well as the teaching. I will give you food and clothing, but you will have to ask another for the teaching. Or, if I give you the teaching, look elsewhere for food and clothing. Choose between the two. But if you choose the teaching, then whether or not you reach Enlightenment in this life will depend solely on your own striving.'

I replied, 'Well, since I came to you for the teaching, I will look elsewhere for food and clothing.'

As I was placing my book in his shrine room, he said, 'Take that filthy book away; it would defile my sacred objects and my shrine.'

'He responds in this way,' I thought, 'because my book contains black magic.'

Carefully, I put it away. I remained with Marpa for several more days. The lama's wife gave me good meals.

Thus spoke Milarepa. Such was the way he met his Master. This is the first chapter describing his good works.

Second Chapter

Ordeals

I went begging throughout the entire valley. In this way I collected twenty-one measures of barley. With fourteen measures I bought a cooking pot with four handles, free of rust, smooth inside and out. With one measure I bought meat and beer, and the remaining measures I poured into a big sack. Then, carrying the cooking pot on top of everything, I returned to the lama's dwelling.

Trembling with fatigue, I dropped the heavy load and the room shook. The lama, who was eating his meal, was so startled he stopped eating.

'Little man,' he said, 'you are too energetic! Do you also intend to bury us under the ruins of the house with your magic? You are obnoxious! Take your barley away.'

And he pushed it away with his foot. While I was dragging the sack outside, I said to myself simply and without evil thought, 'This lama is irritable! I will have to watch my behavior and my way of serving him.' Returning and prostrating myself, I offered him my empty cooking pot. He took it in his hands and held it for a moment, his eyes pensive. Tears fell from his eyes, and he said, 'Your gift is auspicious. I offer it to the Great Master Naropa.'

Marpa raised it in offering. Shaking the handles of the vessel in order to appraise the sound, he made it ring and carried it into his shrine room. He filled it with melted butter from the altar lamps. At this moment I was overcome with emotion and was burning with desire for religion. Again, I begged the lama to instruct me.

He replied, 'Faithful disciples come to me in large numbers from Ü and Tsang. The inhabitants in Yadrok Taklung and those of Ling attack them and steal their provisions and their gifts. Bury these two regions in hail. This will be religious work. Afterward, I shall instruct you.'

I sent a fierce hailstorm to these two regions. Then I asked the lama to instruct me. The lama replied, 'For the few hailstones you have sent, am I to give you a teaching which I have brought back from India with such great difficulty? You want my teaching ... Well then, the mountaineers at Lhobrak Pass attack my disciples coming from Nyal Loro. They laugh at me. You, who call yourself a great magician, cast your spells upon these mountaineers, and if you prove your magic, I shall give you the teaching of Naropa to attain Enlightenment in one life and one body.'

After I had cast my spells, the mountaineers fought among themselves and many of the more belligerent perished by the sword. At the sight of this the lama said, 'It is true that you are a great magician.' From then on he called me Great Magician.

I asked for the teaching on Enlightenment. But he replied, 'Ha! Is it to reward your many crimes that I went to India at the risk of my life? You say you want these teachings which are the living breath of the dakinis and for which, disdaining riches, I offered gold without measure. I hope you are only joking! Anyone else would kill you for that! Now restore the harvest in the land of Yadrok and heal the mountaineers; after that I will teach you. But never come back if you cannot do this.'

In this harsh way the lama rebuked me. Overcome with sorrow, I wept. The lama's wife consoled me.

The next day the lama himself came and said to me, 'Last evening I was very hard on you, but do not be distressed. Be patient. Teaching is very slow work. You have the energy to work, so build a tower which I will give to my son, Darma Doday (Young Man of Sutra). When you have done that I will instruct you and I will supply your food and clothing.'

'During this time, if I die without religion, what will become of me?'

'I guarantee that you will not die during this time. My teaching can be expressed in a few words. If you can meditate with perseverance according to my instructions, you will show whether you can or cannot attain Enlightenment in this life. In my lineage an enlightening energy is transmitted which has no similarity to that of others.'

After these comforting words, I was filled with joy.

Then I said, 'Do you wish to tell me about the plan of the tower?'

All the cousins on Marpa's paternal side had taken an oath among themselves not to build any fortifications. But Marpa had not taken the oath. Now as he was thinking of building a tower, he found at the same time a way to deceive his relatives and a way for me to expiate my evil deeds.

And he said to me, 'Build a tower like this on the eastern crest of the mountain.'

And so I began building a round tower.

When I had half finished, the lama came and said, 'The other day I had not fully considered the matter. Tear down this tower and take the earth and stones back to their places.'

This I did. Another time, on the western crest of the mountain, the lama pretended to be drunk and said to me, 'Make a tower similar to this.'

And so I made a semicircular tower. It was hardly half finished when the lama came back and said, 'It is not yet right. Tear it down and carry the earth and stones back to where you got them.'

This time we went to the top of the mountain to the north and the lama said to me, 'Great Magician, the other day I was drunk and did not give you good direction. Build a sturdy tower here.'

I replied, 'To tear something down while it is being built makes me miserable and is a waste of your wealth. Please think carefully beforehand!'

The lama replied, 'Today I am not drunk. I have thought about it very carefully. This tower will be called Tower of the Tantric Yogin. It should be triangular. Build it. It will not be torn down.'

I began to build a triangular tower. About a third of it had been completed when the lama came and said, 'Great Magician, for whom are you building this tower? Who gave you the instructions?'

'It was the lama himself who ordered this tower for his son.'

'I do not remember having given you such orders. If you are right, I must be crazy. Have I completely lost my mind?'

'I clearly remember suspecting it would be like this and respectfully asking you to think about it carefully. You replied it was fully thought out and that this tower would not be demolished.'

'Very well then, who is your witness? Perhaps you are thinking of shutting us up in your triangular tower, as in a magic triangle, and casting spells on us; yet we have not robbed you of your patrimony, we have not eaten up your father's goods. If that is not so and if you wish for religion, since you have displeased the gods of the region, go and put this earth and these stones back in their places. Afterward, if you want the teaching, I will give it to you. If you will not do this, then leave.'

As he spoke, he was roused to anger.

Overwhelmed by grief and still thirsting for religion, I obeyed. I carried back from the triangular tower, to their places, first the earth and then the stones. It was then that I got a sore on my shoulders. I thought, 'If I show it to the lama, he will only revile me. If I show it to his wife, I will appear to be critical of my task.' And without showing my sore, I tearfully implored the wife of the lama to help me obtain the teaching. The mother went before the lama and said to him, 'The useless work on those towers has only brought grief to Great Magician. Have compassion and grant him the teaching.'

The lama replied, 'Prepare him a good meal and bring him to me.'

The mother prepared the meal and brought me before the lama, who said, 'Great Magician, do not tell lies about something I have not done. Since you desire the teaching, I will give it to you.'

He gave me an exposition on the Triple Refuge and the basic precepts. And he continued, 'This is the general law for everyone. But if you want the secret teaching, here is what must be done.'

And he told me the story of Naropa's liberation and of the way he underwent his terrible ordeals.

'For you this way will be difficult.'

As he was speaking these words, my faith increased so that I shed tears. I swore to carry out everything the lama asked of me.

After several days had passed, the lama took me for a walk. We came to the land protected by the cousins.

The lama said to me, 'Build in this place a square white tower nine stories high with a superstructure and a pinnacle, forming ten stories. It will never be torn down. When you have finished, I will give you the secret teaching. Then you may retire to meditate and during your retreat I will provide for your sustenance.'

'Then,' said I, 'would it not be good for the lama's wife to be witness to all these promises?'

'Very well,' said the lama.

Then he traced on the ground the placement of the walls. I invited the lama's wife to come, and in their presence I said, 'I have already built three towers and have destroyed them. The first time the lama said he had not given it enough thought. The second time he said he was drunk. The third time he wondered if he were crazy, or if he had lost his mind and no longer remembered anything. When I reminded him of the instructions he had given me, he asked me who was my witness and moreover he heaped reproaches upon me. Now that I have called you to hear these new promises, please be my witness.'

The lama's wife replied, 'I am glad to be a witness. But it will be difficult to have my testimony upheld since the lama is very autocratic. First of all, the lama builds without reason and destroys without reason. Furthermore, this land does not belong to us alone; it belongs to the cousins as well. That will be a cause for quarrels. No matter what I say, the father will not listen.'

The lama said to his wife, 'You bear witness. As for me, I will act according to my promise. Great Magician, if you have no trust and if you will not make a pledge, then go away.'

So I laid the foundations for a square tower. While I was putting up the wall, the disciples Ngokton of Shung, Tshurton of Döl, and Metön of Tsangrong playfully rolled a large rock in my direction and placed it as the cornerstone.

When I had built to the second story on both sides of the large door, the lama came and carefully inspected everything. Pointing a finger at the large boulder that had been rolled into place by the three disciples, he said, 'Great Magician, where did this stone come from?'

I replied, 'Your three foremost disciples brought it here for their amusement.'

'Well, you must not put one of their stones in the structure you are building. So take it out and put it where it was.'

'You promised that this tower would not be destroyed.'

'Quite right. Yet it is not fitting for you to be served by my disciples who are practicing the two advanced stages. Do not demolish everything, but take away the stone and put it back where it was.'

Then I demolished the building from the top down and returned the rock to its place.

'Now,' said the lama, 'fetch the stone again and put it back as the cornerstone.'

I put it back. Alone, I had to exert as much strength as the three disciples. Because I had carried away the stone myself and brought it back, I named this stone My Giant Stone.

While I was laying the foundations of the tower on the crest of the mountain, the cousins took counsel and said, 'Marpa is building a tower on the Mountain of Solemn Oath. We must safeguard our land.'

Some of them said, 'Marpa has gone crazy. He has a novice from Latö with great strength who is building towers with no definite plan on every hillock and ridge. When half finished, he demolishes the towers and returns the earth and stones to their places. Likewise he will demolish this one. If he does not tear it down, we can then prevent him from continuing. Let us see what he is going to do.'

Far from demolishing it, I continued to build the tower. By the time I reached the seventh story, I had a sore on my back. The cousins then said, 'This time he is not going to tear it down. The destruction of the previous towers was only a ruse hiding the intent to build this one. We will demolish it ourselves.'

They prepared for war. Then the lama conjured up some phantom soldiers, clad in armor, and put them everywhere, inside and outside the tower. His enemies said, 'Where did Marpa get all these soldiers?'

Filled with terror, they dared not attack, but each one in secret prostrated himself and offered his respects, and they all became benefactors and disciples of Marpa.

At that time, the great Metön of Tsangrong came to request the Yidam Chakrasamvara[1] initiation.

The lama's wife said to me, 'Now try by every means to obtain the teaching.'

In my heart I thought, 'Now that I have built this tower without anyone else bringing a single stone – even the size of a goat's head – a single basket of earth, a single bucket of water, or a single hodful of mortar, I am going to receive the initiation.'

Then, after having greeted the lama, I sat down with the others. The lama called to me, 'Great Magician, what gift do you bring me?'

I answered, 'I rendered you homage by building the tower for your son. You promised to give me initiation and instruction. That is why I am here.'

'You made a little tower which isn't even as thick as my arm. It is hardly worth the Doctrine which I, with great difficulty, brought all the way from India. If you have the price of my teaching, give it to me. Otherwise do not stay here among the initiates of the secret teaching.'

Speaking thus, the lama slapped me, grabbed me by the hair, and threw me out. I wanted to die and I wept the whole night. The lama's wife came to console me.

'The lama has always said that the teachings were brought back by him from India for the good of all sentient beings. Were even a dog to present itself to him, he would teach it the Doctrine, and dedicate the merits of the teaching for the benefit of all. Why he refuses you, I do not know. In any case, do not have bad thoughts because of it.'

Having cheered me up, she left. The next morning the lama himself came. 'Great Magician, do not continue with the tower. Build a shrine room at the base of the tower surrounded by a covered walk with twelve columns. Then I will give you the secret teaching.'

I laid the foundations and built the covered walk. All the while the lama's wife brought me well-seasoned food and so much beer that I became a little drunk. She was full of goodness and she comforted me.

When I was about to finish, Tshurtön Ouangnye of Döl came to ask for the Guhyasamaja[2] initiation.

The lama's wife said to me, 'Now, my son, you should be able to receive the initiation.'

And she gave me a tub of butter, a piece of cloth, and a small copper cooking pot to give to the lama.

Having offered my gifts, I joined the others. The lama asked me, 'Great Magician, what gift have you brought that you place yourself in these ranks?'

'This tub of butter, this piece of cloth, and this copper cooking pot.'

'These things have already been given to me by someone else. Do not give me my own goods! If you have something of your own to give, go and fetch it. If not, do not remain here.'

And, getting up, he cursed me, kicked me, and threw me out.

I wanted to sink into the earth.

Was this punishment for the murders I had committed through sorcery and for the destruction of numerous crops by my hailstorms? Did the lama know that I would never be able to practice the Dharma?[3] Or was it through lack of compassion that he would not teach me? Whatever it may be, of what use is this human body which, without religion, only accumulates defilement? Should I kill myself?

At that moment the lama's wife brought me a portion of the sacrificial cake. She consoled me very much and went away. But I had no desire to eat, and spent the whole night weeping.

The next morning the lama came and said, 'Now finish building the covered walk and the tower. Afterward I will give you initiation and instruction.'

Then I finished the tower and undertook the completion of the covered walk. By that time I had sores on my back. Pus and blood ran from three wounds. I showed my back, which was one mass of sores, to the lama's wife. I begged her to come to my rescue, to ask the lama to teach me and to remind him of the promises he made at the time of laying the foundation of the tower. The mother looked with concern at my sores, and tears poured from her eyes.

'I am going to speak to the lama,' she said.

And going before the lama, she spoke in this way: 'Lama Rimpoche, the work Great Magician is doing has skinned and rubbed all his limbs raw. On his back are three sores streaming with blood and pus. I have heard of, and even seen, horses and donkeys with sores on their backs, but I have never yet seen, nor heard of, such sores on the backs of men. I would be ashamed if other men were to see or hear of such a thing. I am even more ashamed, knowing it was caused by a great lama such as yourself. Because he is truly worthy of compassion, give this child instruction. You said in the beginning that you would give him the teaching when he had built the tower.'

The lama replied, 'That is just what I said. I said that I would give him my teaching when he had built a tower ten stories high. Where are the ten stories?'

'He has built more than the ten stories. He has constructed a lower covered walk.'

'Do not talk so much. If he builds ten stories I will instruct him. Does he really have sores?'

'Not only does he have sores but there is almost nothing left of his back but sores. But you have so much power you can do whatever pleases you.'

Having thus spoken, with great sorrow, she then hastened to me. 'Well then, you had better come with me,' she said.

On the way I thought, 'Is he going to instruct me?'

The lama said to me, 'Great Magician, show me your back.'

I showed it to him and when he had finished examining it carefully, he said, 'My Master Naropa underwent twenty-four mortifications,[4] twelve great and twelve minor trials, all of which surpass yours. As for me, without a thought for my life or my wealth, I gave both to my Master Naropa. So if you seek the teaching, be humble and continue the work on the tower.'

I thought to myself that he was right.

From my clothing he made a pad to protect my wounds and said, 'Since you work in the manner of horses and donkeys, use this pad for your wounds and continue to carry the earth and stones.'

I answered, 'How will the pad for the wounds cure the sores on my back?'

'The pad is to keep the dirt away from your sores.'

Thinking this was an order, I carried the earth in a vessel which I held in front of me, and, as I was making mortar, the lama saw me and thought, 'This submission to everything that is commanded is extraordinary.' And he secretly shed tears.

My sores became infected and I fell ill. I told this to the lama's wife. On my behalf she asked that I be initiated or, at least, that I be permitted to rest and heal my sores.

The lama replied, 'As long as the tower is not finished, he shall have nothing. If he can work, let him do what he can; if he cannot, then let him rest.'

The mother said to me, 'As long as your sores are not healed, rest.'

She fortified me with good food and drink during this time. For a few days I was happy except for my grief at not having obtained instruction. While my sores were healing, the lama came to me and without speaking of the Doctrine, said, 'Great Magician, it is time for you to go back to work on the tower.'

I was about to do this when the lama's wife said to me, 'Between the two of us, let us work out a scheme for you to get the teaching.'

Having reached an agreement with her, I tied my book and few possessions on top of a little sack of flour, as if I were leaving. In order to be seen by the lama, I asked his wife to help me.

She said in a loud voice, 'If you ask the lama, he will give you the teaching. Stay here despite everything.' And she pretended to restrain me.

Seeing this, the lama asked, 'Woman, what are you two doing there?'

She answered, 'Great Magician says that long ago he came from a far-off village to learn the teaching. Instead of the teaching, he has received only abusive words and blows. For fear of dying without religion, he is going to look for another lama and is taking his belongings with him. Thanks to my pleas and promises that he would obtain the teaching, I have been able to delay his departure.'

The lama said, 'I understand.' And he came out and slapped me again and again.

'When you arrived here you at once gave me your body, speech, and mind. And now where are you going? Surely you are not leaving? Since you belong to me, I could cut you, body, speech, and mind, into a hundred pieces. If in spite of that you are going away, tell me, why are you taking my flour?'

Speaking in this manner, he kept slapping me. He grabbed the sack of flour and took it into the house. My despair was like that of a mother who has lost her only son. Following the advice of the lama's wife, and because the lama was so terrible, I went back into the house trembling, and began to weep.

The lama's wife said to me, 'Whatever we may try, the lama will not give you the teaching now, but in the end he will surely give it to you. Meanwhile, I will instruct you.'

She gave me the method for meditating on Dorje Pahgmo.[5] It brought me no inner experience but was very beneficial to my mind and it lifted my spirits. I showed my gratitude to the lama's wife for her kindness.

I thought that she, being the wife of the lama, could purify sins. In the summer when she was milking cows, I held the bucket for her. When she roasted grain, I held the pans for her. Thus everywhere I rendered her service.

At that time I dreamed of looking for another lama. I thought to myself, 'If Marpa does not have the teaching for becoming a Buddha in a single lifetime and single body, certainly no other lama will have it. Even if I do not become Buddha at once, at least I have stopped accumulating actions which lead to rebirth in the lower realms. When I have suffered in the name of religion the same trials as Naropa, the lama will proclaim with great joy that I have become worthy of the teaching. Then I will meditate on it and hope in this way to attain Enlightenment in this lifetime.' Having thought it over, I began bringing up stones and earth.

As I was mixing mortar for the covered walk and shrine room, Ngokton Chodor of Shung and his followers, bringing numerous presents, came to ask for the great initiation of Hevajra.[6]

The lama's wife said to me, 'If the lama is not satisfied with the tower that has been constructed and if he desires riches, offer him a gift and make sure that he grants you the initiation.'

She gave me a large deep blue turquoise that she had kept secretly and said, 'You ask him first, and offer him this. If he refuses, I shall ask for you.'

I offered it to the lama, saying, 'I beg of you, give me instruction on this occasion.'

And I stood among the disciples. The lama examined the turquoise, turning it over and over.

'Where did Great Magician get this?'

I answered, 'The mother gave it to me.'

The lama smiled and said, 'Go and fetch the mistress.'

I begged the mother to come.

The lama said to her, 'Mistress, where did we get this turquoise?'

Having bowed deeply, the mother replied, 'This turquoise is not your concern. When I was given to you in marriage by my parents you flew into a furious rage. Then my parents secretly gave me this turquoise and said to me, "Put this away without showing it to anyone. If ever you and your husband divorce, you may need it." I have given it to this child, for whom I feel unbearable pity. Accept it and grant the initiation to Great Magician. Lama Ngokpa,* you and your followers, who understand his grief at being excluded from initiation, help me in my prayer.'

So saying, she prostrated herself many times. The lama was so terrifying that Ngokpa and his followers did not even dare utter a prayer. They merely made gestures of approval and prostrated themselves along with the lama's wife.

The lama said, 'Through the good offices of my wife, this fine turquoise nearly fell into the hands of a stranger.'

And, tying it around his neck, he continued, 'Mistress, you do not think. If I am wholly your master, I am also the master of your turquoise. Great Magician, if you have some wealth, bring it, and be initiated. This turquoise is mine.'

* Lama Ngokpa is another form of the name Ngokton Chodor of Shung.

Thinking that the mother, in her ardor, would renew he prayer after offering the turquoise, I remained where I was. But the lama was furious and jumped up! 'I sent you away, yet you are still here. What insolence!'

He hurled me to the ground on my face, and everything went black. He threw me on my back and I saw stars. Then he seized a stick, but Ngokpa held him back. Terrified, I jumped down into the courtyard. Although the lama was concerned, he pretended he was still angry.

I was not hurt, but was filled with grief and longed to die. Then the wife of the lama came up to me in tears, saying, 'Great Magician, do not be distressed. There is no disciple more faithful or loving than you. If you want to go to another lama for the Doctrine, I shall prepare whatever is necessary for you. I will give you supplies and gifts.' In this way she comforted me.

Up till then, the mistress had wanted to take part in all the lama's gatherings. But this evening she came and wept with me all through the night.

The next morning the lama sent for me. I went to him, wondering whether he would instruct me. He asked, 'Are you not dissatisfied by my refusal to teach you? Do you not have evil thoughts?'

'I have faith in the lama,' I answered, 'and I have not uttered a single word of rebellion. On the contrary, I believe that I am in darkness on account of my sins. I am the author of my own misery.' I wept. And he continued, 'What do you expect to gain from me by these tears? Get out!'

Then in a state of heart-rending misery I thought to myself, 'I had provisions when I was committing sins. Now that I am practicing religion, I have nothing. If I had even half the gold that I gave away to do evil deeds, I could obtain initiation and the secret teaching. Now, without gifts, this lama will not teach me. Even were I to go to another lama, he too would require gifts. Religion is forbidden to the poor. Without religion, a man is only an accumulator of sins and I would do better to kill myself. What to do? What to do? Shall I go and serve a rich man? Shall I earn wages and obtain gifts to offer for the teaching? Since I did cast my spells, should I now return to my village? My mother would be happy to see me again, and I would be able to earn some money. Either I must search for some other place or seek wealth.'

I thought to myself, 'If I take the lama's flour for provisions it will only enrage him more.' I took my books and left without saying anything, even to the lama's wife. On the way, I remembered her kindness and I cherished it.

Half a day's march from Drowo Lung I stopped to take my meal. I begged for some tsampa and borrowed a pot. Gathering some dry wood, I cooked my meal and ate it. It was now past mid-day and I thought, 'Half my work was service due the lama; the other half was payment for my food. Preparing this one meal was difficult for me. The lama's wife cooked and served my food every day, and I did not even say goodbye to her, evil man that I am! Should I go back?'

But I did not have the courage to go back. As I was returning the cooking pot, an old man said to me, 'Young man, you seem fit for work. Rather than beg, go into homes and recite prayers if you know how to read. If you do not know how to read, work as a servant for food and clothing. Can you read?'

I replied, 'I am not a beggar, and I know how to read.'

'Good. Go and recite the prayers at my house, and I will pay you well.'

I was overjoyed. And while staying there I read the Eight Thousand Stanzas.[7] I then read the story of Taktugnu[8] (Who Weeps Perpetually). I thought, 'Taktugnu, who was also without money, gave his body and his life for religion. He would have torn out his heart and sold it, he would have cut it into pieces. Compared to him, I have given nothing for religion. It is possible Lama Marpa may give me the teaching. If he does not give it to me, his wife has promised to help me meet another master.' This thought gave me courage to return, and I started back.

When I had left the lama, his wife said to him, 'Your indomitable enemy has gone. Now are you happy?'

'Who has gone?'

'Well, upon whom else but Great Magician have you inflicted every misery and whom else have you treated like an enemy?'

At these words, the lama's face clouded and became wet with tears. 'Lamas of the Kagyü[9] Order, dakinis, and protectors of religion, bring back my predestined son.'

Having prayed, he covered his head with his cloak and remained motionless.

At that moment I came before the lama's wife and greeted her. Joyously she cried out, 'Here you are at just the right moment. It appears that the lama will now teach you. I told him of your departure, and he cried out, "Give me back my predestined son." Then he burst into tears. It seems you have softened his heart.'

I thought to myself, 'The mistress is only soothing my heart. If it were really true that he had shed tears, that he had said "predestined son," I would be completely happy. If, on the contrary, he had merely said "Bring him back to me" in the way he has previously refused me initiation and instruction, then I am indeed unfortunate. I have nowhere else to go. Must I be miserable here, without ever obtaining the teaching?'

The mother said to the lama, 'Great Magician has not left us. He has returned. May he come before you?'

The lama replied, 'He did forsake us, but he has not forsaken himself. If you wish, let him come.'

I came before him, and he said, 'Great Magician, if from the bottom of your heart you wish for religion with such impatience and restlessness, you must give your life for it. Complete the three remaining stories of the tower and I will give you the teaching. Otherwise, since it is costly to feed you and since you have somewhere to go to, go now.'

There was nothing I could say, so I left. I said to the lama's wife, 'The lama still refuses to instruct me. If I were sure he would give me the teaching when I finished the tower, I would stay. But, if when the tower is finished, he still decided not to teach me, there would be nothing I could do. I long to see my mother. Therefore, I ask permission to leave for my village. May both the lama and you remain in good health.'

I prostrated myself and, taking my books, prepared to leave.

The mother said, 'My son, you are right. As I have already promised you, I will find a way to have you taught by Ngokton, who is a great disciple of the lama and who is initiated. Stay a little longer and pretend to work.'

With joy I stayed and worked.

Since Naropa had had the custom of celebrating the tenth day of each moon by a great sacrifice of offerings, Marpa also celebrated the tenth day of the moon. From a bushel of barley that she had saved, the mistress brewed three large measures for the libations. She made one measure strong, one light, and one medium. She gave the light beer for sacramental libations. To the monks, to be offered to the lama, she gave more and more of the strong beer. The mistress and myself were pouring it for him. The monks themselves drank the medium beer. The mother, touching the weak beer to her lips, drank very little. I did likewise and did not become drunk. The monks became drunk. As for the lama, he took so much beer, and so much more was offered to him, that he became completely drunk and fell into a deep sleep. Meanwhile, his wife removed the gifts – the jewels of Naropa and the rosary of rubies – from his room. She then forged a message fom the lama. Affixing his seal on a letter prepared in advance, she wrapped them in a precious cloth, sealed it all with wax and gave it to me, saying, 'Act as if these things were sent by the lama. Go and offer them to Lama Ngokpa and ask him to teach you.'

She sent me to Shung. I departed, placing all my hopes in Lama Ngokpa.

Two days later the Lama Marpa said to his wife, 'What is Great Magician doing now?'

'He is on the road. I know nothing more.'

'Where did he go?'

'He told me that even if he finished the work on the tower, you would not give him instruction but would shower him with blows and reproaches. He said that he was going to search for another lama and prepared to leave. I had the thought that I had warned you in vain, since you paid no attention. You would have beaten him again. To avoid this shame, I said nothing to you. I did everything to delay his departure. But, without listening, he left.'

With an angry face the lama asked, 'When did he leave?'

'He left yesterday.'

The lama remained thoughtful for a moment. 'My son cannot be far away yet.'

Now, at that very moment I was arriving at Mount Kyungding in Shung. Lama Ngokpa was expounding an esoteric text entitled 'The Two Divisions'[10] to his disciples. His discourse was interrupted while expounding these verses:

I am the Master of the Dharma.
I am the Assembly of the Hearers.
I am the Master of the Universe and the Object of Realization.

I am the Conditioned and the Unconditioned.
I am the Innate Nature of Spontaneous Bliss.

As he was pronouncing these words I prostrated myself at a distance. He responded by removing his hat, and said, 'This is the manner of greeting used by Marpa's disciples. And the words that he interrupted are of good omen.[11] For this man will be the Master of all the Doctrines. Go and ask him who he is.'

One of the monks went to meet me and, recognizing me, said, 'Why have you come?'

'Since the Lama Marpa is very busy, I am the only one that he has not had time to instruct. I have come here to ask for the teaching. As gifts I bring the jewels of Naropa and his rosary of rubies.'

The monk returned to his master and told him, 'It is Great Magician.' And he repeated my words.

The lama was filled with joy. He exclaimed, 'The jewels and the rosary of the Great Master Naropa in my dwelling! This is as rare and marvelous as the Udumbara[12] flower. We must go out to receive them. For today, let us stop at this auspicious place in our lesson. Monks, fetch a parasol, and quickly, some flags and cymbals, and ask Great Magician to take his place in the procession.'

Since I had remained where I first made my greeting, a monk came to give me this message. I called this place Chaktsal Gang (Ridge of Salutation).

I stepped back and then joined the monks, who formed the procession with parasols, banners, and cymbals. We entered the lama's house. I prostrated myself and gave him the letter with the gifts. With tearful eyes, the lama raised the gifts to his forehead and received their blessing. He placed these sacred objects on the altar, giving them the most prominent place and setting offerings in front of them.

Then he read the letter:

'To Choku Dorje (Diamond of Ultimate Reality): Since I have gone into retreat and Great Magician lacks patience I am sending him to ask you for the teaching. Give him initiation and instruction. As testimony of my permission to do this, I am sending you the jewels of Naropa.'

Lama Ngokpa said, 'Since it is an order from Marpa, I will instruct you. I had thought of sending for you but happily by the grace of Marpa you have come. Many disciples come to me from Kham, from

Tagpo, from Kongpo, and from Yarlung. The evil people of the villages of Yehpo and Yemo of Döl always steal our provisions. Go and strike them all with hail. Afterward you will receive initiation and instruction.'

Then I thought, 'I am destined to perform evil deeds. I can only get the sacred teaching by sending hailstorms, and thereby will again be indulging in harmful deeds. If I do not send hail, I will be disobeying the orders of the lama and I shall not hear the teaching. I cannot avoid sending the hailstorm.'

Having gathered together the ritual objects, I charged some sesame seeds with magical power and brought them along. Arriving in the province of Döl, I set to work and prepared to bring on the hailstorm.

At Yehpo I stayed at the house of an old woman and made myself a shelter nearby. The storm gathered quickly. The thunder rumbled. Dark clouds piled up, one by one, then two by two, and the hailstones began to fall.

The old woman cried out, 'When my crops are struck by hail, what will I have to eat?' And she wept.

I said to myself, 'What I am doing is criminal.' And to the old woman, 'Quickly, draw the shape of your field.'

'It is like this.'

She drew an elongated triangle, which I reproduced. I formed my hand in the mudra[13] of watching and covered the triangle with a wide pan. The apex of the triangle, which protruded a little, was devastated by the wind.

I went out to verify the results with my own eyes. The mountain slopes behind the two villages were transformed into torrents. Only the field of the old woman remained intact and fertile. Nothing remained of all the other fields. The far end of the triangle which had been struck was carried away by the flood. I assured the old woman that from now on her field would always be protected and that she would not have to pay the tithe for protection against hailstorms. She would have to pay it only on the part that the flood had carried away.

I left. On the road I met two shepherds, an old man and a child, whose flock of sheep had been carried away by the flood.

I said to them, 'It is I who have done this. Do not steal from the monks of Lama Ngokpa anymore. If you steal from them again you will be struck by hail each time in the same way.'

They reported these threats and the two provinces respectfully paid homage to the lama. Intending to become his faithful followers, they offered him their services.

At the edge of a thicket, I found many small dead birds. All along the way I gathered up the bodies of birds and rats. I filled the hood and the lap of my rain cloak with them and when I returned to the lama I heaped them all up at his feet.

'Lama Rimpoche, I came here for the holy religion but in truth I have only sinned. Have compassion on me, a great sinner.' Speaking thus, I wept.

The lama answered, 'Brother Great Magician, have no fear. We, the disciples of Naropa and Maitrepa,[14] know the secret formula called "Driving away a hundred birds with a single slingshot," which enables great sinners to achieve Enlightenment instantly.

'In the future all these creatures now killed by the hail will be reborn around you and will form a procession when you attain full Enlightenment. Rejoice that from now on, thanks to me, they will not be reborn in the lower realms. If you do not believe me, I will show you.'

After collecting himself for a moment, he snapped his fingers and immediately the bodies were revivified. In an instant some flew skyward and others raced over the ground and returned to their nests. I thought, 'I have seen a real Buddha. Thus how much better it would be, how much better, if many creatures were to die in this way.'

Then the lama gave me initiation into the mandala of Hevajra. After he had given me this teaching, I moved into an abandoned cave on a steep cliff, facing south, from which the lama's home could be seen. I walled myself in, leaving a small opening through which the lama instructed me. I meditated without respite. But because I had left Marpa without his permission, I had no inner experience.

One day the lama said to me, 'Brother Great Magician, have you experienced any inner signs?'

'No, nothing.'

'What are you saying? Unless my spiritual lineage has become polluted with disharmony, it has the power to bring about an awakening quickly. You have come to me in good faith. But if you did not have the permission of Lama Marpa to leave, why did he send gifts to me? What is going on here? Whatever it is, persevere in your meditation.'

I remained, full of fear. I wondered whether to tell the whole truth. But lacking the courage to speak, I thought, 'In any case Marpa is sure to hear of it.' And I plunged into meditation.

Meanwhile Marpa had completed his son's tower and he sent a letter to Ngokpa: 'Now that my son's tower has reached a point where it needs a wooden frieze, send me as many loads of thin cane as you can.[15] When I have set the frieze and the pinnacle you should come for the consecration of the tower, and also to celebrate the coming of age of Doday Būm (Marpa's son). Bring with you a certain evil-doer who belongs to me.'

Lama Ngokpa came to the small opening of my cell and, showing me the letter, said to me, 'It is just as this letter states. The evil-doer of whom this letter speaks was not sent by Marpa.'

I replied, 'It is true that the order did not come from the lama himself. It is the lama's wife who gave me the letter and the gifts and sent me here.'

'Ah ha! If that is the way it is, we have no reason for working together. Without the lama's permission you will not achieve results. There is nothing to be done. He said to bring you back. Will you or will you not go?'

'May I go with you as a servant?'

'Good. When I have sent the wood for the frieze, I will send someone to find out the day of celebration. Until then, stay in seclusion.'

The one who had gone to verify the day of the celebration returned and, through the opening of my cell, said, 'The ceremony for the consecration of the tower and the coming of age of Marpa's son have been discussed in detail.'

'Did they speak of me?'

'Marpa's wife asked what you were doing. I told her you were in strict seclusion. She asked me what else you were doing besides that. I replied that you were living in a deserted place. She then said, "Maybe he missed this which he left here. When he was with us he used to be very fond of it. Give it to him." This is what she gave me.'

Loosening his belt, he drew out a clay die and handed it to me.

Thinking that this object came from the hands of the lama's wife, I touched it to my forehead with veneration.

The man went away. As I was in a mood to play with the die, I played. Then I thought, 'When I was with Marpa's wife I never played dice. Perhaps now she does not have much affection for me. It was dice which long ago drove my ancestors from their homeland.' And swinging it above my head I threw the die. It broke and out of it fell a roll of paper which read, 'Now the lama will initiate you and give you the teaching. Return with Lama Ngokpa.'

So great was my joy that I danced, leaping from one side of my cell to the other. Then Lama Ngokpa came and said to me, 'Good Great Magician, come out and prepare to leave.'

I obeyed. Lama Ngokpa carried all of his own collection of images, scriptures, and stupas, his gold and turquoise, his silks and his garments, and all the household utensils, leaving behind the gifts given by Marpa. He ordered me to leave an old goat which had a broken leg and could not follow the herd. He took away all his other animals from the stable and the meadow.

When we were ready to leave, he said to me, 'Since you have been helpful to me, take this silk and this turquoise as an offering to Lama Marpa.' His wife also gave me a bag of cheese to offer to Dakmema, the wife of Lama Marpa.

Then Lama Ngokpa, with his wife, retinue of servants, and myself, arrived at the bottom of the Valley of the Birches. Ngokpa said, 'Brother Great Magician, go ahead of us and tell Marpa's wife that we are coming. See if she will send us some beer.'

I went on ahead. First I met the lama's wife. I greeted her and offered her the bag of cheese.

'Lama Ngokpa is coming,' I said. 'Please bring some beer to welcome him.'

Joyfully she responded, 'The lama is in his room. Go and ask him yourself.'

I went. The lama was on his terrace making his devotions, his face turned toward the east. I prostrated myself and offered him the silk and the turquoise. He turned his head away and looked toward the west. I went to this side and prostrated myself again. He looked toward the south.

'O Master,' I cried, 'it is right that as punishment you reject my offerings. But Lama Ngokpa is arriving with his collection of images, scriptures, stupas, gold, and turquoise, with his dzos, his horses, and all his wealth. He only hopes that someone is going to receive him with a little beer. That is why I am asking it of you.'

Bursting with anger, snapping his fingers, the lama shouted in a terrible voice, 'From three collections of sacred books in India I extracted the essence of the four Tantras.[16] When I brought back the teaching, no one came to greet me, not even a little bird. And because Ngokpa is arriving, pushing a few debilitated beasts in front of him, he wishes that I, the great Lotsava,[17] should go to meet him. I shall not go – and now get out!'

I went to tell all this to the lama's wife. She said, 'The lama answered in anger. Ngokpa is a great man and should be met. Let us both go, mother and son.'

I answered, 'Lama Ngokpa and his wife do not expect anyone to go and meet them. They have asked for something to drink so I will go alone and carry it.'

But the lama's wife went to greet them together with some monks carrying a quantity of beer.

Meanwhile, many people of the Southern Cliffs had gathered together, having been invited to a great feast for the coming of age of the lama's son and the consecration of the house.

And Marpa, in their midst, sang this chant of praise and thanksgiving:

I call upon my Master, the Compassionate One;
Excellence abounds in this precious lineage of mine, unstained by flaw or deficiency.
May all be blessed through this excellence.

Excellence abounds in the rapid path of secret transmission,
Without error or deception.
May all be blessed through this excellence.

Excellence abounds in Marpa Lotsava
Guarding the essence of these secrets.
May all be blessed through this excellence.

Excellence abounds in lamas, yidams, and dakinis
Possessing the power of blessing and of aiding true realization.
May all be blessed through this excellence.

Excellence abounds in the spiritual sons and disciples assembled,
In your faith and in your vows.
May all be blessed through this excellence.

Excellence abounds in benefactors far and near,
Accumulating merits through their generosity.
May all be blessed through this excellence.

Excellence abounds in all our actions and endeavors
Achieving enlightenment for the good of others.
May all be blessed through this excellence.

Excellence abounds in gods and demi-gods of the visible world
Remaining faithful to their sacred pledges.
May all be blessed through this excellence.

Excellence abounds in monks and lay people assembled
  in this place
In their aspiration for peace and happiness.
May all be blessed through this excellence.

Thus chanted Marpa. Immediately afterward, the Lama Ngokpa offered him his gifts, saying, 'Lama Rimpoche, since you are already the Master of my whole being, body, speech, and mind, I now offer all my worldly goods, except for a long-haired goat, the decrepit forebear of all my goats, who, unable to come here on her broken leg, has been left behind. Mercifully grant us initiation and profound instruction and the secret teaching written on the scrolls.' And he prostrated himself.

Marpa, appearing joyful, replied, 'But even so, my initiation and profound instructions are the shortest path of Vajrayana which, without having to wait for innumerable kalpas, leads directly to Enlightenment in this life. The precepts written on the scrolls are being kept by me under safeguards according to the strict commands of my own lama and the dakinis. That is why it will be difficult for these precepts to be given you if you do not offer me this old goat, in spite of her age and broken leg. As to the other teachings, I have already taught them all to you.'

All those present burst into laughter, and Ngokpa replied, 'If the goat is brought here and I offer it to you, will you reveal the secret teaching to me?'

'If you bring the goat yourself, and offer it to me, you may have the teaching.'

On the following day, the guests having withdrawn, Ngokpa set out alone.

He returned with the goat on his back and offered it to Marpa, who cried out joyfully, 'You are an initiated disciple such as is worthy to be called faithful to his sacred bond. I have no need of this goat. I only wanted to stress the importance of the teaching that I am giving you.'

He gave him initiation and instruction as promised.

Monks who had come from afar, together with a few close associates who were brought together, arranged a ritual feast. Marpa put a long acacia stick near his seat. Looking at Ngokpa with narrowed eyes and pointing his finger at him, he said, 'Ngokton Chodor, why have you conferred initiation and instruction on this wicked man called Good News?'

Saying this, he glanced toward his stick. Ngokpa was afraid and, prostrating himself, answered, 'Lama Rimpoche, you yourself wrote to me to initiate and instruct Great Magician, and you gave me the jewels of Naropa and his rosary of rubies. Thus I carried out your order. I have no cause to reproach myself and I feel neither shame nor remorse.'

Speaking thus, Ngokpa fearfully raised his eyes. Furiously, Marpa pointed his finger at me and asked, 'Where did you get these objects?'

My heart agonized as though it had been torn out. I was mute with terror. In a trembling voice I confessed that the mother had given them to me.

The lama jumped up and brandishing the acacia stick went out to beat his wife. Having been listening attentively, she got up and ran away.

Taking refuge in the temple, she locked herself in.

The lama shook the door, then returned and sat down. He said to Ngokpa, 'Ngokton Chodor, you acted without my permission. Go this moment and get the jewels of Naropa and his rosary of rubies.'

Then Marpa covered his head with his cloak and remained motionless.

Having prostrated himself, Ngokpa immediately left to fetch Naropa's jewels and his rosary of rubies. I regretted not having fled with the lama's wife.

I felt like crying and, as I tried to hold back my tears, Ngokpa saw me. I asked to go with him as a servant. He replied, 'If I take you away without the lama's permission, it will always be the same thing as today. Since he is angry with us both, stay here for awhile. If later he sends you away without having accepted you as a disciple, then I will have full power to help you.'

'Well then, since Marpa's wife and you are both in trouble because of my sins, and since with this present body I will not receive the Doctrine but only accumulate more sins, I am going to kill myself. May I be reborn with a body worthy of religion!'

As I was about to kill myself, Ngokpa restrained me. And with tears, said to me, 'Worthy Great Magician, not that! According to the most secret teachings of the Buddha, the faculties and the senses of each of us are innately divine. If you die before your time, you commit the sin of killing a god. That is why suicide is such a great crime. Even in the exoteric tradition of the Sutras there is no greater sin than to cut off one's own life. Since you know this, give up the idea of killing yourself. It is still possible that the lama will give you the teaching. But if he does not, another lama surely will.'

While he was speaking in this way, some of the other monks, not being able to bear my misfortune, went up to the lama to see if the moment had come to intercede for me; others came to comfort me. In spite of that, filled with anguish, I thought, 'Is my heart made of iron? For if it were not, it would have burst and I would be dead.'

It is because of the crimes committed in my youth that I endured such suffering while seeking religion. At this moment, there was no one who was not sobbing tearfully. Some of them were overcome by grief and fainted.

Thus spoke Milarepa. This is the second chapter, wherein Mila is purified of the stain of sin and suffering.

Third Chapter

Initiations and Instructions

Then Retchung spoke: 'Master, how were you admitted as a disciple by the Lama Marpa?'

Mila continued:

After the monks had gone back and forth many times between us, the lama broke his silence. His mind now being pacified, he sent for Dakmema, the mistress. Having been invited to come, she appeared before him.

The lama asked her, 'Where have Ngok Choku Dorje and the other monks gone?'

'In accordance with your order to bring back the jewels of Naropa and his rosary of rubies, Lama Ngokpa immediately set out to fetch them, and has now returned.'

She related in detail how Great Magician was imploring Ngokpa to help him and how Ngokpa was consoling him. Lama Marpa shed tears and said, 'Disciples of the secret path must be such as these; indeed they are so. I have compassion for them. Summon all my disciples.'

A monk who was sent to invite Ngokpa said, 'Now the lama is calm. He sent me to ask you to come.'

I exclaimed, 'Happy are those with a good karma! As for me, a sinner, even though the lama is calm, I will not have the good fortune to see him. If I went, he would only curse me and beat me.'

Weeping, I stayed behind. Ngokpa, who stayed with me, said to the monk, 'Go and tell the lama how it is with Great Magician. Ask if he should come before him. If I do not remain near him now, I fear this man may do something terrible.'

The monk related all these events to Marpa. Marpa replied, 'In the past he would have been right. But today, I shall not do the same as before. Great Magician is to be the principal guest. Let the mistress go and fetch him!'

The mistress, both smiling and fearful, said to me, 'Brother Great Magician, the lama now appears to be taking you as a disciple. He seems to be deeply moved by compassion. He said that you are the principal guest, and has sent me to fetch you. He has said no harsh words to me. Let us rejoice and go.'

I wondered if it were true, and, wrongly filled with apprehension, I went in.

Then the lama spoke:

'If everything is carefully examined, not one of us is to be blamed. I have merely tested Great Magician to purify him of his sins. If the work on the tower had been intended for my own gain, I would have been gentle in the giving of orders. Therefore I was sincere. Being a woman, the mistress was also right not to be able to bear the situation, yet her excessive compassion in deceiving with the sacred objects and the forged letter was a serious indulgence. Ngokpa, you were right in the matter you have related. However, go now and bring me those sacred objects and afterward I will give them to you. Great Magician was burning with desire for religion, and he was right to use any means to obtain it. Ngokpa did not know that the mistress had sent someone under false pretenses. This is why he gave Great Magician initiation and instruction. Thus, I shall not look for a way to punish him.

'Although my anger rose like floodwater, it was not like worldly anger. However they may appear, my actions always come from religious considerations which, in essence, conform to the Path of Enlightenment. As for the rest of you who are not yet immersed in religion, do not let your faith be shaken.

'Had this son of mine completed nine great ordeals, his complete Enlightenment, without future rebirth, would have been achieved without leaving any bodily residue. Since, due to Dakmema's weakness, that did not take place, there will remain a faint stain of defilement with him. However, his great sins have been erased by his eight great afflictions of mind and by his numerous small agonies. Now, I receive you and will give you my teaching, which is as dear to me as my own heart. I will help you with provisions and let you meditate and be happy.'

As he was saying these words I wondered, 'Is this a dream or am I awake? If it is a dream, I wish never to awaken.' At this thought my happiness was boundless. Shedding tears of joy, I prostrated myself. The mistress, Ngokpa, and the others thought, 'What skillful means and power the lama has when he wants to accept a disciple! The lama himself is a Living Buddha.' And their faith grew still more. Out of love for me they all cheerfully prostrated themselves before the lama.

At the end, all who had gathered joyfully participated in performing a ritual feast. On the evening of this day, at the very place where we had assembled, we set the offerings before the altar. Marpa said to me, 'I ordain you with the common vow of liberation.' And he cut off my hair.

When my clothes had been changed to a monk's robe, the lama said, 'Your name, Mila Vajra Banner-of-Victory, was revealed to me by Naropa in a dream, even before you came here.'

He bound me by the layman's vow and gave me the Bodhisattva precepts. Through meditation he consecrated the wine of inner offering in the skull-cup of libation.[1] We all saw the wine bubbling with the light of the five colors. Marpa made an offering to his lama and to the yidam, then he drank. He handed me the cup and I drained it.

The lama said, 'This is a good omen. A mere taste of my wine of inner offering is in itself superior to receiving the complete initiation of any other lineage. Starting tomorrow, I shall confer on you the Initiation of Transformation according to the secret path.'

Then an elaborate mandala, Chakrasamvara,[2] with sixty-two deities, was set up for the initiation. When giving the initiation he pointed to the mandala of colored powders. 'This,' he said, 'is just a symbol of the mandala. The real mandala is up there.' He pointed to the sky and we clearly saw the Yidam Chakrasamvara surrounded by the dakas and dakinis of the twenty-four sacred realms, the thirty-two holy places, and the eight great places of cremation.[3] At the same moment, and with one voice, the lama and the deities of the mandala above conferred upon me the initiatory name Pal Zhepa Dorje (Glorious Laughing Vajra).

Giving me the recitation of the Tantra in full, the lama showed me in great detail the ways of practicing in accordance with the profound instruction. Then, placing his hands on my head, he said:

'My son, from the very first moment, I knew you were a disciple capable of receiving the teaching. The night before you came here I learned from a dream that you were destined to serve the teaching of Buddha. The mistress, in a similar but even more remarkable dream, saw two women guardians of a stupa, indicating that the dakinis will protect the teaching of our lineage. In this way, my lama and the guardian deity sent you to me as a disciple. I went to meet you in the guise of a laborer.[4] You drank all the beer I had given you. This beer and the work that you had finished signified that, in penetrating to the heart of the Doctrine, you will grasp the entire teaching. The copper pot you gave with the four handles signified the coming of my four great disciples. Its unblemished surface signified that your mind will become free from blemish and in your body you will have power over the bliss of the fire of Tummo.[5] The empty pot symbolized the meagerness of your food during the time of your meditation in solitude. But in order to sow the seeds of your long life, of well-being for your many disciples, and of your filling your disciples with the sweetness of the teaching, I with my blessing filled the pot with butter from the altar lamps. I made it ring to signify your future renown. To purify you from the darkness of evil, I burdened you with the increasingly terrible work of the towers.

'Each time that I cruelly drove you out from the ranks of the disciples and overwhelmed you with grief, you had no bad thoughts against me. This signifies that your disciples will have first of all the zeal, perseverance, wisdom, and compassion necessary for every disciple. Next, not desiring the wealth of this life, they will endure meditation in the mountains through their ascetic discipline and energy. So finally, through inner experience, spiritual energy, wisdom, and compassion, they will all become perfect lamas. The transmission of this teaching will be like the waxing moon – so rejoice!'

All this he predicted. Encouraging us, he inspired us and gave us joy. This was the beginning of my happiness.

Thus spoke Milarepa. This is the third chapter, in which he obtains initiation and instruction in the secret path.

Fourth Chapter

Meditation

Retchung then said, 'Master, after hearing the Doctrine, did you immediately go into solitude or did you remain with the lama?'

And Mila continued:

The lama told me to meditate with perseverance. He provided me with ample supplies and directed me to meditate in a cave called Tiger Nak at the Southern Cliffs. Then I filled an altar lamp with butter, lit it, and placed it on my head. I meditated day and night in this way, without moving, until the butter in the lamp was exhausted.

Eleven months passed. Then the lama and his wife came, bringing me food for a ritual feast.

The lama exclaimed, 'Well, my son, to meditate for eleven months without letting your cushion get cold is excellent. Open the entrance to your cell and come home for a rest so that you may talk with me, your old father, about your inner experience.'

I thought to myself, 'It has been peaceful here, but I must go out since it is an order given by the lama.'

I began breaking down the entrance. I had hardly begun when I stopped for a moment, not daring to continue further. Just then the lama's wife returned and asked, 'Are you coming, my son?' I replied that I dared not break down the wall. The mother said, 'There is nothing wrong. Such an auspicious event as this meeting with the lama can only have a good result. It is a law of the secret path. Refusing would anger him and spoil the auspicious event, so break open the entrance and come out.'

Knowing that the mother spoke the truth, I tore down the wall and came out.

The lama said, 'We two, father and son, will meditate together. Mistress, prepare a feast.'

As we were making the offering the lama said to me, 'My son, what definite knowledge have you reaped from my special instructions? Let your mind relax and tell me what perceptive and intuitive experiences and understanding you have achieved.'

In an act of faith and ardent veneration toward the lama, I knelt down and joined the palms of my hands. My eyes blurred with tears, I paid homage to him for all that I had understood, and I sang this Song of the Sevenfold Devotions:

O Master, who, to the eyes of impure seekers,
Appears in diverse forms,
And, to the assembly of pure Bodhisattvas,
Manifests as Sambhogakaya Buddha, I salute you.

Sounding the sixty tones[1] of celestial Brahma, you spoke about
The sacred teaching in its eighty-four thousand[2] aspects
Which was understood by people each in their own language.
I prostrate myself before your speech
Which is inseparable from its innate emptiness.

In the clear and lucid space of the Dharmakaya
There is no defilement of discrimination,
Yet it encompasses all knowledge.
I salute the mind of the Immutable Dharmakaya.

Dwelling in the palace of pure emptiness,
Immutable Dakmema, with the body illusory,
You are the Mother who bears the Buddhas of the Three Ages.[3]
Dakmema, I prostrate myself at your feet.

Master, with unfeigned respect, I salute
Your spiritual sons whom you have united,
The disciples who carry out your commandments,
And the multitude of your followers.

I offer my body to you
And whatever else is worthy of sacrifice
In all the realms of the universe.

I repent of all my sins, one by one.
I delight in the virtuous deeds of others.
I implore you to turn the Wheel of the Law far and wide.

I pray that the supremely perfect lama may live
So long as there are sentient beings enmeshed within samsara.
May my spiritual merits benefit all sentient beings.

'Having begun in this manner with the Song of the Sevenfold Devotions, I, your humble follower, wish to express my feeble understanding, made possible by the perfect action and power of spiritual influence arising from the boundless compassion of the lama (who is inseparable from the Buddha Vajradhara) together with the mother and son, and the deep gratitude I owe them.

'Please listen to me out of the unchanging state of your mind. I have understood that this material body, made of flesh and blood along with mental consciousness, is gathered together by the twelve chains of cause and effect – one of which is volition – originating from ignorance. This body is the blessed vessel for those fortunate beings who wish for freedom, but it also leads sinners into the lower realms.

'I understand that in this body lies the vital choice between enormous profit and loss, relating to eternal happiness or misery on the border between good and evil. Relying upon your power of compassion as the venerable guide of sentient beings, I am hopefully endeavoring to achieve liberation from the ocean of existential bondage, from which escape is very difficult.

'Having first sought refuge in the Three Jewels[4] and having scrupulously observed the precepts, I understand that the source of all happiness is the lama, and therefore the first principle is to fulfill all his instructions and maintain, unblemished, a spiritual bond with him.

'Furthermore, a fortunate human existence is a state difficult to acquire. By arousing the mind with great intensity regarding impermanence and death, the consequences of action, and the pain of samsara, one develops a longing for liberation and must pursue it through the observance of moral precepts. Such is the foundation upon which one must build.

'From this point, progressively ascending the Path, it is necessary to observe one's vows as carefully as one guards one's eyes. Even in failure, remedies must be employed. By not seeking one's own liberation on the path of the Lesser Vehicle,[5] one develops Bodhichitta[6] (enlightened mind), which seeks to work toward the liberation of all sentient beings. It is my understanding that the development of an enlightened attitude leads one to rededicate, for the good of all, the fruit of one's action, born of love and compassion.

'In order to embrace the path of the Greater Vehicle,[7] one abandons the path of the Lesser Vehicle. Based upon the foundation of perfect seeing, he enters the supreme path of Vajrayana.

'In order to achieve perfect seeing one needs a perfect master who knows how to transmit fully and unerringly the four aspects of initiation[8] and skillfully explain the hidden meaning with compassion. Initiation awakens one to ultimate reality and from then onward one meditates through all the various stages of the Path. Having endeavored to discover the non-selfhood of personality, which is common to all exoteric traditions, one examines the self by means of logic, the teaching, and analogies and, not finding the self, one understands selflessness. One must then bring the mind into a quiet state. When the mind is calmed by means of such reasoning, discriminating thought ceases and mind reaches a nonconceptual state. If one continues in this state for days, months, and years, so oblivious to the passing of time that one needs to be reminded of it by others, one has then achieved tranquillity of mind.

'This state of tranquillity is maintained by means of continued attention and awareness, not allowing it to become distracted or to sink into passivity. Intensified by the force of awareness, one experiences pure consciousness without differentiation – naked, vivid, and crisp. These are the characteristics of tranquillity of mind.

'Pure consciousness may be regarded as a flash of perfect insight; individuals do not actually experience it until they reach the first stage of Enlightenment. At this stage, one meditates, visualizing the forms of the yidam. In so doing one may experience visions and forms, but these are devoid of substance and are merely products of meditation.

'To sum up: First, a vivid state of mental tranquillity and a sustaining energy together with a discerning intellect are indispensable requirements for attaining perfect insight. They are like the first steps of a staircase.

'Second, all meditation, with or without form, must begin from deeply aroused compassion and love. Whatever one does must emerge from a loving attitude for the benefit of others.

'Third, through perfect seeing, all discrimination is dissolved into a non-conceptual state.

'Finally, with an awareness of the void, one sincerely dedicates the results for the benefit of others. I have understood this to be the best of all ways.

'Just as a starving man cannot be fed by the knowledge of food but needs to eat, so too one needs to experience in meditation the meaning of emptiness. I understand more particularly that in order to arrive at perfect insight it is necessary to practice meritorious deeds and self-purification, without respite, in the intervals between meditations.

'In short, I saw that this meditator's understanding of the emptiness of things, of their unity, of their indefinability, and of their non-differentiation corresponds to the four aspects of initiation according to Vajrayana.

'In order to make this knowledge manifest in myself, I subdued my body, deprived it of food, harnessed my mind, and achieved equanimity in the face of all circumstances including the danger of death.

'I have not come before the lama and the mistress, my father and mother of unsurpassable goodness, to repay them with services and riches. But I offer the best I shall be capable of attaining in my practice of meditation as long as I live, and I ask them to accept the ultimate understanding that I shall attain in the palace of Ogmin:

'Great lama, who is the Buddha Vajradhara,
Mother Dakmema, bearer of Buddhas,
And you, sons of the Victorious Ones,
Inviting you to listen to these few words
Born of understanding and true perception in my mind,
I beg you to bear with patience my faults,
My ignorance, my wrong understanding, and my errors.
Please correct them according to the Dharma.
Under the blessing of the burning rays
Descending from the sun of your compassion,
The lotus of my mind has opened.
With this perfume emanating from experience,
And possessing nothing equal to my gratitude,
To you I render perpetual homage.

May the fruits of my meditation be profitable to all beings,
In striving toward the limits of perfection.
I beg you, listen to the voice of your disciple who dares to
beseech you.'

Thus I spoke. Then the lama said, 'My son, I had great hope and my hope has been realized.' And he was filled with joy.

The mother said, 'This son of mine has the strength of mind for great achievement.'

After many religious talks, the father and mother returned to their house. As for me, I walled up the entrance to my cell and meditated.

About this time the lama visited the northern region of Ü. One evening, after performing a ritual feast at Marpa Golak's house, a dakini explained to Lama Marpa a certain symbolic message given by Naropa which Marpa had not understood. While the lama was contemplating a visit to Naropa, as urged by the dakinis, a young girl appeared to me one night in a dream. She was blue as the sky, and beautiful in her brocade dress and bone ornaments, her eyebrows and lashes sparkling with light. She said to me, 'My son, you already have the Teaching of the Great Symbol (Mahamudra)[9] and instruction in the Six Esoteric Doctrines.[10] These lead to Supreme Enlightenment through continuous meditation. But you do not have the special teaching concerning the Transference of Consciousness to Dead Bodies,[11] which leads to Buddhahood in one moment of meditation. Ask for it,' she said, and she disappeared.

I thought to myself, 'This young girl was dressed in the costume of the dakinis. Is it a warning from the gods? Is it a demon's trick? I do not know. Whatever it is, my Master, who is a Buddha of the past, present, and future, will surely know. He not only knows one thing but all things, from the means for becoming a Buddha down to the formula for putting together a broken jar. If this is a warning from the gods, I must ask for the Doctrine of the Transference of Consciousness to Dead Bodies.'

I broke down the wall of my cell and went before the lama, who cried out, 'Why have you come out of strict seclusion? This could hinder your progress. Why have you done it?'

I described the young girl and what she had said to me in my dream, and I asked, 'Is it a prophetic call or is it the sign of an obstacle? I do not know. If it is a call, I have come to ask for the Doctrine of the Transference of Consciousness.'

The lama reflected a moment and said, 'It is certainly a warning from the dakinis. Before I started back from India, the Master Naropa spoke about the teaching of the Transference of Consciousness to Dead Bodies. Since I was about to leave, I may not have asked for it. So we must search for it through all the books from India.'

We, Master and disciple, searched diligently day and night for the text, Transference of Consciousness to Dead Bodies. We found many works on transference of consciousness, but we did not find the least mention of transference of consciousness to dead bodies. The lama said to me, 'The sign I received in the north of Central Tibet urged me to make the same request. Since there may be other teachings that I do not know, I will go to Naropa and ask for them.'

I reminded him of his age, but did not succeed in dissuading him. He converted his disciples' gifts into gold, filled a pot with it, and left for India.

Naropa had gone away to engage in the exercise of great yogic powers. Marpa, wishing to be with him even at the risk of his life, consulted many omens, and it was revealed that he would find him. Praying fervently, he set out to look for him. He met Naropa in a virgin forest and invited him to come to the hermitage of Puhlla Hari. There he asked for instruction in the Transference of Consciousness to Dead Bodies.

The Master Naropa replied, 'Did you think of this or did you receive a sign?'

'This did not enter my mind, nor did I have a sign. One of my disciples, Good News, received an exhortation from the dakinis and came to ask me for the teaching.'

'What a marvel!' cried Naropa. 'In the dark land of Tibet, this disciple is like the sun rising over the snows.'

He raised his joined hands above his head in veneration and said:

'O disciple called Good News,
I prostrate myself before you,
Like the sun rising on the snow
In the shadows of the somber north.'

With these words he closed his eyes and bowed his head three times. And in India the mountains and the trees inclined three times toward Tibet. To this day, the treetops and the mountains of Puhlla Hari bend toward Tibet. Naropa gave Marpa in its entirety the secret teaching transmitted by the dakinis. Then he interpreted certain omens. For example, Marpa's manner of prostration foretold that his own family line would be short, but that the spiritual lineage molded by the unfolding action of the teaching would be longer than a great river. Marpa then returned to Tibet.

Some time later the monks and disciples were commemorating the anniversary of the death of Marpa's son, Darma Doday, which had taken place as foretold by the omen. When all were assembled for that occasion, the disciples asked Marpa, 'Lama Rimpoche, your son was like a Buddha of the Three Ages. Now our best hope has gone, and you are no longer young. How will the precious Kagyü Doctrine be transmitted? Tell us what our discipline and our task should be.'

The lama answered, 'I, and all the descendants of the Master Naropa, have the power to prophesy through dreams. Naropa has delivered a good prophecy regarding the Kagyü Doctrine. Chief disciples, go now and await your dreams.'

Later, the disciples related their dreams. Even though all had happy dreams, they were unable to extract a premonitory sign. I had a dream of four pillars which I told in the presence of the lama:

'Following the instruction of the Lama Buddha Vajradhara,
Last night I dreamed a dream.
I tell its story to the lama.
Please lend ear to it.

I dreamed that in the vast North of the world
A majestic snow-clad mountain arose,
Its white peak touching the sky.
Around it turned the sun and moon,
Its light filled the whole of space,
And its base covered the entire Earth.
Rivers descended in the four cardinal directions,
Quenching the thirst of all sentient beings,
And all these waters rushed into the sea.
A myriad of flowers sparkled.
Such in general was the dream I had.
I tell this to the Lama Buddha of the Three Ages.

I dreamed that to the East beyond this high majestic mountain
A colossal pillar was standing.
At the top crouched a great lion.
His mane of turquoise flowing everywhere,
He spread his claws upon the snow,
His eyes gazed upward,
And he roamed proudly on the vast whiteness.
I tell this to the Lama Buddha of the Three Ages.

I dreamed that to the South a great pillar was raised.
At the top of this pillar a tigress roared,
Bristling hair covered her whole body.
She smiled three times,
She spread her claws over the forest,
Her eyes gazed upward,
And she floated proudly above the dense woods.
The cedars of the forest were thickly tangled.
I tell this to the Lama Buddha of the Three Ages.

I dreamed that to the West a great pillar was raised.
At the top of this pillar soared a giant garuda.[12]
The garuda's wings were spread,
Its horns rose toward the heavens,
Its eyes gazed upward.
I tell this to the Lama Buddha of the Three Ages.

I dreamed that to the North a great pillar was raised.
At the top of this pillar soared a vulture,
Its pointed wings were spread,
Its nest perched on a crag.
This vulture had a fledgling
And the sky was full of little birds.
The vulture gazed upward
And impelled itself through space.
I tell this to the Lama Buddha of the Three Ages.

I took it as a happy omen
And rejoiced at this good fortune.
I wish you to tell me its meaning.'

I spoke thus, and the lama joyfully answered, 'This dream is a happy dream! Mistress, prepare a ritual feast.'

The mother brought the necessary things and, when she had done so, the disciples and spiritual sons gathered for the feast.

The lama said to them, 'What a marvelous dream Mila Vajra Banner-of-Victory has had!'

The chief disciples asked, 'Since you know how to unravel the portent of dreams, please tell us what this one foretells.'

Then the lama, perfect Master and great Translator, sang this song, which unveiled the dream to the disciples:

'Lord Buddha of the Three Ages,
Master Naropa, I prostrate myself at your feet.
All disciples seated in this place,
Listen to the astonishing omens of the future
Made known by the dream
That I, your old Father, am going to tell you.

The northern land of the world is Tibet
Where the Doctrine of Buddha will spread.
This snow-clad mountain
Is the old Translator Marpa
And the Kagyü teaching.
The summit of snow which touched the sky
Is matchless insight without equal.
The sun and moon turning around its peak
Are meditation radiating wisdom and compassion.
The light filling space
Is compassion dispelling the darkness of ignorance.
Its base covering the whole earth
Is the pervasive action of the teaching as it unfolds.
The four rivers flowing in the four directions
Are the four aspects of initiation and instruction.
These rivers quenching the thirst of all beings
Are for the development and liberation of seekers.
All these waters flowing into the sea
Are the reunion of mother awareness and daughter awareness.
All the varied flowers which sparkled
Are the enjoyment of fruit without blemish.
The dream in general is not ill-fated. It is favorable,
O monks and disciples assembled in this place.

The great pillar rising to the East
On this high majestic mountain of snow
Is Tshurtön Ouangnge of Döl.
The lion dominating the summit of this pillar
Means that Tshurtön has the nature of a lion.
Its flowing mane of turquoise
Is the realization of secret instruction.
Its four claws spread out upon the snow
Are the possession of the Four Infinite Attributes.[13]
Its gaze turned toward the sky

Is the parting from the world of birth and death.
Its proud roaming on the whiteness of the snow
Is the arrival in the realm of liberation.
The dream of the East is not ill-fated. It is favorable,
O monks and disciples assembled in this place.

The great pillar rising to the South
Is Ngokton Chodor of Shung.
The tigress roaring on the pillar's top
Means that Ngokton has the nature of a tiger.
Its hair bristling on its whole body
Is the realization of secret instruction.
The three times it smiled
Is knowledge of the Trikaya.
Its four claws spread over the forest
Are the accomplishment of the four unfolding actions.
Its gaze turned upward
Is a parting from the world of birth and death.
Its proud walk above the dense forest
Is the arrival in the realm of liberation.
The cedars of the forest thickly tangled
Signify a line of heirs and grandsons.
The dream of the South is not ill-fated. It is favorable,
O monks and disciples assembled in this place.

The great pillar rising where the sun sets
Is Great Metön of Tsangrong.
The giant garuda which soared above the pillar
Means that Metön has the nature of a garuda.
Its wings widespread
Are the realization of the secret instruction.
Its horns raised toward the sky
Signify perfection in meditation and insight.
Its gaze turned toward the heights
Is a parting from the world of birth and death.
Its flight across the immensity of space
Is the arrival in the realm of liberation.
The dream of the West is not ill-fated. It is favorable,
O monks and disciples assembled in this place.

The great pillar rising to the North
Is Milarepa of Gungthang.
The vulture which hovered over the pillar
Means that Mila is like unto the vulture.
Its pointed wings outspread
Are the realization of the secret instruction.
Its eyrie in the cliff
Means that his life will be harder than the rock.
The fledgling born of this vulture
Means that he will be without rival.
The small birds filling space
Signify the propagation of the Kagyü Doctrine.
Its gaze turned toward the heights
Is a parting from the world of birth and death.
Its flight toward the immensity of space
Is the arrival in the realm of liberation.
The dream of the North is not ill-fated. It is favorable,
O monks and disciples assembled in this place.

The work of the old one is finished.
For you, disciples, your hour has come.
If the word of this old man is prophetic,
The perfect teaching, transmitted,
Will spread far and wide in the future.'

So he spoke. Then all those present were filled with joy. The lama revealed to his chief disciples the treasure of the Doctrine and the special instruction. He instructed us in them by day, and at night we joyfully meditated on them.

One evening, when he was giving the Initiation of Anatmata,[14] the lama began to ponder on what particular instruction he should give to each of his disciples destined to fulfill the task of spreading the teaching. He decided to consult the omens of the dawn.

The next day, in the light of dawn, he saw his chief disciples. Ngokton Chodor of Shung was commenting on the text of the Yidam Hevajra. Tshurtön Ouangnge of Döl was meditating on the Transference of Consciousness. Great Metön of Tsangrong was meditating on Purity of Awareness.[15] As for me, I was meditating on the fire of Tummo. Thus the lama knew what the special task was for each of us.

He then entrusted Ngokpa with the transmission of the six modes and the four methods[16] of explaining the Secret Teaching which set the teaching out like a row of fine pearls, and gave him the six jewels of Naropa, his rosary of rubies, a sacrificial spoon and strainer, and the Sanskrit commentary on the Hevajra Tantra. Then he said to him, 'Work for the good of all beings by giving discourses on the teaching.'

Tshurtön Ouangnge of Döl was entrusted with mastery of the Transference of Consciousness, likened to a bird flying through an open skylight; he gave him a lock of Naropa's hair, the fingernails of Naropa, pills[17] of nectar, and a crown called the Five Classes of Buddha.[18] Then he said, 'Work toward mastery of the Transference of Consciousness.'

Great Metön of Tsangrong was entrusted with the mastery of the Purity of Awareness, which is like a fire lighted in the darkness; he gave him the bell and vajra of Naropa, the damaru of Naropa and his kapala[19] lined with mother of pearl. And he said to him, 'Free yourself from the intermediate state of Bardo.'

To me he entrusted the secret oral instruction of the Fire of Tummo, comparable to a well-set wood fire, and gave me the hat of Maitrepa and the garments of Naropa. Then he said, 'Go and wander in the barren mountains and in the snows, and practice perfect seeing and meditation.'

Finally, to all the monks assembled for a ritual feast, he said, 'Just as I made the gift of my instructions to you, as foretold by the omens, I have entrusted to each of my foremost disciples his respective task as well as the great benefit of my teaching. Because my son, Darma Doday Būm, is no longer here, I have entrusted to you as a paternal heritage the Kagyü Teaching and the transmission of my illuminating energy. Therefore, be full of zeal, and the benefit of all beings will increase.' Then the chief disciples departed, each to his own region.

The lama said to me, 'As for you, stay near me for a few years. I will give you special initiation and instruction. It may be necessary for you to consolidate your inner experience in the presence of your lama. Therefore, remain in complete seclusion.'

As prophesied by Naropa, I withdrew to the cave called the

Dzangpūhk Drok. The father and mother gave me provisions, including a share of every ritual feast they celebrated. And this they did with great tenderness.

Thus Milarepa spoke. So ends the fourth chapter, in which Milarepa through meditation with the lama brings to germination the seed of his awakening.

Fifth Chapter

Meditation

Then Retchung asked, 'Master, what circumstances led you to leave Marpa? Lama Marpa asked you to live near him for a few years. How long did you stay?'

The Master replied:

I did not stay there many years. Certain circumstances led me to visit my village. While in seclusion I did not normally fall asleep but early one morning I dozed off and had this dream: I had come to my village of Kya Ngatsa. My house, Four Columns and Eight Beams, was cracked like the ears of an old donkey. The rain had leaked throughout the house and had damaged the sacred books, Castle of Jewels.[1] My field, Fertile Triangle, was overrun with weeds. My mother and my relatives were dead. My sister had left to wander and beg. Because our relatives had risen up as enemies against mother and son, I had, from my youth, been separated from my mother and had not seen her again. This thought caused me immense pain. I called to my mother and sister by name and wept. I awoke and my pillow was wet with tears.

I became thoughtful and evoked the memory of my mother. I shed many tears and resolved to do everything necessary to see her again. Then day broke. I tore down the door of my cell and went to see the lama. He was asleep. I approached him, and bowing humbly at the head of his bed, I sang this song:

'O Master, Buddha Immutable,
Send this poor mendicant to his homeland
In the valley of Kya Ngatsa.
Mother and children, hated by our relatives,
We have been separated for years.
My love can no longer endure the separation.
Let me see my mother just once more and I will return
without delay.'

Such was my request. The lama awoke. At that moment the sun rose and through the window its rays fell on his head. At the same time the lama's wife entered, bringing his morning meal. The lama spoke.

'My son, why have you so suddenly broken the strict seclusion of your retreat? It might engender inner obstacles and open the way for Mara.[2] Go back and remain in your solitude.'

Once more I told him about my dream and implored him:

'O Compassionate Master, Buddha Immutable,
Send this poor mendicant to his homeland.

In my village of Kya Ngatsa,
Nothing is left of my possessions,
Yet there is much to make me fearful.

I wish to see if my house, Four Columns and Eight Beams,
Is in ruins or still standing;

To see if rain now falls drop by drop
On the sacred texts, Castle of Jewels;

To see if the rich field, Fertile Triangle,
Is overrun by weeds;

To see if the mortal body of my old mother
Is now in good health;

To see if my sister, Peta Happy Protectress,
Is now a wandering beggar;

To see if Zessay, bound to me by karmic link,
Can now be wed to someone else;

To see if my maternal uncle and neighbor, Yung the Victorious,
Is still alive;

To see if my aunt, Demoness Who Equals Tigers,
Is dead or alive;

To see if the family priest, Konchok Lhabūm,
Is still there.

But above all it is my mother,
Who begat me, body and mind,
For whom my longing is unbearable.

Let me go just once to my homeland,
And I shall quickly return to you.'

I prayed thus and the lama answered:

'What are you saying, my son? When you first came to me you declared that you were no longer attached, either to your homeland or to your neighbors. Now you want quite a few things. If you go to your village it is not certain that you will see your mother. As for the others, I do not know if they are there. You have passed several years in the region of Ü and Tsang, and a number of years here with me. If you wish to leave, I shall let you go. But if you count on returning, know that your coming here to make your request and finding me asleep foretells that we shall not see each other again in this life.

'However, the sun rising in space foretells that you will make the Buddha's teaching shine as splendidly as the sun. Most important of all, the rays of the sun striking my head foretells that the Kagyü Teaching will be spread far and wide. The arrival of the mistress bringing the meal signifies that you will be nourished by spiritual food. Now, it is only for me to let you go. Dakmema, prepare a special offering.'

The lama set up the mandala and the mother arranged the offerings. The lama bestowed upon me by means of esoteric symbolism the Initiation of the Path of Awakening according to the most secret oral transmission of the dakinis and also gave me the complete instruction of the path of Enlightenment. These are transmitted from one teacher to one disciple only and therefore remain unknown to others. Then the lama said:

'In truth, these instructions were given to me by the Master Naropa, who commanded that they be transmitted to you. And you in turn must pass on this oral transmission to one of your closest disciples, designated by the dakinis, placing him under pledge of maintaining the single line of transmission which must continue for thirteen spiritual generations. If you give away these instructions in return for food, riches, or simply to please others, you will incur the wrath of the dakinis. Keep them in your heart, and practice them yourself. If there comes to you a predestined disciple, even if he has no gifts to offer, bind him to you by initiation and instruction in order to preserve the teaching. To impose trials on a disciple, as Tilopa did on Naropa, or as I did on you, will be profitless for undeveloped minds. Give the teachings with discernment.

'However, in India there are nine other forms of oral transmission of the invisible dakinis which are not so restrictive as the one-to-one transmission between master and disciple. Of these I have given you four. Concerning the five others, someone of our lineage should go and ask for them from the descendants of Naropa. They will be profitable to sentient beings. Learn them as well as you can.

'If you think that you have not received my whole teaching because you had few gifts to offer me, know that I am not concerned with gifts. It is the offering of your endeavor toward realization and your zeal that have brought joy to me. Be ardent and raise the banner of perfection.

'Among the instructions of the Venerable Naropa, there is the secret oral transmission of the dakinis which none of the other great disciples has received. I have given it all to you as though pouring it from a full pitcher.'

My Master swore by the yidam that his teachings were not false and his instructions not incomplete. Having taken this oath, Marpa sang:

'I prostrate myself before you who are full of compassion,
  and I pray.
Contemplating the lives of the Masters, one sees that
Even a desire for more instruction is a distraction.
Keep the essence of the teaching safe in your heart.

Too many explanations without the essence
Is like many trees without fruit.
Though they are all knowledge, they are not ultimate truth.
To know them all is not the knowing of truth.

Too much elucidation brings no spiritual benefit.
That which benefits the heart is our sacred treasure.
If you wish to be rich, concentrate on this.

The Dharma is the skillful means for overcoming mental
  defilement.
If you wish to be secure, concentrate on it.

A mind that is free from attachment is the Master of Contentment.
If you want a good master, concentrate on this.
The worldly life causes tears; abandon laziness.

A rocky cave in the wilderness was the home of your spiritual
Father.
A deserted and solitary place is a divine abode.

Mind riding upon mind is a tireless horse.
Your own body is a sanctuary and celestial mansion.
Undistracted meditation and action is the best of all medicines.
To you who have the true aim of Enlightenment
I have given instruction without concealment.

Myself, my instruction, and yourself,
The three are placed in your hand, my son.
May they prosper as leaves, branches, and fruit,
Without rotting, scattering, or withering.'

Thus he sang. Then, placing his hands on my head, he said, 'Son, your departure breaks my heart. Impermanence is the mark of all composite things, we can do nothing about it. Yet stay here for a few days. Ponder on the instructions and if you have some uncertainties, clarify them.'

And so I stayed several days in accordance with the lama's orders and clarified my confusions and doubts concerning the instructions. Then the lama said, 'Mistress, prepare a sacred feast with the finest of offerings. Now Mila is on the point of leaving and I must bid him farewell.'

The mother offered a sacrifice to the lama and the yidam, made offerings to the dakinis and guardian deities, and prepared a special feast for the brotherhood of initiates. In our midst, the lama showed the forms of Yidam Hevajra, of Chakrasamvara, of Guhyasamaja, and others: the symbols of the vajra and handbell, the precious wheel, the lotus, the sword, and other symbols; the three letters Om, Ah, and Hūm[3] – white, red, and blue – and all the visible and invisible spheres of light.

Then he said, 'These are miraculous psychophysical transformations. To display them casually serves little purpose. I have shown them on the occasion of Milarepa's departure.'

Having seen the lama as a Living Buddha, I was filled with great joy. I thought that I also would try to achieve such miraculous power through my meditation.

The lama asked me, 'Son, have you seen and do you believe in these transformations?'

'I am so overwhelmed that I could not but believe. I thought that I should try to be able to do likewise through meditation.'

'Well, if that is so, son, you may now leave. Since I have identified all things with illusion, practice accordingly. Take refuge in the solitude of the barren mountains, the snows, or the forests. In the solitude of the mountains there is Gyalgyi Sri (Glorious Victory) of Latö, which has been blessed by the greatest saints of India. Go there to meditate. There is Mount Tisi,[4] which the Buddha spoke of as Gangchen (Snowy Mountain) and which is the palace of the Yidam Chakrasamvara. Go there to meditate. There is Lachi Gangra, which is the Gandavari, one of the twenty-four sacred regions. Go there to meditate. There is the Riwo Palbar of Mangyül and the Yolmo Gangra of Nepal, which are the holy places prophesied in the Mahayana Sutras. Go there to meditate. There is Drin Chuwar, dwelling place of the dakinis who protect the region. Go there to meditate.

'Meditate in every other favorable solitary place. Raise a banner of meditation in each.

'Adjacent to each other in the east there remain the great sacred places, Devikoti and Tsari. The time to open them has not yet come. In the future your spiritual descendants will establish themselves there. But you, yourself, go first and meditate in these foreordained sacred places. If you meditate, you will serve your lama, you will show your gratitude to your father and mother, and you will achieve the aims of all sentient beings. If you cannot meditate, there will only be an increase in evil actions during a long life. For this reason, devote yourself to meditation, wholly rejecting the bonds of passion of this life, and abandon association with pleasure-seeking people.'

As he said these words, his eyes overflowed with tears. 'We, father and son, will not see each other again in this life. I will not forget you. Neither will you forget me. And so, rejoice that in the Beyond, we will doubtless meet in the Realm of the Dakinis.[5] One day in your practice of a certain exercise you will encounter an obstacle. When that time comes, look at this which I now give you. Do not look at it before.' And the lama gave me a scroll of paper sealed with wax.

I imprinted in my heart these last encouraging words of the lama. Later, the memory of each of them strengthened my devotion.

Finally, the lama said, 'Mistress, prepare for the departure of Mila Vajra Banner-of-Victory tomorrow morning. Even though the occa-

Milarepa with Marpa directly above; Tilopa, upper left; Naropa, upper right. Events surrounding the birth depicted below. This painting and others from this series are housed in the Ethnographic Museum, Stockholm, Sweden. The full series, in black-and-white reproductions and with explanatory comments are published in *The Cotton-Clad Mila* by Toni Schmid, Statens. *(Etnografiska Museum, Stockholm, 1952.)*

Milarepa's dream of the four pillars, foreshadowing his supreme station in the Kagyüpa lineage. Also depicted, upper left, is Milarepa's return to his village of Kya Ngatsa where he finds the bones of his mother. *(Ethnographic Museum, Stockholm.)*

The central figure depicts Milarepa emaciated by his austerities. Also depicted are the attack by the aunt and uncle, the visit of the hunters and the first visits of Zessay and Peta. *(Ethnographic Museum, Stockholm.)*

The Life of Milarepa, 16th century. The Nasli and Alice Heeramaneck Collection. *(Los Angeles County Museum of Art.)*

The ordeal of the towers and other aspects of Milarepa's apprenticeship under Lama Marpa. *(Ethnographic Museum, Stockholm.)*

Milarepa with scenes from both the *Life* and *The Hundred Thousand Songs*. Included are an encounter with the robbers in Milarepa's cave and the discourse to Peta, Milarepa's sister. *(Ethnographic Museum, Stockholm.)*

Death and Nirvana. Various elements of Part II, Chapter Nine are portrayed, including the yearning of the disciples for the miraculous stupa. *(Ethnographic Museum, Stockholm.)*

A rare photograph of Milarepa's Tower.

sion will be sad, I wish to accompany him.' And to me he said, 'Come and sleep near me this evening. Father and son will have one more talk.' And so I slept near the lama. When the mother came in she was weeping and lamenting.

The lama said to her, 'Dakmema, why do you weep? Because Mila has obtained the instructions of the oral tradition from his lama and because he is going to meditate in the barren mountains? Is that any reason for tears? A true cause for tears is the thought that all sentient beings who are potential Buddhas are still not aware of it and die in misery; and what is especially a cause for tears is the thought that once they have reached the human condition, they still die without the Dharma. If it is for this you cry, you should cry unceasingly.'

The mother replied, 'All that is very true. But it is difficult to feel such compassion unceasingly. My own son, who achieved wisdom and the understanding of samsara and nirvana and who would have fulfilled the aim of himself and others, has been separated from us by death. Now this son, full of faith, fervor, wisdom, and compassion, who obeyed everything that was required of him, absolutely without fault, will leave us while still living. This is why I do not have the strength to bear my grief.'

Having thus spoken, she redoubled her lamentations. As for me, I was choked with sobs. The lama himself shed tears. Master and disciple alike suffered in our mutual affection and our tears stopped all words.

The dawn of the next day appeared. Bringing ample provisions, the Master, with about thirteen disciples, accompanied me for half a day's journey. All this time they walked along with the sadness of loving hearts, speaking words of affection and showing signs of love.

Then at a mountain pass from where the Ridge of Religion could be seen, we sat down to take part in a ritual feast. And the lama, taking my hand in his, said:

'My son, you are going into Ü and Tsang. At Silma Pass in Tsang there is a strong chance of meeting brigands. I had thought of not letting you leave without a good companion, but the time has come when you must go alone. Now I invoke my lama and yidam and command the dakinis to keep my son free from harm on the way. For your part, it is important that you take care during the journey. Go from here to Lama Ngokpa. Compare your instructions and see if there are any differences. After that, set out quickly. Do not stay more than seven days in your own district, and go immediately into solitude. It is for your own good and for that of all sentient beings.'

On leaving, I offered the lama this Song of Departure for Tsang:

'O Master Buddha Vajradhara, the Immutable One.
For the first time I go to Tsang as a beggar.
For the first time I go to my homeland as a mere seeker.

By the grace of my father and compassionate lama,
At the summit of Silma Pass in Tsang,
The twelve dakinis of the mountain will come to meet me.

I invoke the Master, the Blessed One.
I put my confidence in the Three Jewels.
My escorts are the dakinis of the three stages of the Path.[6]

I go with enlightened attitude as a companion.
Eight armies of gods[7] and their followers will welcome me.
I have nothing to fear from a hostile enemy.

Even so, it is to you I turn,
I beg you to meet and guide me in this life and the next.
Turn all danger away from me.
Protect my body, speech, and mind.

Bring about the realization of my vows.
Initiate me into the power of compassion,
Strengthen me in knowledge of the Tantra and in
transmitting it.

Grant me a long life devoid of illness.
You who know the joys and sorrows of this mendicant,
Bless me that I may have the strength
To live in solitude in the mountains.'

Thus I prayed and the lama answered, 'My son, it shall be so. Keep in your memory the last words coming from your old father's heart. Do not forget them.'

Then, having placed his hand on my head, he sang this song:

'Salutation to all Venerable Lamas,
May my fortunate son, seeker of the Dharma, attain to the
Dharmakaya.

Through the indestructible, silent voice of mantra with its
  nectar-like flavor,
May you attain Sambhogakaya.

May the tree of your enlightened mind, with its root in
  human awareness,
Be covered with the leaves of Nirmanakaya.

May the adamantine words of your lama
Live in your heart, never to be forgotten.

May the blessing of the yidams and dakinis
Penetrate to the very roots of your life.

May the guardian deities of religion
Ceaselessly watch over you.

May this profound and auspicious prayer
Be quickly realized.

May the compassion of all seekers
Sustain you in the past, present, and future.

On Silma Pass in Tsang
The twelve goddesses[8] will come to meet you.

Tomorrow, on your way,
The dakas and dakinis will urge you onward.

In the beloved field and house of your homeland
Is the guru of ephemeral illusion.

In your aunt, your sister, and relatives
You have a master who dissolves illusion.

In the wilderness cave
You have an open market where you can barter samsara for
  nirvana.

In the monastery of your heart and body
You have a temple where all Buddhas unite.

From the offerings of fresh food
You will make nectar pleasing to the dakinis.

By harnessing the vital centers of energy
You will harvest precious fruit.

In your village where people have little love for you
You will practice virtue without distraction.

In strict seclusion, without man or dog,
You will have the torch to quickly see the signs.

In the freedom of obtaining food without begging
Is the heavenly blessing of a peaceful heart.

In the crystal palace of the gods
You will be witness to your own victory.

In practicing the supreme Dharma whole-heartedly
You will achieve the pure spiritual bond.

To help you carry out my instructions
You will have the treasure of Enlightenment.

In the sacred teachings which are the living heart of the
  dakinis
You will find the frontier between samsara and nirvana.

For the disciples of Marpa the Translator,
There will be many avenues of renown.

Through the persevering heart of Milarepa
There will stand the pillar of the Buddha's teaching.
May he who guards the pillar of the Dharma
Be blessed with a noble lineage.
May he be blessed by the Kagyü lamas.
May he be blessed by the excellent yidams.
May he be blessed by Hevajra, Chakrasamvara, and Guhyasamaja.
May he be blessed by the sacred Dharma.
May he be blessed by the dakinis.
May he be blessed by the dakinis of the three stages of the Path.
May he be blessed by the guardian deities.
May he be blessed by dakini Dusolma.[9]
May he be blessed by good disciples.
May he fulfill the words of his lama.

May future disciples be blessed for all generations.
May all those blessings be constant and unchanged.'

'Keep these words in your memory and practice without forgetting.' Speaking thus, the lama expressed great joy. After that the mother gave me ample provisions, clothing and new boots. Then she said:

'My son, these things that I give you as an earthly farewell are only material things. Since it is the end of our reunion as mother and son in this life, I wish your departure to be joyous. I pray that in the Beyond we may be reunited in the Dakinis' Realm of Ugyen. As a spiritual farewell, I ask you not to forget these words spoken from your mother's heart.'

She gave me a kapala and a vase filled with ritual wine, and sang this song:

'I prostrate myself at the feet of the most gracious Marpa.
My son, who has the power of perseverance and endurance,
Who is gentle and steadfast in affection,
O most fortunate son,
Drink the nectar of the lama, a wine of perfect wisdom,
To your deepest satisfaction,
And then depart.
May we meet again in the Pure Land of the Buddha
As friends reunited.

Without forgetting us, your father and mother,
Call to us ceaselessly in your distress.
Depart after enjoying the teachings that feed the heart.
Eat your fill and assimilate them.
May we meet again in the Pure Land of the Buddha
As friends reunited.

Without forgetting your compassionate father and mother,
Remember their kindness and persevere in your practice.
Wear the cloak of the dakinis' deep breath,
Let it warm you on your journey.
May we meet again in the Pure Land of the Buddha
As friends reunited.

Without forgetting helpless sentient beings,
Let your mind settle in the path of enlightened awareness.
Engender an urge to bring about universal emancipation
And carry the burden of the Dharma
With a great strength as you depart.
May we meet again in the Pure Land of the Buddha
As friends reunited.

My son, I, fortunate Dakmema,
Speak to you from my heart.
Keep my words in your heart and do not forget them.
Your mother will remember you.
Mother and son, minds and hearts in harmony,
May we meet again in the Pure Land of the Buddha
As friends reunited.

May my prayer be fulfilled.
May you repay the kindness of your lama through the practice of the Dharma.'

Speaking thus, she shed many tears. And all those present wept and displayed their grief. As for me, I prostrated myself before the father and the mother, touching my head to their feet. I asked for their blessing. I kept walking backward until I could no longer see the lama's face. All those present tearfully watched me. I was reluctant to leave. At last, seeing that the lama and mother were out of sight, I set out and, after crossing a little valley, I looked back. The lama and his followers, still in the same place, seemed to form a brown mass in the distance. I wondered if I would ever return. Then I reflected, 'I have finally obtained complete instruction. I will never again have anything to do with profane deeds. I need never be separated from my lama, so long as I can visualize him in meditation above the crown of my head. I even have his promise that we will meet again in the Pure Land of the Buddha. Once I have seen the mother who bore me, body and mind, I may still return to the lama.'

This thought ended my sadness and I set out again. I arrived at the house of Lama Ngokpa. We compared our instructions. In explaining the Tantra, he was greater than I. In actual practice I was not far behind, but in the secret transmission of the dakinis I surpassed him.

After paying respects, I left for my village. I arrived there in three days.[10] I was elated to realize I had the yogic powers that made this possible.

Thus spoke Milarepa. This is the fifth chapter, wherein he masters all the general teachings; wherein, as urged by prophetic dreams, he obtains secret oral instructions transmitted from one master to one disciple; and wherein he leaves the lama to go to his own village.

Sixth Chapter

Meditation

Then Retchung asked, 'Venerable Master, when you arrived in your native land, did you find your mother alive or was it as you had dreamed?'

The Master answered, 'Just as in my bad dream, I was not fortunate enough to see my mother again.' Retchung then said, 'Tell me, Master, in what condition was your house and whom did you meet first?' And Milarepa continued:

The first people I encountered were some herdsmen. That was in the upper valley from where I could see my house. Pretending ignorance, I asked them the name of the region and who the landowners were. They answered truthfully. Then pointing out my own house, I said, 'And that place down there, what is it called? What is the owner's name?'

One of the herdsmen said, 'That house is called Four Columns and Eight Beams. It has no living owner, only a ghost.'

'Are the inhabitants dead or have they left the village?' I asked.

'At one time the master of this house was one of the wealthiest in the region. He died prematurely, leaving an only son, who was still young. Because the father made his will unwisely, the cousins seized all the son's property. When the son grew up, to punish them for seizing his wealth, he brought misfortune on the village by casting spells and sending hailstorms.'

'Perhaps the inhabitants fear his guardian deity, and dare not look at the house and field, let alone approach them,' I said.

The herdsman continued, 'The house contains the mother's corpse and is haunted by her ghost. His sister abandoned her mother's body and disappeared, no one knows where. As for the son, he is either dead or lost. It is said there is a sacred book in the house. Hermit, if you dare, go and see for yourself.'

'How much time has passed since these events?'

'The mother died about eight years ago. Nothing but a memory remains of the curses and the hail. I have only heard about it from others.'

So the villagers did indeed fear my guardian deity.

I thought they would not dare harm me. But the certainty that my old mother was dead and my sister wandering filled me with sorrow. Weeping, I hid myself and waited until the sun went down. When it was dark, I went into the village.

It was truly as in my dream. My field was overgrown with weeds. I went into my house, which had been built like a temple. Rain and dirt had fallen on the sacred books, Castle of Jewels. Rats and mice had made nests there, covering the books with their droppings. At this sight, I became pensive; and my heart was filled with sadness.

I entered the main room. The ruins of the hearth mingling with dirt formed a heap where weeds grew and flourished. There were many bleached and crumbled bones. I realized that these were the bones of my mother. At the memory of her I choked with emotion and, overcome with grief, I nearly fainted.

Immediately thereafter, I remembered the lama's instructions. Unifying my consciousness with that of my mother and with the enlightened mind of the Kagyü lamas, I seated myself upon my mother's bones and meditated with a pure awareness without being distracted even for a moment in body, speech, or mind. I saw the possibility of liberating my father and mother from the suffering of the cycle of birth and death.

Seven days passed and I emerged from my meditation. I began to reflect: Being convinced of the futility of samsara, I will have a reliquary made from the bones of my mother, and as payment I will give the books, Castle of Jewels. After that, I will go to Horse Tooth White Rock and dedicate myself to meditation both night and day for the rest of my life and will kill myself if I so much as think of the Eight Worldly Reactions. If I succumb to the law of desire, may the guardian deities of religion take my life. I repeated this terrible oath again and again from the depths of my heart.

I gathered together the bones of my mother and the books and paid homage to them, after having cleansed them of the dust and bird droppings. The books were not too damaged by rain and could still be read. On my back I took the first part of the books which was undamaged, and the bones of my mother I carried in the folds of my chuba. I was filled with the futility of samsara. Overcome with immeasurable sorrow, I sang this Song of Equanimity, pledging myself to the essential purpose of the Dharma:

'O Venerable, Compassionate, and Unchanging One,
In accord with the prophecy of Marpa the Translator,
Here in the demonic prison of my homeland
I find a teacher of ephemeral illusions.

Bless me, that I may absorb the truths
Offered by this teacher.
Everything that exists
Is transitory and in constant movement.
And especially this world of samsara
Is devoid of essential purpose and value.

Rather than engage in futile actions
I must devote myself to the essential purpose of the Dharma.
At first when there was a father,
There was no son.
When there was a son, there was no longer a father,
Our meeting was illusion.
I, son, will practice the true Dharma.
I go to meditate at Horse Tooth White Rock.

When there was a mother, there was no son.
Now that I have come, my old mother is dead,
Our meeting was illusion.
I, son, will practice the true Dharma.
I go to meditate at Horse Tooth White Rock.

When there was a sister, there was no brother.
Now that her brother has come, she has wandered away,
Our meeting was illusion.
I, son, will practice the true Dharma.
I go to meditate at Horse Tooth White Rock.

When there were holy books, there was no veneration.
Now that I venerate them, they are damaged by rain,
Our meeting was illusion.
I, son, will practice the true Dharma.
I go to meditate at Horse Tooth White Rock.

When there was a house, there was no master.
Now that the master has come, it is in ruins,
Our meeting was illusion.
I, son, will practice the true Dharma.
I go to meditate at Horse Tooth White Rock.

When there was a fertile field, there was no master.
Now that the master has come, it is overgrown with weeds,
Our meeting was illusion.
I, son, will practice the true Dharma.
I go to meditate at Horse Tooth White Rock.

House, homeland, and fields
Are of a world without true benefit.
Let the ignorant take them.
As a hermit I go to seek liberation.
Compassionate Father, Marpa the Translator,
Bless this mendicant so that he may meditate in solitude.'

Thus, having expressed my suffering, I left for the home of the tutor who had long ago taught me to read. He was dead, so I offered the first part of the Castle of Jewels to his son, saying, 'I will give you the rest of this sacred book. Make earthen figurines with the bones of my mother.'

He answered, 'Your guardian deities will surely follow your book, so I do not want it, but I will help you mold the figurines.'

'My guardian deities will not follow my gifts.'

'Then all is well,' he said.

With my help he made the figurines with the bones of my mother.[1] We then performed the consecration ceremony and installed the figurines in a stupa. Afterward I prepared to leave.

The son of my tutor said, 'Stay here for a few days and talk, and I will attend to your needs.'

I answered, 'I have no time for talk. I yearn to meditate.'

'Then stay tonight. Tomorrow when you leave I will give you provisions.'

I consented to stay, and he continued, 'When you were young, you vanquished your enemies by magic. Now that you are in the prime of life, you profess a religion which is marvelous. Someday you will become a great saint. From which lama did you receive instructions, and what were they?' He asked me very detailed questions.

I answered, 'I have obtained the teaching of the Great Perfection. But above all, I met Marpa.'

'That is amazing! If this be so, it would be good if you were to repair your house, marry Zessay, and continue in the footsteps of your lama.'

I answered:

'The Lama Marpa took a wife for the benefit of sentient beings. But I have neither the intention nor the ability to act as he does. To do so would be like a hare imagining it could follow in the footsteps of a lion. It would fall into an abyss and surely die. Saddened by the cycle of birth and death, I wish for nothing but to meditate and obey the teachings of the lama. The very basis of his teaching is that this meditation be practiced in solitude. It is in this way that I shall continue in his path. Only by meditation can I fulfill his hopes. It will serve the cause of the teaching and will help all sentient beings. It will even save my father and my mother, and will bring about the realization of my own aim. I only know how to meditate, and I can do nothing else.

'I have no other thought. I came back to my village chiefly because my parents had owned a house and property here. The disappearance of all my worldly goods has intensified my wish to meditate until it is now like a flame burning in my breast.

'Others have not known such misfortune. For those who do not think of the sufferings of death and the lower realms, the sensory pleasures of life may be enough. As for myself, all these things compel me to meditate with complete disregard for food, clothing, or recognition.'

Shaken by sobs, I sang this song:

'I prostrate myself at the feet of Marpa, the Perfect One.
Bless this mendicant that he may be free from attachments.

Alas! Alas! Misery, misery!
When I think of those who trust in worldly things,
I am filled with sadness.

To indulge in worldly things stirs up misery at its very source.
Swirling continuously, one is thrown into the pit of samsara.
What can they do, those trapped by sorrows and tribulations?
There is no other course than devotion to the Dharma.

Venerable Marpa, Immutable, Upholder of Ultimate Truth,

Bless this mendicant that in solitude he may live.
In the city of ephemeral illusion,
The traveler from afar has been grieved.

In the strange land of Gungthang
My flocks of sheep and the land they grazed upon
Are today the prey of evil-doers.
This, too, is an example of ephemeral illusion,
An example which summons me to meditation.

The main hall at Four Columns and Eight Beams
Today is like the upper jaw of a lion.[2]
My house with its four angles, four walls, and pinnacle
Is today like the ear of a donkey.
This, too, is an example of ephemeral illusion,
An example which summons me to meditation.

My good field, Fertile Triangle,
Today is devoured by weeds.
My cousins and my next of kin
Are today my enemies,
Having made war against us.
This, too, is an example of ephemeral illusion,
An example which summons me to meditation.

Today, my good father, Mila Banner of Wisdom,
Is no more, no trace remains.
My mother, White Jewel, descendant of Nyang,
Is nothing but crumbling bones.
This, too, is an example of ephemeral illusion,
An example which summons me to meditation.

The family priest, Myriad Gems of Heaven,
Is now a domestic servant.
The holy books, Castle of Jewels,
Are today a nesting place for rats and mice.
This, too, is an example of ephemeral illusion,
An example which summons me to meditation.

My maternal uncle, Yung the Victorious,
Lives today amidst my enemies.
My sister, Peta Happy Protectress,
Has wandered away without leaving a trace.

This, too, is an example of ephemeral illusion,
Which summons me to a life of meditation.

Venerable Marpa, Compassionate and Immutable,
Bless this mendicant that he may meditate in solitude.'

In grief, I sang this song.

The son of my tutor cried out, 'It is amazing, and yet it is true!' And he sighed deeply. His wife was sobbing uncontrollably. I had seen the plight of my village, and I could not help but affirm again and again my determination to continue meditation. I kept this wish deep in my heart and, constantly practicing meditation, I had no cause for remorse.

Thus spoke Milarepa. This is the sixth chapter, in which Milarepa, convinced of the futility of samsara, resolves to dedicate himself to meditation.

Seventh Chapter

Meditation

Retchung asked, 'Master, where did you practice asceticism and meditation?'

Milarepa continued:

The next day, my tutor's son said to me, 'Take these provisions, and remember us in your meditation.'

He gave me a sack of barley flour and some excellent dried meat. I withdrew to a good cave on the hill behind my house to meditate. As I was sparing with my provisions, my body began to weaken. Nevertheless, I was able to withstand several months of ardent meditation.

When my provisions were exhausted and I had nothing left to eat, I felt I could not hold out much longer.

I thought, 'I will beg for meat from the herdsmen in the highlands and for grain from the farmers in the valley. By carefully rationing my food, I will be able to continue my meditation.' And so I went to beg from the herdsmen.

At the entrance to a tent, I called out, 'Please give a hermit some food.'

I had chanced upon the encampment of my aunt. As soon as she recognized me, she became furious and set her dogs on me. I defended myself with stones and staff. Then my aunt, seizing a tent pole, shouted at me, 'Disgraceful son of a noble father! Dishonor to your family! Destroyer-demon of your village! Why have you come here? Such a son – born to such a good father!'

Speaking in this way, she threatened me. I drew back, but as I was starved and weak I tripped over a stone and fell into a pool of water. Although I was nearly dead, my aunt continued to curse me. I got up as best I could and, leaning on my staff, I sang this song to her:

'I prostrate myself at the feet of Marpa the Compassionate.

In the evil land of Tsayi Koron,[1]
We, mother and children, were hated by our relatives.
We are scattered like beans with a stick.
Uncle and aunt, it is you who have scattered us.
Remember that!

While I wandered to the ends of the earth begging,
My mother was killed by the sword of poverty and sorrow.
My sister wandered away to beg for food and clothing.
As I had never stopped loving my mother and sister,
I returned to the prison of my homeland,
And found my beloved mother dead
And my unhappy sister wandering to the ends of the earth.
Sadness and bitterness overflowed in my breast.

With this suffering of mother and children,
O cousins, have you not plotted to overwhelm us with grief?
Yet it is this intolerable grief
Which has called me back to the religious life.
While cut off in a mountain retreat, and meditating
On the teachings of Marpa the Compassionate,
My body, though a mere illusion, was deprived of food.

Setting out to beg,
Like an insect dying at the opening to an anthill,
I found myself at the doorway of my aunt's tent.
She sent a ferocious dog to welcome me.
With weakened body I fought it off.
Her curses, evil words, and slander
Caused my heart to overflow with grief.

Armed with a tent pole,
She rained blows upon my body, causing great pain and suffering,
And nearly deprived me of my precious life.
Although I have good cause for anger,
I shall fulfill the teachings of the lama.

O aunt, forget your anger,
And give me provisions for my retreat.
O noble Marpa, Merciful Lord,
Bless your disciple, and calm his anger.'

Thus I sang these harmonious lamentations, which shamed even my aunt. Accompanied by a young girl, who was weeping, she went into their tent.

The aunt sent the young girl to me with a pat of butter and a partly spoiled cake of cheese. I went to beg at the other tents where I knew none of the people, but everybody, knowing who I was, looked at me curiously and gave me bountiful alms. Carrying these offerings with me, I left quickly.

I knew that my uncle would act in the same way as my aunt, and I thought to myself, 'I must avoid going in his direction.' But while asking for alms from the peasants in the valley of Tsa, I arrived at the door of the house where my uncle was living.

Even though I looked like a decaying corpse, he recognized me, and shouted, 'Ah, you are just the one I wanted to see.'

And he threw a murderous stone, nearly hitting me.

As for me, I recognized my uncle and fled. He threw stones at me with all his strength, and I kept running. He then went for his bow and arrow.

'Unnatural son! A disgrace to your family! Have you not brought about the ruin of your village?' And he shouted to the villagers, 'We have now got hold of our enemy. Come quickly.'

With these words, he shot arrows at me. Some young men from the village also began to throw stones. I decided to threaten them with black magic, as I feared they might do something terrible to me because of my sorcery in the past. I cried out, 'Father Lamas of the Kagyü lineage! O you ocean of guardian deities, drinkers of blood! The Dharma-practicing hermit is surrounded by enemies. Come to my rescue.' And to the villagers I said, 'I may die, but my guardian deities are deathless.'

Terrified, the men seized my uncle and stopped harassing me. The stone throwers asked for forgiveness. Each of the others brought an offering. Only my uncle refused to give anything. But, as my stay in the region would have aggravated their anger, I decided to leave.

In the evening I had a dream foretelling a happy event if I were to remain for a few days. So I stayed, and Zessay learned of my arrival in the village. She came to see me, bringing provisions and some excellent beer. She embraced me and burst into tears. She told me how my mother had died and that my sister had become a wanderer. Overcome with grief, I too shed many tears.

I said to her, 'Why, after all this time, have you not married?'

She replied, 'They were afraid of your guardian deity, and no one would have me. If anyone had proposed, I would have refused. That you have taken up religion is astonishing. What are you going to do with your house and your field?'

I understood her idea and I thought to myself, 'That I did not marry her is only by the grace of Marpa the Translator. From the worldly point of view I must tell Zessay that there is no hope of marriage with me, but from the religious point of view I shall say earnest prayers for her.'

And I said to her, 'If I find my sister again, I will give her my house and my field. Meanwhile, make use of the field yourself. If it becomes known for certain that my sister is dead, you may keep the house and the field.'

'But do you not want them yourself?'

'In accordance with my ascetic practice, I will seek food as do the mice and birds, so I have no need of a field. My abode will be an empty cave, therefore I do not need a house. Even if one were Master of the Universe, at the moment of death one must give up everything. If one renounces everything now, one will be happy here and hereafter. That is why, quite the opposite of what others do, I have now given up everything and everybody. Do not expect me to be a man in the worldly sense.'

She replied, 'So, your practice is opposed to that of other religious people?'

'First of all, those who think only of worldly goals are content with studying a few religious books. They rejoice in their own success and in the failure of others. In the name of religion, they amass as much wealth and fame as they can. They take holy names and put on yellow robes. I turn away from them and always will.

'But other devotees, if their minds and practice have not been so corrupted, are in agreement with me, no matter what robes they wear, and I cannot turn my back on them. I shun only those who do not follow the essence of the Dharma.'

'I have never seen a religious devotee like you. You look even worse than a beggar. What kind of Mahayana is this?'

'It is the best of all. It throws the Eight Worldly Reactions to the winds in order to realize Enlightenment in this lifetime. This appearance of mine conforms with that tradition.'

Zessay replied, 'As you say, your way and theirs are quite opposite; one of them must be false. If they are both equally true, I would prefer their way to yours.'

'I do not like what you worldly people like. Even those monks in yellow robes who follow the same path as I do seem not entirely free from the Eight Worldly Reactions. Even if they are free, there is an immeasurable difference in the time it takes to attain Enlightenment. This is what you do not understand. If you can, practice the Dharma. If you cannot, then go on living as you are and take possession of my house and field.'

Zessay answered, 'I want neither your house nor your field. Give them to your sister. As for me, I shall practice the Dharma, but I cannot follow a path like yours.' Having said this, she went away.

My aunt learned that I no longer had any use for my field and my house. A few days passed and she thought, 'Since he says that he will follow the instructions of his Master, I will see if I can get this field for myself.'

She came to me, bringing barley flour, beer, and some dried meat. 'The other day I acted stupidly,' she said. 'But since you are a holy man, you will forgive me. Now I, your aunt, will cultivate your field and bring you provisions.'

I answered, 'Very well, aunt, bring me a sack of barley flour each month and keep the rest for yourself.'

'I will do that.'

For only two months she brought the barley flour to me as agreed. After that, she came to me on one occasion, and said, 'People say that if I cultivate the field, my nephew's guardian deities will cast evil spells upon us. But you would not let that happen, would you?'

I answered, 'Why should they do that, since it is beneficial for both of us that you cultivate the field and bring me my provisions?'

'Very well, nephew, since it makes no difference to you, it will ease my mind if you take an oath.' I did not know how she would feel about all this in the future, but I took the oath since to make others happy is the Dharma. Then she was happy and returned home.

I made a serious effort to meditate, but I was completely unable even to attain the blissful experience of inner warmth and, while I was wondering what to do, I had this dream: I was plowing a strip of my field. The earth was hard and I asked myself if I should give it up. Then the venerable Marpa appeared in the sky and said to me, 'My son, strengthen your will, have courage, and work; you will furrow the hard and dry earth.'

Speaking in this way, Marpa guided me and I plowed my field. Immediately a thick and abundant harvest sprang up. I woke up full of joy, and I thought, 'Since dreams are nothing more than projections of hidden thoughts, not even fools believe they are real. I am more foolish than they are.' Even so, I took this dream to mean that if I persevered in my efforts in meditation I would attain a new quality of inner experience, and I sang this song to elucidate the meaning of my dream:

'I beg you, Compassionate Master,
Bless the mendicant that in solitude he may live.
I cultivate the field of fundamentally non-discriminatory mind
With the manure and water of faith,
And sow the seed of a pure heart.
The powerful thunder of my invocations reverberates,
And the rain of your blessings falls effortlessly.

Upon the oxen of a mind free from doubt
I put the yoke and plow of skillful means and wisdom.
Steadfastly I hold the reins without distraction.
Cracking the whip of effort, I break up the clods of the five
poisons.
I cast away the stones of a defiled heart,
And weed out all hypocrisy.
I cut the stalks and reap the fruit of action
Leading to liberation.

I fill the granary with the fruit of excellent instructions,
Without the support of mental concepts.
This excellent grain, roasted and ground by the dakinis,
Is the hermit's food for inner growth.
This is the meaning of my dream.

Realization does not arise out of words.
Understanding does not come from mere suggestions.
I urge all those who work for Enlightenment
To meditate with perseverance and effort.
Endurance and effort overcome the greatest of difficulties.
May there be no obstacles for those who seek Enlightenment.'

Having sung these words, I resolved to go and meditate at Horse Tooth White Rock.

The same day, my aunt brought me three loads of barley flour, a worn-out fur coat, a garment of good linen, some dried meat, and some butter and fat. And she said to me: 'Here is the price of your field. Take it and go someplace where I will never see you or hear of you again. People are beginning to say, "After all the misery Good News has caused, now you are having dealings with him. Rather than let him kill the rest of us with his black magic, we will do away with both of you." That is why it would be good for you, my nephew, to go to another village. In any case, if you stay, they have no real reason for killing me. But as for you, nephew, they will not hesitate to kill you.'

I knew very well that the people of the village had not said that. I thought to myself, 'What if I did not act according to the Dharma? In principle I have not taken an oath against casting spells on anyone who takes my field away from me. Moreover, particularly for a yogin, an oath is a dream without reality. There is nothing to prevent me from sending hailstorms the minute she turns her back. But such things I shall not do. For how can one practice patience if there is no one to be angry with? If I were to die tonight, what would I do with my field and all this?

'It is said that patience is the best means of attaining Bodhi [Enlightenment]. My aunt is the support of my meditation. It is thanks to my uncle and my aunt that I have entered the path of liberation. As a token of my gratitude I will pray unceasingly for their Enlightenment. In this life I can give them not only my field, but also my house.'

And, explaining my thought to my aunt, I said to her, 'As I have no other means for attaining Enlightenment in this life except to follow the instructions of my lama, please take not only my field, but also my house.' And I sang this song:

'Venerable Lama, in your hands are the joys and sorrows
Of this mendicant whom you have guided into the mountain solitude.

For one tortured by the karma of universal samsara,
Defilement bursts the vital artery of liberation.

What human beings cultivate are evil deeds.
If indulged in, they will suffer the miseries of the lower realms.

Love of kith and kin is a citadel of demons.
Were I to build it, I would be sucked into a furnace.

If one accumulates food and wealth,
It becomes the possession of others.

Everything one accumulates
Becomes the property of one's enemies.

Tea and beer when craved are poisons.
If I drink them, I will burst the vital artery of liberation.

The price my aunt paid for my field is her avarice.
To have any part of it would cause me to be reborn among the hungry ghosts.

The words of my aunt are words of anger.
Were I to speak the same language, we would destroy one another.

Aunt, take my house and field.
Take them and may you be happy.

Through my devotion to the Dharma, you will be released from blame,
And I will make my way to the temple of ultimate truth.

It is through compassion that I overcome the demons.
Slander is thrown to the wind, and I turn toward higher aims.

O Gracious Lama, immutable in essence,
Bless this mendicant that he may fulfill his life in the mountain solitude.'

After this song, my aunt replied, 'You, nephew, are a true and sincere seeker. That is marvelous!' And she departed, full of joy.

Disturbed by this event, I was overwhelmed by a terrible sadness. At the same time, I was happy and relieved to have disposed of my house and field. Once more I thought of going to meditate according to the dictates of my heart at the cave of Horse Tooth White Rock. Since I had consolidated my contemplative practice here in this cave where my aunt visited me, I called it Cave of the Foundation.

The next morning, taking the payment for my field and some other small things which remained, I arrived at Horse Tooth White Rock without anyone knowing, and stayed there in a pleasant cave.

I placed a small hard mat as a cushion for meditation and took up my abode. Then I made a vow not to descend to an inhabited place:

'So long as I have not attained the state of spiritual illumination,
I will not descend to enjoy alms, or offerings dedicated to the dead, even if I die of hunger in this mountain solitude.
I will not descend for clothing even if I die of cold.
I will not indulge in worldly pleasures and distractions, even if I die of sadness.
I will not descend to seek medicine, even if I die of sickness.
Without allowing myself to be distracted in body, speech, and mind, I will work to become Buddha.
O lama and yidam, bless me, that I may fulfill all these vows.
May the dakinis and guardian deities of the Dharma support me with their power of action.
It is better to die than to live as a human being who breaks vows by not striving toward self-realization.
O ocean of guardian deities, destroy my life instantly upon any violation.
O lama and yidam, bless me so that I may meet with religion in my next life and be reborn in a human body capable of striving toward Buddha-hood.'

Having made these vows, I sang this Song of Promises and Prayers:

'O Son of Lord Naropa, bless the mendicant so that he may
Achieve in solitude the path of liberation.

Shelter me from the distracting forces of Mara
And increase the depth of my meditation.

Without being attached to the lake of inner tranquillity,
May the flower of transcendent insight bloom within me.

Without arousing fleeting thoughts of discrimination,
May the leaves of my non-conceptual state spread.

Let not doubt inhabit my cell,
But may the fruit of awakening grow ripe.

Let not the Maras[2] dare to create obstacles.
May an absolute certainty arise in my mind.

Without hesitation on the path of skillful means
May the son follow in the footsteps of the father.

O Compassionate Lama, immutable in essence,
Bless the mendicant that he may attain perfection in the solitude of the mountains.'

Having thus prayed, I sustained myself solely on a thin soup with a little roasted barley flour, and began meditation.

Even though a definite awareness arose in my mind concerning Mahamudra (the Great Symbol), I could not control my breath because of the weakening of my body; no blissful Fire of Tummo warmed me and I experienced intense cold. Then I invoked my lama with great concentration, and one night I perceived, in an inner state of lucidity, a multitude of women officiating at a sacrificial feast, who surrounded me and said, 'Marpa has sent us to tell you that if you do not feel the Fire of Tummo, you may use these methods of body, speech, and mind until the blissful warmth arises within you.'

They demonstrated yogic postures. I sought physical bliss through the sitting position known as the six interwoven hearths. I sought control of vocal energy through the force of the vital element in air. I sought and meditated on mental harmony through the vital powers of the self-releasing snake's coil, and soon the Fire of Tummo began to spread through me.

A year passed.

Then I had a desire to go out and refresh myself. I prepared to leave. But I recalled my earlier vow and reminded myself with this song:

'O Marpa, Manifestation of Dorje-Chang, Upholder of Ultimate Truth,
Bless the mendicant so that he may complete his retreat in solitude.

Milarepa, O proud one, may this song be your reminder and your help.
You are cut off from companions and their pleasant talk.

Empty are the views of the valley you long to see.
Nothing external can lift your heart.

Do not indulge in wandering thoughts, but let the mind be tranquil.
If you indulge, you will succumb to unwholesome thoughts.

Do not be distracted, do not be distracted, but attentive.
If you are inattentive, your devotion will be carried away by the wind.

Do not leave, do not leave, but stay where you are.
If you leave, your foot will stumble against a stone.

Do not seek pleasure, but control yourself.
Seeking pleasure will serve no purpose.

Do not sleep, do not sleep, but meditate.
If you sleep, the five poisons of corruption will overwhelm you.'

Having thus scourged myself, I meditated without distinguishing night from day. The quality of my practice improved and three more years passed in this way.

Each year I consumed one of my sacks of meal. And if I had had nothing else to sustain me, it would have been the end of my life. When men of the world, having found one-tenth of an ounce of gold, rejoice over it and then lose it, they despair. But that cannot be compared to dying without having attained Enlightenment. For a life which leads to Enlightenment is more precious than a billion worlds filled with gold. I thought, 'What shall I do? It is better to die than to break my vow. I shall not go down to the village. I will not break my vow. But since it is for a religious aim, I must find just enough food to sustain my life.'

I went out in front of the White Rock cave where the sun was warm and the water excellent. Here were many nettles – an open place with a distant view. Joyfully, I stayed there.

Sustaining myself with nettles, I continued my meditation. Because I had no clothes on my body and no other nourishment whatever, my body, covered with grayish hair, became like a skeleton and my skin turned the color of nettles. When this happened, I took the scroll that the lama had given me and placed it on my head. From that time, although I did not eat anything, my stomach felt full and there was the taste of food in my mouth. I was tempted to break the seal of the scroll to look at it. But an omen warned me not to open it yet. So I let it be.

About a year passed. Some hunters from the market of Kirong who had had no luck hunting suddenly came to my cave. Upon seeing me, they cried, 'It is a ghost!' and they ran away. I called out to them that I was a man and a hermit.

'That is hard to believe,' they said, 'but let us see.'

Returning, they rushed into the cave and demanded, 'Where is your food? Give it to us. Later we will return it in kind. If you refuse, we will kill you.' With these words, they threatened me.

'I have nothing but nettles,' I told them. 'Lift me up and see. I have no fear of being robbed.'

'We will not rob you.'

'What would happen if we were to lift up the hermit?' said one.

'It might bring us a blessing,' said another.

One after the other lifted me up and dropped me down again. Although my body, disciplined by asceticism, was filled with pain, I felt a terrible and unbearable pity for them. I wept.

One of the hunters, who had stood by without hurting me, said to the others, 'Wait! This man seems to be a real seeker. Even if he were not, you do not prove your manhood by harassing such a bag of bones. It is not his fault that we are hungry. Stop what you are doing.' And he said to me, 'You are a wonderful yogin. Since I have not tormented you, place me under the protection of your meditation.'

The others said, 'And we who lifted you up, protect us also.'

One of them said, 'Yes, but there are different kinds of protection, believe me.' He burst out laughing and left.

Although I did not think of using sorcery, they eventually received retribution at the hands of my guardian deities. The regional chief punished the hunters. The leader was killed, and all the others had their eyes torn out, with the exception of the one who had said, 'Do not harm the hermit!'

After a year had passed and when all my clothes were worn out and the old fur coat given to me by my aunt in payment for my field was in tatters, I thought of sewing together the empty flour sack and the rags of my clothes to make a cushion. But I said to myself, 'If I were to die this evening, it would be wiser to meditate than to do this useless sewing.' Meanwhile, having given up the idea of sewing, I spread the tattered fur over my cushion and pulled up the edges of the fur to cover my lower body. The upper body I covered with pieces of the sack wherever it was necessary. When this cloth fell apart, I began to think that my renunciation was going too far and that I must sew it together. But there was neither needle nor thread. I knotted the three parts of the sack to cover the upper, middle, and lower parts of my body and fastened these with bits of jute rope. I wore this by day; by night I put the scraps of fur over my cushion for as long as they lasted. And in this fashion I passed another year meditating.

The voices of many men were heard. Some hunters, laden with game, arrived at the entrance to my cave. Seeing me, they cried out, 'It's a ghost!' and the nearest one ran away. Those farther away said, 'There are no ghosts to be feared in the daytime. Take a good look. Is it still there?'

Some old hunters came forward and they too became frightened. I explained to them at length that I was not a ghost but a hermit meditating in the mountains, and that lack of food was responsible for the condition of my body.

'We shall see if it is true,' they said, and they went into the cave.

There was nothing there but nettles. Deeply moved, they offered me a large supply of meat along with other provisions, and said, 'What you are doing is wondrous. Please save the creatures that we have killed, let them be reborn in the higher realms. As for us, wash away our sins.'

Having spoken, they paid their respects and left.

'What good luck,' I said to myself joyfully. 'Now I can eat like a human being.'

After I had eaten cooked meat, my body began to feel tranquil bliss. My health improved, my sensitivity was keener, and my practice was strengthened. I experienced a blissful state of emptiness as never before. I saw that the few gifts received in the mountain retreat were far more beneficial to me than a hundred offerings enjoyed in towns and villages.

I ate the meat sparingly, but what I saved eventually became infested with maggots. I intended to eat it after picking them out, but then I thought to myself, 'This is neither my fate nor my right. It is not fair to rob the maggots of their food. I no longer want it.' I left the meat as food for them, and returned to my ascetic diet of nettles.

One night a man came in search of food. He searched the entire cave. I burst out laughing and said, 'Just try to find something in the middle of the night, when I can find nothing even in broad daylight.'

Then also laughing, the man went away.

Another year passed. One day some hunters from Tsa, not having shot any game, arrived at my cave. I was clothed in the sack gathered in three places by rope, and I was in deep meditation. At the sight of me, one of the hunters pointed at me with his arrow and said, 'Is it a man or a ghost? Is it a scarecrow? Judging by its clothes, it appears to be a ghost.'

I smiled and said, 'It is me, I am a man.'

They recognized me by the gap in my teeth.

'Are you Good News?'

'I am he.'

'In that case, give us something to eat now. We will pay you back later. It has been many years since you came to the village. Have you been here all that time?'

'I have been here all along. I have nothing good for you to eat.'

'Give us what you eat yourself. That will be enough for us.'

'Very well, make a fire and cook some nettles.'

When they had made the fire and cooked the nettles, they asked for meat.

I replied, 'If I had meat, my food would be nourishing. I have not had any for many years. Use more nettles instead.'

'Then we want bones.'

'If I had bones, my food would not be so tasteless. I have done without them for years. Just use more nettles.'

'But we cannot do without salt.'

'Use the nettles as salt.'

'It is certain that with such a way of eating and dressing you will never look normal. You are not a man. Even a servant eats his fill and wears warm clothing. There is no man on earth more miserable or pitiful than you.'

'Please! Do not speak that way. I was born the most fortunate of men. I have met Lama Marpa of the Southern Cliffs. From him I obtained the instructions which allow me to attain Buddha-hood in this life and with this body. By renouncing the world and meditating in this solitary mountain, I am trying to reach a goal in eternity. I have sacrificed food, clothing, and status, thereby destroying the enemies, passion and prejudice, in this very life. There is no worldly man braver or with higher aspirations than I. Although you were born in a country in which the teaching of the Buddha has been spread, you have not even the urge to listen to the Dharma, let alone meditate. There is no conduct more dangerous than piling up faults little by little, and handful by handful – it fills the depth and duration of hell. Now forever at peace, I shall have supreme bliss and from now on I am assured of happiness. Therefore, listen to my song.' And I sang to them this Song of the Five Happinesses:

'I prostrate myself at the feet of Marpa the Compassionate.
Bless my renunciation in this life.
Horse Tooth White Rock is the Fortress of the Middle Way.
At the summit of the Fortress of the Middle Way,
I, the cotton-clad Tibetan hermit,
Have renounced food and clothing in this life
To become a perfect Buddha.

I am happy with the hard cushion beneath me,
I am happy with the cotton cloth which covers me,
I am happy with the cord of meditation which ties my knees,[3]
I am happy with this phantom body, neither starved nor satiated,
I am happy with my mind which has gained insight into reality.
I am not unhappy; I am happy.

If it seems to you that I am happy, do as I have done.
If you do not have the good fortune to be religious,
Consider the true and lasting happiness
Of all beings, of you and of me,
And do not mistakenly pity me.

Now the sun is setting,
Return to your homes.
Since life is short and death strikes without warning,
I who strive toward Buddha-hood
Have no time for useless words.
Therefore, leave me to my contemplation.'

The hunters replied, 'You have said many beautiful things. Certainly you have the gift of speech. But, however commendable your example may be, we cannot follow it.' And with these words they went away.

*

Each year at Kya Ngatsa a great festival was held for the casting of figurines.[4] On this occasion, these hunters sang the Song of the Five Happinesses. My sister Peta, who was begging at the feast, heard the song. She cried out, 'Whoever spoke these words is a Buddha!'

One of the hunters laughingly said, 'Well, well, she is singing her brother's praises.'

Another added, 'Whether your brother is a Buddha or an ordinary man, this is his song, and he is on the point of dying of starvation.'

Peta replied, 'My father and mother died long ago. Our cousins turned against us. My brother wanders to the ends of the earth. I myself am a beggar and will never see him again, so I do not wish to make merry.' As she said these words, she wept.

Zessay came up to her and said, 'Do not cry. Your brother is alive. I saw him some time ago. Go to Horse Tooth White Rock and see if he is there. If he is, then we will all be reunited.'

Persuaded that this was so, Peta took a full jar of beer, which she had begged from door to door, and, with a small vessel filled with flour and mixed condiments, she arrived at Horse Tooth White Rock. She looked at me from the threshold. My body was wasted by asceticism. My eyes were sunk in their sockets. All my bones protruded. My flesh was dried out and green. The skin covering my fleshless bones looked like wax. The hair on my body had become coarse and gray. From my head it streamed down in a frightening flood. My limbs were about to fall apart.

At this sight, my sister, terrified, thought at first that I might be a ghost, but the words she had heard, 'Your brother is dying of starvation,' made her hesitate.

'Are you a man or a ghost?' she asked.

'I am Mila Good News.'

She recognized my voice. She came in and embraced me. 'Brother, elder brother!' she cried. And overcome with feeling, she fainted.

I had recognized Peta. I was at the same time joyful and sad. I did my best to revive her. After a few moments she recovered consciousness. She placed her head on my knees and, covering her face with her hands, said between sobs, 'Our mother died of grief and loneliness for her son, and no one even came to bury her. I gave up all hope and left the house. I went to another province to beg. I wondered if you, too, were dead or, if alive, whether you had found some happiness. But look at you! Such is my brother's destiny! And such is the sister's suffering! There is no one on earth more wretched than we too, brother and sister.'

She called to our mother and father by name, and she wept. All my attempts to comfort her were useless. Then I, also filled with sadness, sang this song to my sister:

'Obeisance to the venerable lamas.
Bless the mendicant that he may fulfill his task in solitude.

O sister, sentient being of the world,
All joys and pains are ephemeral.
But since you grieve in this way now,
I am certain that for you there exists a lasting happiness.
For this reason, listen to the song of your elder brother.

To give thanks due
To all sentient beings who are my parents,
I do religious work in this place.
This place is like a lair of savage beasts;
At the sight of it, others would be roused to indignation.

My food is like the food of dogs and swine;
At the sight of it, others would be moved to nausea.

My body is like a skeleton;
At the sight of it, a savage enemy would weep.

My behavior appears to be that of a madman,
And my sister blushes with shame.
But my awareness is truly Buddha;
At the sight of it the Victorious One rejoices.

Even though my bones have pierced my flesh on this cold stone floor, I have persevered.
My body, inside and outside, has become like a nettle,
It will never lose its greenness.

In the solitary cave, in the wilderness,
The recluse knows much loneliness.
But my faithful heart never separates
From the Lama-Buddha of the Three Ages.

By the force of meditation arising from my efforts,
Without doubt I will achieve self-realization.

And when one has attained deeper experience and illumination,
Happiness comes of itself in this life
And Enlightenment in the next.
This is why I ask my sister Peta,
Instead of being overcome with frustration and sorrow,
To strive with perseverance toward the Dharma.'

Peta answered me, 'If this be so, your words are astonishing and it is difficult to believe that they are true. For if they are true, other followers of the Dharma would have practiced, partly if not fully, the same path, but I have never seen anyone so miserable as you.'

Having spoken, she gave me the food and the beer. I ate and drank, and at that moment my mind became crystal clear. On that evening my practice was greatly enhanced.

The next day, after the departure of Peta, my body, unaccustomed to such food, knew both ease and discomfort. As my mind began to wander between positive and negative thoughts, I meditated with all my strength, but obtained no results.

Several days later, Zessay came to see me with Peta, bringing meat, butter, tsampa, and a great deal of beer. I had gone to look for water and met them. As I was naked, they blushed on seeing me, and they wept for my misery. They offered me the meat, butter, and flour, they poured the beer, and while I was drinking, Peta said, 'From whatever point of view one looks at my elder brother, one cannot call him a man. You should ask for alms and little by little eat the food that humans eat. I will give you what you need to make clothes.'

Zessay said, 'Whatever you do about asking for food, I too will give you clothing.'

I answered them, 'I do not know when I shall die, and I have neither time nor desire to go begging to obtain food. Were I to die of cold, I would have little regret since it would be for religion. I would not find satisfaction by indulging in food, drink, and laughter with relatives and friends gathered around me, and by wearing fine clothes and having ample food obtained at the expense of my meditation. Therefore, I want neither your clothing nor your food. I will not listen to you nor will I go begging.'

Peta answered, 'Well then, elder brother, what do you think will satisfy you? Is there nothing better than your misery?'

I answered, 'The three lower realms are infinitely more terrible than my misery. Many are the beings who seek such suffering. Here is how I shall attain happiness through fulfillment of my aim.' And I sang this Song on Fulfillment of My Aim:

'I invoke my lama in his manifestation
To bless the mendicant so that he may complete his retreat
in solitude.
My happiness unknown to my relatives,
My misery unknown to my enemies,
If I could die in solitude,
The aim of this yogin will be fulfilled.

My growing old unknown to my friends,
My growing sick unknown to my sister,
If I could die in solitude,
The aim of this yogin will be fulfilled.

My dying unknown to men,
My rotting corpse unseen by vultures,
If I could die in solitude,
The aim of this yogin will be fulfilled.

Without a vigil around my corpse,
Without lamentation over my death,
If I could die in solitude,
The aim of this yogin will be fulfilled.

With no one to ask where I have gone,
With no one to say that I am here,
If I could die in solitude,
The aim of this yogin will be fulfilled.

In this solitary cave in the mountains
May this wish about the mendicant's death
Be fulfilled for the benefit of all beings,
Thus my aim will be realized.'

Zessay said to me, 'Your present conduct is in accord with your earlier words. And I marvel at this.'

Peta spoke again. 'No matter what my brother says, I cannot bear his complete lack of food and clothing. Good food and clothing will not keep you from meditating, so I am going to bring you materials to make a cloak. Since you do not wish to ask for alms, then, according to your desire, die of misery unattended in the wilderness. But if you do not die, I will bring what you need to make clothing.'

They left, and I ate the good food they had brought. The sensation of pleasure and pain and the feelings of hunger increased so much that I could no longer meditate. I thought that there was no greater obstacle for me than this inability to meditate. Breaking the seal of the scroll that the lama had given me, I looked at it. It contained the essential instructions to overcome obstacles and improve practice, instructions for transforming vice into virtue, and more especially the advice to take good food at this time.

I understood that, through the force of my former perseverance in meditation, my nerves had absorbed creative energy. Due to my inferior food the energy remained inactive. Peta's beer had stimulated my nerves to some extent and Zessay's beer and food had completed the process. Following the directions on the scroll, I worked hard on the vital exercises recommended for body, breathing, and meditation. As a result, the obstructions in the smaller nerves as well as those in the median nerves were cleared away. I attained an experience of joy, lucidity, and pure awareness similar to what I had known about in theory. In fact it was an extraordinary experience of illumination which was very powerful and stable. Having overcome the obstacles, I realized imperfections as perfections; even through discriminating thought, I perceived the inherent simplicity of the Dharmakaya.

I understood that in general all things related to samsara and nirvana are interdependent. Furthermore I perceived that the source consciousness[5] is neutral. Samsara is the result of a wrong point of view. Nirvana is realized through perfect awareness. I perceived that the essence of both lay in an empty and luminous awareness. More particularly, this special experience of my illumination was the fruit of my previous meditations and the immediate effects of the food and the profound instructions of the lama. I also had a very special understanding that the methods of the Esoteric Path (Vajrayana) are for the transformation of all sensory experience into spiritual attainment.

Because I owed all this to Peta and Zessay, I expressed my appreciation in meditation so that their merit would contribute to their Enlightenment. And I sang of the Essence of Interdependence:

'I prostrate myself at the feet of Marpa of the Southern Cliffs.
May he bless the mendicant so that he may fulfill his retreat in solitude.

The services rendered by my benefactors
Have sown the seed for their illumination and mine.
This body, difficult to obtain, easy to destroy,
Has regained health, thanks to nourishment.

The fertility of this solid earth,
And the rain of that blue immensity,
These two interact for the benefit of all beings,
And the essence of this interaction lies in the sacred law.

My illusory body nurtured by my father and mother,
And the teaching of the holy lama,
These two interacting brought me to the true Dharma.
And the essence of this interaction lies in the sacred law.

This rocky cave in a deserted land,
And my devotion to the noble path,
These two interact for the fulfillment of my aim.
The essence of this interaction lies in Ultimate Reality.

Milarepa's perseverance in meditation,
And the faith of the beings of the three cosmic planes,
These two interacting herald success in my service to all beings.
And the essence of this interaction lies in compassion.

The great yogin meditates in the rocky cave,
And benefactors bring him food.
These two interacting lead them together toward Enlightenment.
And the essence of this interaction lies in sharing merits.

The compassion of the good lama,
And the disciple's perseverance in meditation,
These two interacting ensure the upholding of the Dharma.
And the essence of this interaction lies in their solemn commitment.

Initiation leading to a rapid transformation,
And invocation with intense trust and devotion,
These two interacting will bring us together soon.
And the essence of this interaction lies in blessings.

O Lama Vajradhara, immutable in essence,
You know the happiness and difficulties of this mendicant.'

Thus I sang and, redoubling my efforts, I meditated.

During the day I had the sensation of being able to change my body at will and of levitating through space and of performing miracles. At night in my dreams I could freely and without obstacles explore the entire universe from one end to the other. And, transforming myself into hundreds of different material and spiritual bodies, I visited all the Buddha realms and listened to the teaching there. Also, I could preach the Dharma to a multitude of beings. My body could be both in flames and spouting water.

Having thus obtained inconceivably miraculous powers, I meditated joyfully and with heightened spirit.

I was actually able to fly through space, so I flew to the Cave of the Eagle's Shadow, where I meditated. Then an intense Fire of Tummo radiating warmth and bliss arose in me, immeasurably superior to any such experience I had had in the past. As I returned to the Horse Tooth White Rock, I passed over a small village called Langda, where a man was plowing with his son. This man was the older brother of someone who had been killed when my uncle's house collapsed. The son was leading the oxen while the father was guiding the plow and tilling the field. The son saw me and cried out, 'Father, look at that fantastic thing! A man flying through the air!'

The father stopped and looked up. 'It is no great wonder. It is the son of that wicked woman, White Jewel of Nyang; it is that cunning, obstinate Mila, wracked by starvation. Don't let his shadow fall on you. Keep on plowing.' The father kept moving around, fearful of being touched by the shadow.

His son said to him, 'If a man can fly, obstinate or not, there is no greater spectacle than that! So look, father!' And the son went on looking at me.

I thought that I should now work for the good of sentient beings. As I was reflecting on this a prophecy of the yidam came to me: 'Devote yourself wholly to meditation in this life, in accordance with the lama's instructions. There is nothing greater than serving the teachings of the Buddha and thereby saving sentient beings through meditation.' Again I thought, 'If I meditate as long as I live,

I will be setting the best example for future disciples to renounce the world and meditate.' And I was certain that both the tradition of the Dharma and sentient beings would derive much benefit from that.

Then I thought, 'I have stayed in this place too long and have talked too much about my knowledge of the Dharma to those who visited me. People saw me flying after my experience of illumination. If I stay here any longer I will fall under the influence of the world. There exists a risk of encountering Mara's obstacles, and the Eight Worldly Reactions will disturb my meditation. I must go and meditate at Chuwar according to the prophecy of the lama.'

Then, carrying the pot in which I had cooked the nettles, I left Horse Tooth White Rock. But I was weakened by privation during long meditation and my foot, rough and cracked, stumbled on the uneven ground outside the cave, and I fell. The handle of the pot broke off, and the pot rolled down the slope. I ran to stop it. From the broken pot the layers of residue deposited by nettle broth broke loose in a single green piece which had the form of the pot.[6] I consoled myself with the thought that all composite things are impermanent. Understanding that this too was an exhortation to meditate, I first marveled at it; then, becoming certain, I sang:

'At the same moment I had a pot and I did not have a pot.
This example demonstrates the whole law of the impermanence of things.
In particular, it shows the human condition.
If this is so, I, the hermit Mila, will strive to meditate without distraction.
The precious pot containing my riches
Becomes my teacher in the very moment it breaks.
This lesson on the inherent impermanence of things is a great marvel.'

As I was singing, several hunters arrived to take their mid-day rest. They said to me, 'Hermit, your song is melodious. Now that you have broken the earthenware pot, what are you going to do with the nettle pot? How did your body become so thin and so green?'

I answered, 'From the fact of having nothing to sustain it.'

'What a marvel! Well, get up and come over here.' And they gave me part of their meal.

During the meal a young hunter said, 'You are a capable man. If instead of this misery you had lived a worldly life, you could have ridden an excellent horse, the equal of a young lion. Girded with armor, you would have vanquished your enemies. Rich and opulent, you would have had the good fortune to protect your kindly kinsmen. Failing that, had you engaged in business, you would have had the pleasure of being your own master. At worst, even as somebody's servant, with good food and clothing you would have been healthier in body and mind. You did not know this before, but now do something about it.'

An old hunter said, 'Indeed, he seems to be a good hermit. There is no danger that he will succumb to our worldly advice. So hold your tongue.' To me he said, 'O you whose voice is so agreeable, please sing us a song for our spiritual benefit.'

I replied, 'In your eyes I may seem exceedingly miserable. You do not know that there is no one happier and more sensible than I in the world. Since I live in the highest happiness you can conceive of, listen to this Song of the Galloping Horse of the Yogin:

'I prostrate myself at the feet of Marpa the Compassionate.
In the mountain hermitage which is my body,
In the temple of my breast,
At the summit of the triangle of my heart,
The horse which is my mind flies like the wind.

If I try to catch him, with what lasso will I catch him?
If I try to tie him, to what stake will I tie him?
If he is hungry, what fodder will I give him?
If he is thirsty, what shall I mix with his water?[7]
If he is cold, within what walls will I shelter him?

If I catch him, I will catch him with the lasso of the unconditioned.
If I tie him, it will be to the stake of deep meditation.
If he is hungry, I will nourish him with the lama's precepts.
If he is thirsty, I will water him at the perpetual stream of mindfulness.
If he is cold, I will shelter him within the walls of Emptiness.

For saddle and bit, I will use skillful means and wisdom.
I will equip him with the strong martingale of immutability.
I will hold the reins of life-sustaining energy.

The child of awareness will ride him.
For a helmet, he will wear the enlightened attitude of Mahayana.
His coat of mail will be fashioned from listening, questioning, and meditation.
On his back he will wear the shield of patience.
He will hold the lance of perfect seeing.
At his side will be fastened the sword of knowledge.

If the arrow of his source consciousness bends,
He will straighten it without anger.
He will fletch it with the feathers of the four boundless attitudes.[8]
He will tip it with the sharp point of insight.
To the bow of the emptiness of things he sets the deep nock of compassionate skillful means.

Measuring the infinitude of non-duality,
He will loose his arrows throughout the world.
Those whom he will strike are the faithful ones.
That which he will kill is their clinging to self.

And thus, as enemy, he will subdue desire and delusion.
As friend, he will protect the sentient beings of the six realms.
If he gallops, he will gallop on the plains of great bliss.
If he persists, he will attain the rank of Victorious Buddha.
Going backward, he cuts the root of samsara.
Going forward, he reaches the high land of Buddha-hood.
Astride such a horse, one attains the highest illumination.

Can you compare your happiness to this?
I do not wish for worldly happiness.'

So I spoke and the hunters, showing veneration, went away.

When I arrived at Dingri, by the Chuwar road going through Peykhu, I sat down by the side of the road and watched what was going on. Some pretty young girls wearing jewels passed me on their way to Nokme. Seeing my emaciated body, one of them said, 'Look! What misery! May I never be reborn as such a creature.'

Another one said, 'How pitiful! A sight like that depresses me.'

I thought to myself, 'I have compassion for these ignorant beings.' And, feeling pity, I stood up and said to them, 'Daughters, do not speak in this way. There is no reason for you to be so distressed. You could not be born like me, even if you wished. It is astonishing that you feel compassion, but your compassion comes from pride and a wrong understanding. Listen to my song.' Then I sang to them:

'I invoke the Compassionate Marpa,
Grant me your blessing.

Sentient beings engulfed by their bad karma
Show no respect to others, but only to themselves.

Unfortunate girls, you have faith only in ordinary life.
Your self-esteem and wrong perception burn like fire.
I feel pity for such immature beings.

In these dark days of the Kali Yuga[9]
Deceitful people are honored like gods.
Hypocrites are prized more than gold
And the faithful are rejected like stones on the road.
I have pity for such confused beings.

You proud young girls, my sisters, and
I, Milarepa of Gungthang,
We are disturbing to each other.
Let us compare our pities and by tilting the lance of compassion
See which will be victorious in the end.

To those ignorant ones indulging in idle talk
Milarepa replies by teaching the Dharma.
He returns wine for water,
He returns good for evil.'

So I spoke. The young girl who had been moved to pity for me replied, 'It is he who is called Milarepa. We are all full of self-esteem. We have said many unwise things. Now, let us ask his forgiveness.'

I gave special advice to this girl. Then she offered me seven shells and all the girls prostrated themselves and asked for pardon. In response to their request for instruction, I sang this song:

'I invoke the Compassionate Lama,
I offer the sacred Dharma in brief song.

Above, in the celestial mansion of the Devas,
Conventional Doctrine is preferred; true Doctrine is ignored.

Below, in the palace of the serpent gods,
Worldliness is preferred; the profound teaching is ignored.

In the middle, on man's Earth,
False teachers are preferred; authentic teachers are ignored.

In the four regions of Ü and Tsang
Teaching is preferred; meditation is ignored.

In the dark days of Kali Yuga
Wicked people are preferred; the good are ignored.

In the eyes of these beautiful girls
The handsome man is preferred; the hermit is ignored.

In the ears of these young girls
This brief song sounds pleasant; the profound Dharma unpleasant.

These are my instructions in song.
This is my response to the gift of the seven shells.
This is the celebration of your forgiveness.'

So I sang. The girls believed in me, and went their way. Then I too left for the region of Drin. I had heard of the caves of Chuwar and Kyipūhk, and I stayed at the cave Castle of the Sun, at Kyipūhk, and meditated there.

Some months passed and my meditation deepened. People came once or twice and brought me food and drink. This I saw as a distraction and I thought, 'Now my inner experience is increasing. If I attract too many people it will create obstacles in my contemplative life. I must go to an isolated wilderness. According to the lama's instructions, I must go to Lachi.'

While I was having such thoughts, Peta came to Horse Tooth White Rock bringing the cloth she had woven for me from the wool and goat hair she had collected. Not finding me there, she went to look for me, questioning everyone.

She was told at Upper Gungthang that a hermit resembling a nettle worm had left Peykhu for South Latö. Thereupon, Peta decided to leave for that region. At Dingri she saw Lama Bari Lotsawa dressed in rich garments of silk, seated upon a high throne and sheltered beneath a canopy. When his monks blew on the trumpets, a great crowd of men surrounded him and deluged him with offerings of tea and beer.

Peta thought to herself, 'This is the way other people treat their lama. My brother's religion is one of misery for which other people have only contempt. Even his relatives blush for him. If I find my brother, I must urge him to enter this lama's service and I must convince him to do so.'

With this thought in mind, she questioned some of the men regarding my whereabouts. She learned that I was at Drin and decided to go there. Arriving at Kyipūhk, where I was staying, she said to me:

'My elder brother's religion provides him with nothing to eat and nothing to wear. This is shameful and I will no longer stand for it. Make a loincloth from this material which I have woven. Other monks have a lama named Bari Lotsawa. They have erected a throne for him sheltered under a canopy. They dress him in fine silk and offer him tea and beer. Then his monks take up trumpets and sound them to assemble a large crowd of people who offer him gifts beyond belief. He is useful to both his followers and relatives and satisfies their wishes. Religion of this kind is excellent. Try to see if this lama will take you into his service. Even were you the least of his monks you would be happy from now on. Otherwise, this religion and my impoverished condition will not sustain our life.'

While speaking she wept. I answered, 'Do not speak like that. My nakedness and my unconventional behavior embarrass you. But I am content with this body of mine which enabled me to encounter religion. So I have nothing to be ashamed of. Since I was born naked, I have no cause for shame.

'Those who knowingly, and without restraint, commit sins break their parents' hearts. Those who live off the lama's wealth and temple offerings, and those who injure beings by crafty means to achieve their own aims – all these only injure themselves and others and displease the gods and holy men. They are a cause for shame both in this life and the next. If you are ashamed of my nakedness you should be more ashamed of your big breasts, which you did not have when you were born from your mother. You think that I meditate without food or clothing through lack of alms? It is not so. Inwardly, I fear the sufferings of samsara and the lower realms as a man fears being hurled alive into the flames. When I see how people indulge in pleasure and in the Eight Worldly Reactions, I am disgusted, like a man gorged with food who vomits it up. I am as horrified as though I were seeing blood-stained hands that had murdered my own father. This is the reason for my renunciation.

'In the following instructions of Lama Marpa of the Southern Cliffs, I was advised to renounce indulgence in the Eight Worldly Reactions: "You must renounce food, clothing, and fame. You must withdraw to one solitary place after another. And you must, above all else, meditate with intense devotion and determination, abandoning the aims of this life." It is these instructions that I am carrying out. And in so doing not only do I assure the happiness of those who follow me but also lasting happiness for all other beings. The hour of death being uncertain, I have renounced the works of this life and the ways of pursuing the Eight Worldly Reactions. If I tried, not only could I join the lowest rung of Lama Bari Lotsawa's retinue but I could even become like him. But wishing to attain Enlightenment in this life, I ardently dedicate myself to meditation. Peta, you too, renounce the Eight Worldly Reactions and follow me to the snows of Lachi to meditate. The sun of happiness will shine on you in this life and the next if you can renounce the Eight Worldly Reactions and meditate. Listen to your brother's song:

'Lama, Protector of beings and Embodiment of the Buddhas of the Three Ages,
Unstained by the Eight Worldly Reactions,
You who bless your spiritual descendants,
Marpa the Translator, I prostrate myself at your feet.
Listen to me, sister Peta, young maiden,
Consumed by the desires of this earthly life.

First, a parasol with pinnacle of shining gold;
Second, encircled with fringes of Chinese silk;
Third, the frame adorned as beautifully as the tail of a peacock,
Fourth, a handle made of red sandalwood;
These four things your elder brother could obtain, if he so wished.
But these things ensue from the Eight Worldly Reactions
And your brother has abandoned them because the sun of happiness has risen for him.

Abandon the Eight Worldly Reactions, O my sister, Peta.
Abandon them and follow me to the snows of Lachi.
Let us go together to the snows of Lachi.

First, the brightly painted little monastery, high above the village;
Second, the eloquent discourses of a young lama;
Third, a good butter tea, warming on the splendid stove;
Fourth, the young monks, eager to serve;
These four things your elder brother could obtain, if he so wished.
But these things ensue from the Eight Worldly Reactions
And your brother has abandoned them because the sun of happiness has risen for him.
Abandon the Eight Worldly Reactions, O my sister, Peta.
Abandon them and follow me to the snows of Lachi.
Let us go together to the snows of Lachi.

First, the rites and rituals, divination and astrology;
Second, the abbess, high priestess skilled in hypocrisy;
Third, those who organize ritual feasts for sensual pleasure;
Fourth, sweet chanting to deceive the female devotees;
These four things your elder brother could obtain, if he so wished.
But these things ensue from the Eight Worldly Reactions
And your brother has abandoned them because the sun of happiness has risen for him.
Abandon the Eight Worldly Reactions, O my sister, Peta.
Abandon them and follow me to the snows of Lachi.
Let us go together to the snows of Lachi.

First, the majestic castle with its soaring tower;
Second, intense cultivation of the fertile fields;
Third, provisions and treasure amassed by avarice;
Fourth, the crowd of servants deepening the involvement in samsara;
These four things your elder brother could obtain, if he so wished.
But these things ensue from the Eight Worldly Reactions
And your brother has abandoned them because the sun of happiness has risen for him.

Abandon the Eight Worldly Reactions, O my sister, Peta.
Abandon them and follow me to the snows of Lachi.
Let us go together to the snows of Lachi.

First, the arched neck of a great stallion;
Second, the ornamented saddle, glittering with jewels;
Third, the warrior brilliant in his armor;
Fourth, the passion to subdue the enemy and protect the friend;
These four things your elder brother could obtain, if he so wished.
But these things ensue from the Eight Worldly Reactions
And your brother has abandoned them because the sun of happiness has risen for him.
Abandon the Eight Worldly Reactions, O my sister, Peta.
Abandon them and follow me to the snows of Lachi.
Let us go together to the snows of Lachi.

In not renouncing the Eight Worldly Reactions,
In not going to the snows of Lachi,
Your sisterly affection distracts me.
Worldly talk disturbs my practice.
From the moment one is born, he does not know when he will die.
I do not have time to put off my practice till later.
I will exert myself to meditate without distraction.
The instructions of my Father Lama benefit the mind.
By meditating according to these instructions,
I shall achieve the great tranquillity of liberation.
That is why I go to the snows of Lachi.

Sister, choose if you wish the Eight Worldly Reactions,
Accumulate sins small and large.
Bind yourself to the whole cycle of existence,
And even try to reach the three lower realms.
But if you fear the round of birth and death,
Abandon the Eight Worldly Reactions.
Let us go to the snows of Lachi.
Brother and sister, let us go together to the snows of Lachi.'

Thus I sang, and Peta replied, 'What my brother calls the Eight Worldly Reactions, people call worldly happiness. We have no happiness to give up. Your high-sounding words are an excuse to cloak your realization that you will never be like Lama Bari Lotsawa. I will not go to Lachi to buy misery and deprive myself of food and clothing. I do not even know where Lachi is. Rather than running away and hiding in the rocks like a deer pursued by hounds, stay in one place and your practice will intensify and also it will be easier for me to find you. People in this region seem to revere you. So, stay for a few days, even if you do not live here permanently. Make yourself a loincloth from this material. I will soon return.'

I promised to stay there a few days. When my sister had gone to Dingri, I made a hood to cover my head and sewed a sleeve for each of my fingers and for my feet. Then I sewed a sheath for my sexual organ.

My sister returned at the end of a few days and asked, 'Brother, have you sewn the cloth?'

'I have.'

I put them on and I showed her the sheaths I had made for each of my extremities.

She exclaimed, 'Look at him! My brother has nothing human left in him! Not only is he completely without shame, but he has also ruined the cloth that I wove with such labor. Is it because he has no time to do anything but meditate, or is it because he has too much time?'

I answered, 'I am the holy man who seeks the essential good from this precious human life. Knowing what real shame is, I remain faithful to my vows and precepts. Sister, you alone blush at my nakedness. Even if I wished to cut off my sexual organ, I dare not. I fashioned a modest covering for it just as you asked me, even though it interrupted my meditation. Since I consider all the parts of my body to be of equal worth, I made these sheaths. Your cloth has not been destroyed. But I see now that you feel more ashamed than I. If you blush at my organ, blush equally at your own. If for you it is better to get rid of an object you consider shameful, get rid of your own.'

As I said these words, her face darkened. I continued, 'Moreover, worldly people do not know how to feel shame. They feel ashamed of things which are natural while unashamedly indulging in evil deeds and hypocrisy which are truly shameful. Listen to your brother's song about shame:

'Homage to the venerable lamas,
Bless this mendicant that he may understand shame.

Maiden Peta, bound by false modesty,
Listen for a moment to your brother's song.

You who feel ashamed through ignorance
Blush at things which are not shameful.
But I, a hermit, know what shame really is.
Living normally in body, speech, and mind,
How can discriminative shame arise?

Knowing that we are born as men and women,
The differences are clear to everyone.
Real concern for modesty and decency
Is not to be found among worldly people.
Shameful is the bride, bought for silver,
Shameful, too, the child in her arms.

Greed and hatred and evil deeds,
Robbery, trickery, and fraud,
The betrayal of friends,
All these are the results of distorted perception
And are truly shameful. But few abstain from them.

All great hermits who have renounced this life
Devote the whole of their lives to the Dharma.
Through the secret practice of the profound Vajrayana,
Which is the quintessence of all vital practices,
There is no reason to feel false shame.
Therefore, Peta, do not create your own misery.
Bring your mind back to its natural purity.'

So I sang. Peta, with a sullen face, offered me the tsampa and meat which she had obtained by begging. Then she said, 'No matter what I say, my brother does not listen to me. But I will not forsake you. Eat these things and I will try to get more.'

She prepared to leave. I wondered how I could bring her to the Dharma. I said to her, 'Even if you do no religious work, live here without committing sins as long as these provisions last.' During the time that she stayed with me, I explained as much as I could about the law of karma.

My sister gained a definite understanding of the Dharma and her desire for worldly things began to decrease.

*

In the meantime my uncle died, and thereafter my aunt began to feel sincere remorse. Looking everywhere for me, she arrived at Drin, leading a dzo loaded with provisions. She left the dzo there and, carrying as much as she could, found her way to my cave.

Peta, standing on a ledge, caught sight of her. As soon as she recognized our aunt, she exclaimed, 'Because our aunt inflicted all kinds of sufferings on our mother and ourselves, it is better not to meet her.'

Then Peta pulled back the log which bridged the entrance to our cave. At that moment the aunt arrived at the other side.

'Niece,' she said, 'do not pull back the log. Your aunt is here.'

Peta answered, 'That is just why I pulled it back.'

'Very true, my niece. But now a terrible sense of remorse has arisen in me. Brother and sister, I have come to find you, so put back the bridge. If you do not replace it, at least tell your brother that I am here.'

I was on the other side of the crevasse and had climbed to the top of a rock, where I remained. The aunt prostrated herself and repeatedly begged to see me. I thought to myself, 'If I do not eventually meet with her, I will not be acting in accordance with the Dharma; but first I must rebuke her.'

So I said, 'In principle, I have given up all attachment to relatives, and especially to my uncle and my aunt. First, you plunged us into misery. Even after I set out upon the religious path and came begging, you brutally assaulted me. That is why I do not concern myself with you. The song I am going to recite will tell you why. Listen!' And then I sang this Song of Shame to my aunt:

O Compassionate One, merciful to all beings,
Marpa the Translator, I prostrate myself at your feet.
Be the support of this mendicant who has no other protection.

O my aunt, do you remember what you have done?
If you have forgotten, I will remind you with this song.
In the wretched land of Kya-Ngatsa,
We, mother and children, lost our noble father.
Then all our wealth was taken from us and we were given misery in return.
We were scattered like beans with a stick
By you and by our uncle too.
From that day on, I gave up all attachment to my relatives.

But when I wandered to the ends of the earth
I yearned to see my mother and sister, so I returned home.
My mother was dead and my sister gone.
Under the weight of sadness and despondency,
I devoted myself wholly to meditation.

Because I was starving, I left my cave to beg
And found myself at my aunt's tent.
Recognizing the poor hermit,
She was prompted to anger and violence.
She called her dog and set him upon me.
Using a tent pole as a stick,
She beat my body as one flails a sheaf of grain.
I fell face down into a pool of water.
As I was about to lose my precious life,
She screamed at me, "Monster of evil,"
And reviled me as the shame of the family.
My heart, crushed by these terrible words,
Was torn with pain and roused to fury.
Breathless and stunned, I could not speak.
With countless deceptions, she took my house and fields,
Even though I no longer wanted them.
A demon's mind lives in my aunt's body.
From that day on, I abandoned all my feelings for her.

Then, when I arrived at my uncle's door,
He, with evil in his heart, shouted terrible words at me:
"The demon of destruction has come!"
And he called the neighbors to help kill me,
He cursed me with all sorts of vile words.
Showers of stones were thrown at me,
And a stream of arrows descended on me.
My heart was struck with unbearable pain.
At that moment I was close to death.
A butcher's heart is in my uncle's body.
From that day onward I abandoned all my feelings for him.

To this poor hermit, relatives are more cruel than enemies.
Later, when I was meditating in the mountains,
The faithful Zessay, who could not forsake me,
Came to me out of her love.

With affectionate words, soothing to my mind,
She consoled my wounded heart.
With nourishing food and drink
She eased my thirst and hunger.
I am deeply grateful to her.

Even so, except for devotees of the Dharma,
I have no reason to see anyone, even Zessay,
And still less reason to see my aunt.
So leave now while it is still day.'

So I spoke. My aunt, weeping and repeatedly prostrating herself, implored me, 'Nephew, all along you have been right. I beg your forgiveness and I sincerely confess my guilt. My remorse is terrible. I never completely lost my feeling for you, nephew and niece, and so I came looking for you. Please let me see you. If you do not grant my wish, I will kill myself.'

I could not bear to refuse her. But as I was about to put the log in place, Peta whispered to me many reasons why I should not see my aunt. Not heeding her, I replied, 'Normally, a man's mind is defiled by drinking from the same source as one who has betrayed human trust. But my aunt has not betrayed any sacred trust and because I am a devotee of the Dharma, I will receive her.'

Speaking thus, I put the log in place. I received my aunt according to her wish. I spoke to her at length about the law of karma. She turned her whole attention to Dharma practice. Afterward, she became a yogini who achieved her own liberation through meditation.

At this moment, Shiwa Ö Repa (Repa Calm Light) asked the Master, 'Master, when you were receiving religious instruction, did you show great devotion to the lama? Your perseverance in meditation was so inconceivably great that in comparison our practice is mere pretense. This will not lead us to liberation. What can we do?' So saying, he wept.

The Master answered:

'Considering all the misery of samsara and of the lower realms, my devotion and perseverance do not seem great. Thoughtful people who accept the great law of cause and effect are capable of such perseverance. Those who do not believe in the Dharma have little understanding and are incapable of abandoning the Eight Worldly Reactions. That is why it is important to believe in the law of karma.

When one has continually shown signs of disbelief, even in the obvious aspects of karma, it is far more difficult to understand and believe in the emptiness of things, regardless of ample explanations based on the Buddha's words and rational considerations. If one believed in the emptiness of things one would perceive the interdependence of cause and effect as being inherent in Emptiness itself. Moreover one would achieve greater devotion to the application of noble principles. The foundation of all Dharma practice lies in belief in the law of karma, and therefore it is very important for you to devote yourself wholeheartedly to the elimination of harmful deeds and to the practice of virtue.

'Even though I was at first incapable of understanding the meaning of Emptiness, I trusted the law of karma. This is why, after having accumulated many crimes, I thought I would not be able to escape the lower realms. My fear was so great that I was compelled to venerate my lama and dedicate myself to meditation.

'You also must live alone in mountain solitude and carry on the practice of esoteric teaching according to my instructions. And I, an old man, assure you that you will achieve liberation.'

Then Bodhi Raja of Ngandzong asked:

'Lama Rimpoche, it seems to me that you are either the incarnation of Vajradhara Buddha and that you engage in all these actions for the benefit of sentient beings, or you are a great Bodhisattva who has attained the state of "Non-returning" and who has accumulated immense merit for many aeons. In you, I see all the characteristics of a true yogin who sacrifices his life for the Dharma practice. We human individuals cannot even conceive the extent of your asceticism and your devotion to your lama, let alone practice it ourselves. If we dared to practice in this way, our bodies could not bear such an ordeal. That is why it is certain that you were a Buddha or Bodhisattva from the very beginning. And so, although I am incapable of religion, I believe that we sentient beings will be led toward liberation from samsara through seeing your face and hearing your words. Revered Master, I beg you to tell us if you are the incarnation of a Buddha or a Bodhisattva.'

The Master replied:

'I never heard whose incarnation I am. Maybe I am the incarnation of a being from the three lower realms, but if you see me as Buddha you will receive his blessing by virtue of your faith. Although this belief that I am an incarnation springs from your devotion to me, actually there is no greater impediment to your practice. It is a distortion of the true Dharma. The fault lies in not recognizing the true nature of the achievement of great yogins. The Dharma is so effective that even a great sinner like myself has reached a stage not far from Enlightenment due to my belief in karma, my subsequent renunciation of the aims of worldly life, and due especially to my single-minded devotion to meditation.

'More particularly, if you receive initiation and the secret instruction which brings spontaneous awakening unclouded by conceptualizations, and if you then meditate under the guidance of an enlightened lama, you will undoubtedly attain Enlightenment.

'If you commit the ten harmful deeds and the five deadly sins, without doubt you will be reborn into the torments of the lowest realms. This is because there is no belief in karma and but little devotion to the Dharma.

'Whoever wholeheartedly believes in karma and dreads the suffering of the lower realms, a great longing for illumination will arise in him. This will lead him to devote himself to a lama, to meditation, and to maintaining a deeper insight. It is possible for every ordinary man to persevere as I have done. To consider a man of such perseverance as the reincarnation of a Buddha or as a Bodhisattva is a sign of not believing in the short path. Put your faith in the great law of cause and effect. Contemplate the lives of enlightened teachers; reflect upon karma, the misery of the cycle of existence, the true value of human life, and not knowing the hour of death. Devote yourselves to the practice of the Vajrayana.

'I deprived myself of food, clothing, and recognition. I strengthened my mind. And without concern for the hardships imposed on my body, I went to meditate in the solitude of the mountains. Then the virtue of the spiritual state manifested itself. Follow my example with your whole heart.'

Thus spoke the Master. This is the seventh chapter, in which he tells how he obeyed the instructions of his lama, how he renounced this life, practiced terrible austerities, and withdrew to meditate in the mountains.

Eighth Chapter

Retreats

Then Retchung asked, 'Master, there is nothing more marvelous than the essence of your life which is indeed a matter for joyous laughter. But its outer form gives cause for unhappiness and tears. Please tell us about those aspects of your life which cause laughter.'

The Master replied, 'The form of my life which is cause for joyous laughter is my perseverance in meditation resulting in my service to the Dharma in guiding human and non-human beings to achieve liberation.'

Retchung asked, 'Master, who were the first of these human and non-human beings?'

The Master replied, 'First, non-human beings came to torment me, and after them came the first human disciples. Then the goddess Tseringma[1] came to me in human form. Finally other human disciples appeared. I now foresee that the goddess Tseringma and my disciple Upa Tonpa (Gampopa) from Ü will propagate my teaching.' Thus spoke the Master.

Repa of Seban then asked, 'Master, your principal places of retreat were Lachi and Chuwar. Besides the caves that you mentioned earlier, where else have you meditated?'

Milarepa replied, 'At Mount Yolmo Gangra in Nepal; in six well-known caves open to view, in six unknown caves, in six secret caves, and in two others, making twenty in all. In addition there were four widely known large caves and four unknown large caves. This includes all my places of meditation, except for some smaller caves where conditions were favorable. As a result of my meditation I have achieved total awakening wherein the object meditated upon, the action of meditating, and the subject who meditates merge into one, so that now I no longer know how to meditate.'

Then Retchung said, 'Master, because you have completely eradicated the stains of discrimination, your humble disciples are deeply grateful to you for the joy of having achieved real understanding and authentic experience. For the spiritual benefit of future disciples, please identify each of these known, lesser known, and unknown caves as well as the large caves.'

The Master answered:

'The six outer well-known caves are: the middle cave of Dakar Taso Umadzong (Horse Tooth White Rock), Minkyug Dibma (Shadow of the Pleiades), Lingpa Dakmar Dzong (Red Rock), Ragma Jangchub Dzong (Ragma Cave of Enlightenment), Kyangphen Namkha Dzong (Banner of the Sky), Dagkya Dorje Dzong (Gray Rock Vajra). The six unknown caves are: Chonglung Kyung (Eagle of Chonglung), Kyipūh Nyima Dzong (Upper Castle of Joy), Khujuk Enpa Dzong (Lonely Cuckoo), Shelpūhk Chushing Dzong (Crystal Bamboo Tree), Betse Doyon (Sensory Pleasure of Betse), Tsikpa Kangthil Dzong (Base of the Wall). The six secret caves are: Gyadak Namkha Dzong (Rock and Sky), Takpūhk Senge Dzong (Lion and Tiger), Beypūhk Mamo Dzong (Secret Cave of the Goddess), Lapūhk Pema Dzong (Lotus of the Grotto), Lango Ludu Dzong (Elephant Gate of Serpent-Gods), Trogyel Dorje Dzong (Wrathful Vajra King). The two other caves are: Kyipūhk Nyima Dzong (Sun Castle of Joy) and Potho Namkha Dzong (Sky of Peaks).

'The four widely known large caves are: Nyanang Dopa Pūhk (Stomach-like Cave of Nyanang), Lachi Dudal Pūhk (Demon Conqueror of Lachi), Dringi Diche Pūhk (Tongue of the Dri in Drin), Tisi Dzutrul Pūhk (Miracle Cave of Mount Kailas). The four unknown caves are: Tsai Kangtsuk Pūhk (Cave of Firm Root), Rongi Osey Pūhk (Luminous Clarity of Ron), Ralai Zaok Pūhk (Silk Cave of Goat Mountain), Kuthangi Pūhkron Pūhk (Pigeon Cave of Kuthang).

'If you meditate in these caves you will have solitude and favorable conditions. Go there and meditate and you will have the blessings of my lineage.'

When the Master had spoken in this way, all the disciples and followers, men and women, felt in their hearts an abhorrence of samsara and an urge for liberation, and were deeply moved by a faith and compassion that knew no bounds.

As a deep aversion arose in them to the earthly vanities of the Eight Worldly Reactions, they dedicated themselves in body, speech, and mind to the teachings of the Buddha and the welfare of sentient beings. They vowed to cease their wanderings and to meditate in mountain solitude with intense determination, perseverance, and asceticism. The guardian deities promised to protect the teaching.

The best among the lay followers renounced worldly life, and many men and women who had followed the Master meditated and awakened to the true nature of reality. Lesser followers took vows to meditate for several months or several years. Even beginners vowed to abstain from at least one vice and to practice at least one virtue for the rest of their lives. Everyone fulfilled his or her vows.

I have recorded the exact words spoken by the Master, showing how he brought great benefit to all who follow the path of meditation.

I am now going to enlarge a little on the Master's life.

There were three large groups of followers: the malevolent non-human beings whom the Master conquered, those dedicated disciples whom the Master guided toward liberation, and lay followers at all levels from different regions for whom the Master turned the Wheel of the Law.

First, concerning the conquest of non-human beings: the Master gave the Demon King Binayaka at the Red Rock of Chonglung the teaching on the Six Ways of Being Aware of One's Lama.[2] Following Lama Marpa's instructions, the Master went to Lachi to meditate. In the course of compelling the great god Ganesha (King of Obstructing Forces) to accept the precepts, the Master sang of Lachi Chuzang. The following year, when he traveled to Neti in Lachi, he sang his famous Song of the Snows. In accordance with the lama's instructions, and wishing to go to Mount Peybar in Mangyül and to Yolmo Gangra in Nepal, he passed through Gungthang. Attracted by Lingpa Cave, he stayed there for some time and sang a song to the Demoness of the Lingpa Cave. At Ragma, Cave of Enlightenment, close to Mount Peybar, he sang the song that pacified the Goddess of Earth and a local spirit inhabiting the Ragma Cave.

While living at Kyangphen Namkha Dzong (Banner of the Sky), the Master worked for the benefit of many human and non-human beings. From there he went to Mount Yolmo Gangra and lived in Takpūhk Senge Dzong (Cave of the Lion and Tiger) in the forest of Singala, doing work beneficial to many human and non-human beings. Meanwhile he received a sign directing him to go back to Tibet, to meditate in mountain solitude and work for the benefit of all beings. Having returned to Tibet, he dwelt in a cave in Gungthang and sang the Song of the Pigeons.

Second, concerning how he met his spiritual sons: While the Master was living in the cave Dagkya Dorje Dzong (Gray Rock Vajra) and was meditating for the benefit of sentient beings, his yidam predicted the coming of all his disciples, particularly of the disciple Retchung Dorje Drakpa, whose mission would be to bring the secret oral instruction of the dakinis from specified places. And when the Master was at Ralai Zaok Pūhk (Silk Cave of Goat Mountain) in Gungthang, he met his spiritual son, Retchung. Later Retchung went to India to be cured of an illness, and on returning, the Master and his disciple met again.

In the cave Ronpuhi Osey Pūhk (Cave of Luminous Clarity) he met Tsakūph Repa, and on going to Ragma Jangchub Dzong (Cave of Enlightenment), he met Sangye Kyab Repa (Enlightened Protector). He then went to the Cave of Nyanang, where he met Shakyaguna of Kyo, who was already a devotee, and set him upon the path of liberation by giving him initiation and instruction.

On the way to Tago in the north, he met a woman, Pey Dar Būm (Hundred Thousand Glorious Flags), at Losum below Chung.

On his return he met Repa of Seban at the Inn of Yeru in the north.

While proceeding to Gyalgyi Sri of Latö, he met Repa of Digom.

Having gone to beg during the autumn, he met Shiwa Ö Repa (Calm Light) at Chumig Ngulchu Būm (Hundred Thousand Beads of Mercury).

Then, at Bachak Gora in Chenlūng, he met Repa of Ngandzong (Evil Cave).

While living at Lachi, he was urged by the dakinis to fulfill a certain prophecy of the lama. On the way to Mount Kailas, he met Dampa Gyakpūhwa. When he came to Mount Lowokere, he met Repa of Karchūng. While passing the winter on the snowy slopes of Ditse (Summit of Di) in Purang, he met Darma Ouangchuk Repa. In the spring, having gone to Mount Kailas, he sang of Kailas, where he defeated the Bön priest Naro Bönchūng in a contest of miracles.

He then returned to Dagkya Dorje Dzong (Gray Rock Vajra), where he met Repa of Rongchūng. Directed on his way by the dakinis, he came to Beypūhk Mamo Dzong (Secret Cave of the Goddess). Staying there for several days, he was sought out by a herdsman called Lukdzi Repa, who later became a sage. He then met Repa the Hermit of Shen at Lapūhk Pema Dzong (Lotus of the Grotto). These two men served him later, while he was living at the Lango Ludu Cave (Elephant Gate of Serpent-Gods) and at the Secret Cave of the Goddess.

While traveling to Chorodig, he met a woman named Retchungma. And at Nyishang Gurta of Mon, he met Repa the Hunter. It was he who spread the renown of the Master in Nepal. Prompted by a message from the goddess Tara,[3] the King of Khokhom honored the Master.

At the invitation of Retchung and Repa the Hermit of Shen, the Master dwelt in a cave called Dho Nyenyon-pūhk in Lachi, and the following year he lived on the cliff of Chonglung.

When he had gone to Chuwar, he instructed his disciples in three propitiatory rites for invoking the goddess Tseringma. Going down to Drinding, he met Dorje Ouangchuk Repa. When Master and disciples were dwelling in the Beypo Cave at Nyanang, he met the Indian saint Dharma Bodhi, who paid homage to the Master. Since Milarepa's fame was increasing, Darlo, a master of metaphysics, became envious and challenged him to a debate. The Master victoriously answered with higher spiritual wisdom and with the performance of miraculous feats. Afterward he sang songs about Retchung and Tibu. During this time he met Repa of Megom at the Stomach-like Cave. At Naktra (Black Stripes), a cave of Nyanang, he met a young girl called Sallay Ö Rema (Shining Light).

Then the Master withdrew to the Cave of Red Rock on a high ridge. He had foreknowledge that Retchung was returning from India and he went to meet him. This was a special occasion for the Song of the Yak Horn and the Song of the Wild Ass.

Then having gone to Chuwar, he met Repa Hermit of Len from Dagpo. On the hill of Trode Tashigang (Blessed Happiness), he met Gampopa Dao Shonnu, the incomparable monk physician from Dagpo, who was a Master of the Vajrayana. A great Bodhisattva, he reincarnated in human form for the benefit of sentient beings, as was prophesied by the Buddha. Gampopa became the Master's greatest disciple.

Since the Master was living at Omchung (Little Tamarisk) in Chuwar, he met the monk Lotön, who at first opposed him and later became his disciple. Then, while living at the Cave Kyipūhk Nyima Dzong (Sun Castle of Joy), he met Dreton Trashibar. During the period when the Master engaged in the exercise of great yogic powers, a monk called Charuwa of Likor followed and served him.

As prophesied by the dakinis, the Master had among his disciples eight spiritual sons, thirteen close disciples, and four sisters. All these twenty-five became awakened Masters. There are extensive accounts of his meetings with each of these disciples, very rich in exchange and experience (The Hundred Thousand Songs of Milarepa).

Third, concerning disciples and lay followers from many regions, the Master told how he met great disciples at unknown and secret caves. He recorded these meetings, but did not specify in what order they occurred. Included were accounts of the Master's answers to questions put to him by monks and lay followers. When he was with Gampopa, he told the story of how he had encountered a priest of the Bön[4] religion. Then, having gone to Nyanang, he gave initiations and conducted the ritual of empowerment and consecration. At Tsarma, he met two women disciples, Shen Dormo and Legse Būm. There he gave instruction on Chidrö Thigtsakma[5] for preparing oneself for death.

He then went with Retchung to Lachi, stopped at the cave Dudül Pūhk (Demon Conqueror), and wandered about in the vicinity.

He continued his journey and visited the cave Nampūhkma of Ramdig (She Who Pierces the Sky).

Finally, while dwelling in the Stomach-like Cave of Nyanang, at the request of lay followers, the Master related some episodes in his life and sang of Retchung's departure for the Ǔ Province. Urged by the dakini named Sengdhongma (Lion Face), he met with Dampa, an Indian saint, at Thongla.

At Leshing he performed for his mother, in order to repay her kindness, a special rite called Compassionately Guiding the Dead through the Bardo State. At Tsarma he gave his last instructions to the lay disciples and to other inhabitants of Nyanang. During his journey to Chuwar, he met Lhaje Yangde, an inhabitant of Dingri. When he arrived at Chuwar, he sang about the second departure of Retchung for the Ǔ Province. He met the benefactor Tashi Tsek at Lharo in Drin. At Dakkhar in Drin he met Zessay Būm (his former betrothed), Khujuk, and other lay followers.

On top of Red Rock on a high ridge, he vanquished the four Maras. It was there that he answered questions put to him by a devotee of Vajrayana. He brought immense joy to all his disciples and performed bodily transfigurations.

Innumerable people received teachings, both known and unknown, during the period in which the Master set in motion the Wheel of the Law. Guided by the Master, the most highly developed disciples achieved Enlightenment. The less developed disciples were brought to the stage of awakening and shown the path to liberation. The least developed he set on the path to Bodhichitta. Through a diligent application of the Bodhisattvas' precepts, they were brought to a firm level of awareness. Even in the very least developed ones he sowed the seed of virtue and assured them of attaining the peace of the higher realms in their lives.

With compassion limitless as the sky, the Master protected innumerable beings from the misery of samsara and of the lower realms by bringing the light of the Buddha's teaching.

All these aspects of the Master's life are amply expounded in the Gur Būm (The Hundred Thousand Songs).

This is the eighth chapter, in which the Master renders service to the teaching of the Buddha and to all sentient beings through the fruit of his meditation.

Ninth Chapter

Nirvana

At the time when these words were being fulfilled, there was a very rich and influential lama named Geshe[1] Tsakpūhwa who lived at Drin. At first, he made a show of honoring the Master. But later, succumbing to envy and wanting to embarrass the Master before the crowd of his benefactors, he pretended to be troubled by doubts and asked him many questions.

During the first month of autumn in the year of the Wood Tiger, the Master had been invited to preside at a wedding feast at Drin. Geshe Tsakpūhwa also attended. He prostrated himself, hoping that the Master would return his prostration in the presence of the gathering. The Master had never prostrated himself before anyone, nor returned anyone's prostration except in the case of his lama, and, following his custom, he did not return the prostration.

The geshe thought, 'What! A Master as learned as myself paying homage to an ignorant fool and receiving no homage in return! I shall make him pay for my embarrassment.' And, handing him a text on Buddhist logic, he said, 'Master, would you be kind enough to clear up my uncertainty and explain this to me, word by word?'

The Master replied, 'You know very well the conceptual meaning of this text. But real spiritual meaning is found in abandoning the Eight Worldly Reactions and the personal ego, through destroying false perceptions of reality by realizing the single flavor of samsara and nirvana, and through meditating in mountain solitude. Apart from that, arguing over words, and pointing out what comes after what, is totally useless if one does not practice the Dharma. I have never studied logic. I know nothing about it and if I ever did, I have forgotten it now. I will tell you why. Listen to this song:

"I prostrate myself before Marpa the Translator,
May he bless me and keep me from dispute.

The blessing of my lama penetrated my mind.
I have never been overcome by distractions.

Having meditated on love and compassion,
I forgot the difference between myself and others.

Having meditated on my lama,
I forgot those who are influential and powerful.

Having meditated constantly on my yidam,
I forgot the coarse world of the senses.

Having meditated on the instruction of the secret tradition,
I forgot the books of dialectic.

Having maintained pure awareness,
I forgot the illusions of ignorance.

Having meditated on the essential nature of mind as Trikaya,
I forgot my hopes and fears.

Having meditated on this life and the life beyond,
I forgot the fear of birth and death.

Having tasted the joys of solitude,
I forgot the need to please my relatives and friends.

Having assimilated the teaching in the stream of my consciousness,
I forgot to engage in doctrinal polemics.

Having meditated on that which is non-arising, non-ceasing, and non-abiding,
I disregarded all conventional forms.

Having meditated on the perception of phenomena as the Dharmakaya,
I forgot all conceptual forms of meditation.

Having dwelt in the unaltered state of naturalness,
I forgot the ways of hypocrisy.

Having lived in humility in body and mind,
I forgot the disdain and arrogance of the great.

Having made a monastery within my body,
I forgot the monastery outside.

Having embraced the spirit rather than the letter,
I forgot how to play with words.

As you are a Master, explain the treatise yourself.'

Thus he spoke.

The geshe continued, 'This may be the hermit's way, but if I were to challenge it with my learned arguments, your discourses would go no further. I had hoped you were a noble man. That is why I prostrated myself before you.'

These words did not please the benefactors. With one voice they said to him, 'Master Geshe, however learned you may be, there are many more like you on earth. You are not equal to the Master, not even to a pore of the skin of his body. Just preside and be silent. Increase your wealth as much as you can, since you do not possess even the smell of religion.'

In spite of his growing irritation, the geshe could not protest since everyone supported Milarepa. His face darkened and he thought, 'Milarepa acts and jests like a madman who knows nothing. Through his lies and imposture he is degrading the teaching of the Buddha, and living on gifts obtained by deceit. I, who have got so much knowledge and am the richest and most influential man in this region, now count for less than a dog in religious matters. I must do something about this.'

Then he mixed some poison with curdled milk. Promising his concubine the gift of a large turquoise, he sent her with the poison to Drin Cave, where the Master was staying.

The Master knew that his foremost disciples were already enlightened and that, even if he were not to take the poison, his time to die had come. He knew also that, unless the woman were given the turquoise before he drank the poison, she would never get it. So he said to her, 'I shall not drink this now. Bring it back later, and then I will drink it.'

Wondering if the Master suspected her, the woman, worried and ashamed, went back to Geshe Tsakpūhwa.

'Because of his clairvoyance,' she said, 'the Master suspected me and refused to drink.'

The geshe replied, 'If he really had clairvoyance, he would not have told you to bring it back. He would have told you to drink it yourself. Since he did not, that proves he does not possess clairvoyance. Take this turquoise. Go find the Master and make sure he drinks the poison.'

He gave her the turquoise, and she answered, 'Everyone believes he is clairvoyant, so it must be true. That is why he did not take the drink in the first place, and I am sure he will not take it now. What's more, I am too afraid to do it. I will not go! I do not want your turquoise.'

The geshe answered, 'Laymen believe he is clairvoyant because they have not read the scriptures, and because they have been led astray by his lies. In my books, men gifted with clairvoyance are not like that. I assure you that he is not clairvoyant. Once I have seen proof that you have given him the drink, we shall be married. We have been living together for a long time and, as they say, there is not much to choose between eating a little garlic or a lot. Besides having this turquoise, you will be entrusted with the care of all my possessions, both within my household and without, and we will share all our joys and sorrows and be one family. So do your best.'

Hoping that these promises would be fulfilled, she then mixed some poison with curds and took it to the Master, who was now staying at Trode Tashigang. The Master smiled and took the vessel in his hands. She thought, 'The geshe is right, he does not seem to have clairvoyance.' Even while she was thinking this, the Master said to her, 'So you have been given the turquoise for the deed you are carrying out?'

Overwhelmed with confusion, she prostrated herself, and said in a weeping and trembling voice, 'I do have the turquoise, but I beg you, do not take the drink. Give it back to me. I am a thoughtless evil-doer.'

'What are you going to do with it?'

'I myself will drink it since I am guilty.'

The Master continued:

'First of all, I have too much compassion to let you drink it. It would violate the essence of the Bodhisattva precepts[2] and would bring with it grave spiritual consequences. My mission is complete and my life is coming to an end. My time has come to go to another realm. By itself the drink could not harm me in the least. It does not matter whether I drink it or not. But if I had drunk it the first time, you would not have received the turquoise as payment for your crime. Now that the turquoise is in your hands, I will drink, both to satisfy the geshe's desire and to be sure that you earn the turquoise.

'As for the geshe's other promises, they will not be fulfilled. He said many things about my behavior. There is no truth in what he said, so both of you will experience terrible remorse. When this happens, in order to purify yourself, strive toward self-realization in this life. Even to save your life, do not commit any similar crimes. Call upon me and my spiritual sons with a sincere heart. Both you and the geshe have always cut yourselves off from happiness and sought out sorrow. This time I will see if I can purify you of your evil karma. Speak to no one of this while I am alive. Afterward, everyone will hear about it. Although you have neither seen with your eyes nor heard with your ears the truth of my previous sayings, keep well in mind these words I speak now. The moment will come when you will see that they are true.'

Having thus spoken, he drank the poison.

When the woman related all this to Geshe Tsakpūhwa, he answered, 'Not all that he says is true, just as not all food is fit to eat. It is enough for me that he has taken the poison. Now remember, keep quiet about it.'

Meanwhile the Master spoke. 'Men of Nyanang and Dingri, and all benefactors and followers, prepare a ritual feast and gather round me. Let all other men in the region, who have not seen me but wish to meet me, come also.'

All the disciples spread the word. Many of those who heard these words did not believe the Master had actually said them. But faithful laymen and disciples who followed the teaching, as well as other people who wished to meet the Master, gathered at Chuwar. Then for many days the Master spoke to them of the doctrine of karma on the ordinary level and of the essential nature of reality on a higher level.

During this time, several of the chief disciples clearly saw that the sky was filled with gods listening to the words of the Master. Many others, intuitively feeling that the sky and the earth were filled with gods and men listening to the teaching, experienced a state of great joy. In plain view of everyone, a rainbow canopy appeared in a limpid sky. Sacrificial offerings, parasols, and innumerable banners took form in the five-colored clouds, filling the atmosphere. There fell a rain of flowers in five different colors. Exquisite music could be heard and there was the fragrance of exotic perfumes.

The lesser disciples, having perceived these miracles, asked the Master, 'We have the impression that the sky and earth are filled with gods and men listening to the Dharma, and we are overcome with joy. What is the cause of these miracles?'

The Master replied, 'Good human disciples like you, enlightened yogins and lay devotees, are few, but celestial listeners fill the entire space of the skies and are offering me the five objects[3] of sensory joy, and this is what evokes well-being in you. This is the reason for the signs around you which some of you sense and others perceive directly.'

'Well then,' they said, 'why don't we all see the signs?'

'Among the gods there are many who have achieved awakened states of "non-returning" and others who have attained awakened insight. One needs subtle vision to see the gods, or else one needs intense yearning for virtue and awareness, and a mind unstained by delusion and defilement. If you are able to see the chief gods, you will see their followers. If you strive in this way, you will see the nature of your own mind, which is the ultimate god.' And he sang this Song on How to See the Gods:

'Homage to Marpa, the Compassionate One!
Blessed be your lineage, may it be noble.

The celestial listeners
Come from the joyful realm of the gods
To hear the hermit Milarepa,
And fill the boundless sky.

Except for those who possess the five levels of vision,[4]
No mortals can see them.
I see them all clearly.
But common folk see only the celestial offerings.

The sky is filled with rainbows and light;
A shower of celestial blossoms falls;
Fragrant incense fills the air and harmonious music resounds.

'Joy and happiness abound in all those present due to the compassion of the Kagyüpa lamas. Those of you, under their protection, who wish to see the gods and dakinis who are listening to my teaching, first hear my song:

'Owing to karma accumulated in past lives,
You have delighted in evil since the day you were born.
You have no longing for virtue.
Even in old age your minds are impure.
You will surely reap the fruit of your actions.

If you ask yourselves whether your sins will be purified,
Your longing for virtue wipes away your defilements.
But he who knowingly commits evil
Obtains a crumb of food at the price of shame.

He who poses as a guide for others
And himself knows not where to go,
Harms himself as well as others.

If you sincerely wish to avoid suffering,
Avoid all evil intent toward other beings.

In your devotion to lama and yidam,
Feel remorse for your past sins.
Vow never to commit them again.
This is the instruction for purifying yourself.

Most sinners are clever,
They lack high aim and indulge themselves.
If they have no spiritual impulse,
It proves they are still burdened with defilements.

Strive unceasingly for purification,
Dispel ignorance and accumulate merit.
If you do so, you will not only see
The Dharma-loving gods who come to listen,
But you will even perceive within yourself
The Dharmakaya, the holiest and highest of all gods.
If you see that, you will also see
The whole truth of samsara and nirvana
And you will free yourself from karma.'

Among the godly and human listeners assembled at that place, the most highly developed of them realized the true meaning of the Dharmakaya. The less highly developed experienced awareness of non-duality in a lucid and joyful state, and were set upon the path of liberation. Among the least developed, there was not one who did not embrace the practice of Bodhichitta.

Then the Master said to them, 'O you monks and disciples, gods and men, and all assembled here, our coming together in pursuit of the Dharma has been due to our spiritual aspirations in previous lives. Now that I am old, I do not know if I will see you many more times. Try your best to practice the teaching I have given you. Do not waste your time. If you follow my instructions, you will be the first of my disciples to be reborn in the Pure Land of my Buddhahood. Therefore rejoice!' Thus he spoke.

The lay devotees from Nyanang wondered if this kind of talk by the Master indicated his intention to depart from the world for the benefit of beings in other realms. They fervently begged him, were that so, to leave for the Realm of Ultimate Reality from Nyanang. If it were not so, they entreated him to come back there once again. Tearfully beseeching him in this way and overcome with intense veneration, they clasped his feet, uttering cries and groans. Likewise the followers from Dingri earnestly begged the Master to come to their country.

The Master said, 'I am old, and I will go neither to Nyanang nor to Dingri. I will wait for my death near Drin and Chuwar. Intensify your longing for liberation. We will meet again in the Realm of Ultimate Reality.'

'If the Master is not coming, may he bless each of the places he has visited so that they may have peace and prosperity. May he bless the land so that it will have spiritual harmony. May he bless all sentient beings and those who have met him and heard his name and his teaching.'

The Master replied, 'I am indebted to you for the provisions you have given me out of veneration, and I have repaid you by compassionately giving you the teaching. As a yogin who has achieved the special power of blessing, I shall bless you all so that you may have peace and happiness throughout your lives.' And he sang this song:

'I prostrate myself at the feet of Marpa the Translator,
Father protector of all beings, who has realized his aim.

O my disciples, assembled here, listen to me.
You have been kind to me,
And I have felt compassion for you.

May Master and disciples, thankful to each other,
Meet in the Buddha's Pure Land.

May all the followers and benefactors here present
Have happiness and long life.

May their spiritual aspirations be fulfilled,
Without harmful thoughts arising.

May this region be blessed,
May it be free from sickness and war,
And endowed with rich harvests and increasing good fortune.
May the followers always devote themselves to the Dharma.

May I meet again in the Buddha's Pure Land
Those who saw or heard me,
Those who remember my story,
Those who have only heard of it and of my name.
May those who emulate my life and meditate,
Those who ask for, narrate, and listen to my story,
Those who read and venerate it,
Those who follow my example in their lives,
May they find me in the Buddha's Pure Land.

May men of the future,
If they are capable of meditating
With the asceticism I have practiced,
Be spared all impediments and errors.

May those who practice the Dharma through asceticism
Harvest immeasurable merits.
To those who encourage others to follow this path,
Immeasurable gratitude is due.
May those who hear my story receive immeasurable blessings.
Through these three immeasurable blessings,
May those who only hear my story achieve liberation,
May those who meditate upon it fulfill their aim.

May those who meditate in my caves,
May those who enshrine the few objects I possess,
May they all bring happiness wherever they may be.

May I embrace all space
Just as space embraces earth, water, fire, and wind.
May the eight orders of gods and nagas,[5]
And the host of local gods, not create obstacles.

May the wishes of the devotees
Be fulfilled in harmony with the Dharma.
May all sentient beings, even the least of them,
Be guided by me toward liberation.'

Upon receiving these blessings, the lay devotees were overjoyed. The people from Nyanang and Dingri, still fearful that the Master might die, came to ask for his blessing and devoted themselves to the Dharma as never before. Each returned to his home and immediately the rainbow and the other visions disappeared. The people of Drin, supported by Calm Light Repa and other great disciples, implored the Master not to abandon them. The Master went to live in Drin, in a cell built for him at the top of a rock, shaped like the hood of a snake, called Rekpa Dukchen (Poisonous to Touch), in order to subdue the serpent-god Dolpa Nakpo (Black Executioner). While there, he instructed the benefactors of Drin. At the end of his discourse the Master said, 'Monks, if some of you have doubts about my instructions, hasten, because it is not certain that I will live much longer.'

The monks first conducted a ritual feast and then received the complete instructions. Among the rows of monks gathered around the Master were Repa of Digom and Repa of Seban, who said, 'Judging from your words, we do not believe that you will soon pass into nirvana. Perhaps your life is not yet over.'

'My life is over and my mission has been completed. Signs of my death will soon become apparent.'

A few days later, the Master showed signs of his illness. Repa of Ngandzong said to him, 'Master, for this sickness, we, your disciples, will sacrifice offerings to the lamas, yidams, dakinis, and guardian deities. We will also perform the ritual of longevity and give you treatment and medicine.'

Repa of Ngandzong called other disciples to help with preparations for the ritual. The Master then said to him:

'For a hermit, sickness is usually an exhortation to spiritual practice. Without performing any ritual, he must transform all experiences of adverse conditions into sublime attainment and must be able to face sickness and even death itself. In particular, because I, Milarepa, have already performed all the rituals in accordance with the instructions of my compassionate lama, Marpa, I have no need for the first or the second ritual. Because I have transformed adverse conditions into favorable factors, I have no need for ceremonies, propitiatory rites, or drum calls. Spirits of evil who appeared before me have been subdued and transformed into protective forces to aid us in the realization of the Fourfold Power of Action.[6] I do not want the remedy of six medicinal herbs,[7] because the sickness of five poisons[8] has become in me the dawn of the Five Aspects of Transcendental Awareness.[9] And so I need no remedies.

'Now that my time has come, my earthly body has been transformed into a more subtle form, dissolved into a totally awakened state of emptiness. Worldly men experience the consequences of their defilements through the cycle of birth, old age, sickness, and death. They cannot avoid it through remedies or rituals. Inexorably they must confront it. Nothing can stop it, neither the power of kings, nor the deeds of heroes, the beauty of woman, the wealth of the rich, the speed of the cowardly, nor clever entreaty. If you are afraid of this suffering and desire happiness, I know an effective means to remove misery and achieve permanent peace.'

'Please give this to us.'

'Very well. The nature of samsara is such that wealth which has been accumulated is dispersed, houses that have been built are destroyed, unions are broken, and all that is born must die. Since inevitably one suffers for one's acts, one must abandon worldly aims and give up accumulating, building, and uniting. The best remedy is to realize the ultimate truth of reality under the direction of an enlightened lama. Furthermore, I have very important instructions to give you later as my last testament. Do not forget.'

Calm Light Repa and Repa of Ngandzong continued to urge, 'Master, were you in good health, you would fulfill the aims of many more sentient beings. Even if you do not grant our wish, we implore you to perform a ritual according to the secret tradition, to take some medicine, and also to allow us to offer prayers for your long life, so that at least we have no remorse.'

The Master replied:

'Had my time not come, I would do as you both have asked. But performing such a rite to invoke a yidam in order to prolong life without concern for the benefit of sentient beings is like asking a king to step down from his throne to sweep the floor.

'Never use the secret method of the Vajrayana for your worldly aims. In mountain solitude I unceasingly performed the highest rites for the sake of unenlightened creatures, so there is no need for any other ritual.

'Since my inner consciousness is not a separate entity from the All-Embracing Emptiness, there is no need for any prayers for longevity. Marpa's remedies extirpated the five poisons at their roots. These remedies were enough.

'But if you have no capability for turning adversity into favorable conditions for achieving your aims, and if your time to depart has not yet come, then it is not wrong to take medical treatment and apply spiritual remedies in order to surmount obstacles, since a possibility of doing so still exists. It was thus long ago that the Buddha, with the thought of suffering creatures in mind, showed his hand to Shonnu[10] the physician and took his remedies. Even though he was a Buddha, when his time came, he died. My time has also come. That is why I will not take these remedies.'

Then the two Repa disciples asked, 'If you must leave for the sake of other beings, how shall we perform the devotional ceremonies, funeral rites, and the cremation of your body? How shall we make the figurines from the ashes and build a stupa? Who will guide the order of our tradition? How shall we commemorate your death? What offering should be made to you on your anniversary? Tell us how we should pursue our search through listening, questioning, and meditating.'

The Master replied:

'With the guidance of the Compassionate Marpa, I have completed the work of liberation. It is not at all certain that an awakened hermit, whose body, speech, and mind have attained to the highest state, will persist in the form of a corpse. Do not cast figurines or build a stupa. I have no monastery, hence there is no established center for the Order. Adopt as your abode of solitude both the arid and the snow-covered mountains. Consider the beings of the six universal realms as your followers and give them spiritual protection and compassion. Rather than molding figurines, meditate four times a day. Rather than building a stupa, develop higher perceptions of the cosmic universe and raise the banner of meditation. The best commemoration of my death is to have veneration for your lama.

'Concerning the way of pursuing your inner search, reject all that which increases self-clinging and inner poison, even if it appears to be good. On the contrary, practice all that which counteracts the five poisons and helps other beings, even though it appears to be bad. This is essentially in accord with the Dharma. However learned you may be, if you lack deep experience and knowingly indulge in harmful deeds, you will only throw yourself deeper into the lower realms through self-delusion. Since life is short and the time of death unknown, devote yourself wholly to meditation. Act wisely and courageously according to your inborn sense of discrimination, even at the cost of your life. In a word, act in a way you will not be ashamed of.

'If you follow these directions attentively, even if you go against the letter of the sacred books, you will not be going against the intentions of the Buddhas of the past and will also fulfill the wish of this old man. Such is the essence of all listening, questioning, and meditating. If my wish is fulfilled, you will complete the work of your liberation. On the other hand, all efforts to satisfy worldly desires are useless.'

After he had said this, he sang the Song of Spiritual Gain:

'I prostrate myself at the feet of Marpa the Translator.
Disciples gathered in this place,
Listen to this song of final instruction.
By the compassion of Marpa of the Southern Cliffs,
The aged hermit Milarepa
Has accomplished the whole of his task.

All of you, disciples and monks,
If you heed my words,
You will accomplish in this life
A great task for yourselves and others,
And so achieve the intentions of past Buddhas and myself.
All other actions
Go against the needs of oneself and others,
And fail to satisfy my wish.

Without the guidance of a lama who has lineage
What benefit is there in seeking initiation?
Without the inner consciousness of the Dharma
What is the use of memorizing the Tantras?
What is the use of meditating according to instructions
If you do not renounce worldly aims?

What good are ceremonies
Without attuning your body, speech, and mind to the Dharma?

What good is meditating on patience
If you will not tolerate insult?
What use are sacrifices
If you do not overcome attachment and revulsion?
What good is giving alms
If you do not root out selfishness?
What good is governing a great monastery
If you do not regard all beings as your beloved parents?

What use is there in building stupas
If faith does not grow in your mind?
What use is there in molding figurines
If one cannot meditate in the four divisions of the day?[11]
What good is it to commemorate my death
If you do not invoke me with deep veneration?
What good to lament my death
If you do not heed my instructions?
What good to view my dead body
Without venerating me when alive?

Without disgust for samsara and the urge for liberation
What good is the virtue of renunciation?
Without learning to love others more than oneself
What good are sweet words of pity?
Without uprooting delusion and desire
What profit in serving the lama?
What good are great numbers of disciples
If they do not listen to my words?

Give up all useless action,
It can only bring you harm.
A hermit who has fulfilled his goal,
I no longer need to strive.'

The disciples were deeply moved by these words.

Since the Master showed increasingly grave symptoms of illness, the Geshe Tsakpūhwa brought a little meat and beer, and pretending to inquire about his health, said to the Master, 'It is really a pity that such an illness befalls a saint like the Master. If it is possible to share it, divide it among your disciples. If there is a way to transfer it, give it to a man such as myself. But since that is impossible, what should be done?'

The Master smiled and said, 'You know very well that my illness has no natural cause or provocation. And in any case, illness in an ordinary man is not the same as illness in a spiritual man. I should accept it as a special opportunity for inner transformation. For this reason, I bear my sickness as an ornament.' Having thus spoken, the Master sang:

'Samsara and nirvana are perceived as one single reality
In the State of Ultimate Awareness.
To perceive the Ultimate Reality,
I mark everything with the Great Seal of Emptiness.[12]
This is the quintessence of non-duality.
I work on myself with no regard for obstacles.

Sickness, evil spirits, harmful deeds, and delusion
Are my ornaments, hermit that I am.
In me, they are the nervous system, vital fluids, and
psychic energies.
For me, generosity and the other virtues
Are the one hundred and twelve signs of Buddhahood.
May the sinner be absolved of his crimes.
This sickness greatly becomes me;
I could transfer it, but have no reason to do so.'

The geshe thought, 'He suspects that I gave him the poison, but he is not sure. Although he has reason to transfer his sickness, he cannot.'

So he said, 'If I knew the source of the Master's sickness, and if it were an evil spirit, I would exorcize it. Were it a physical disorder, I would cure you. But I do not know what you have. So if you can transfer your disease, transfer it to me.'

And the Master said, 'A certain being is possessed by the demon of egotism, which is the worst one of all. It is he who has caused my illness. You could neither exorcize the demon nor cure me. If I shared my sickness with you, you could not bear it for an instant. I shall not transfer it.'

The geshe thought, 'He cannot transfer it. He is pretending.' So he insisted, 'Transfer it anyway.'

'Well then, I will not transfer it to you, but I will transfer it to that door. Watch carefully.'

And he transferred it to the door of the cell. Immediately there was a loud crack and, shaking violently, the door began to break apart. At this moment the Master was without illness.

The geshe suspected that it was a magician's trick and said, 'Very strange! Now transfer it to me.'

'Good! I will give the geshe a little taste of it.'

The Master withdrew the sickness from the door and gave it to Tsakpūhwa, who collapsed in pain. Paralyzed and choking, he was on the verge of death. Then the Master took back a large part of the sickness and said, 'I have only given you half of my sickness and you could not bear it.'

Full of remorse for having inflicted such suffering, the geshe threw himself sobbing at the Master's feet.

'O Precious Master, O Saint, it is just as you said, one who was possessed did this evil to you. I offer you my house, wealth, and property. Help me to free myself from the consequences of my actions. I sincerely beg for your forgiveness.'

Milarepa was very pleased and took back the rest of the sickness and said, 'All my life I have had no desire for house, wealth, and property. Now that I am approaching the end of my life, I certainly have no need for them, so take back your gifts. Never again act contrary to the Dharma, even at the cost of your own life. I will invoke my lama to keep you from suffering the consequences of your action.' And the Master sang:

'I prostrate myself at the feet of Marpa, the Enlightened One.
May the five inexpiable sins[13]
Be wiped out through remorse.

May the sins of all beings be wiped out
By virtue of my merits
And those of the Buddhas of the three periods of time.

May all your sufferings
Be assumed and transformed by me.
I have compassion for him who offends
His master, teacher, and parents.

May the consequences of his karma
Be assumed and transformed by me.

In all times and circumstances
May he avoid the company of the sinful.

But in lives to come
May he meet with virtuous companions.
May he avoid bad thoughts, destructive of merit.
May he abstain from harming others.

May all creatures attain to Bodhichitta.'

At these words the geshe was overwhelmed with joy and said, 'In the future I will do nothing contrary to the Dharma, but will meditate to the end of my life, as the Master has commanded. Formerly, I sinned for the sake of wealth. Therefore I no longer want my worldly goods. If the Master refuses them, let his disciples accept the goods to provide for their needs during meditation.'

The disciples accepted the gifts, which were used later at Chuwar each year to commemorate the Master's death. The Geshe Tsakpūhwa then renounced the world and became a devotee.

The Master said, 'I came to live in this place in order to accept the remorse of this sinner and help him to achieve liberation from the consequences of his crime. For a hermit to die in a village would be like a king dying in a hovel. Now I am going to Chuwar.'

Repa of Seban said, 'As the Master would be exhausted by his sickness, we will carry him in a palanquin.'

The Master replied, 'There is no reality in my sickness. There is no reality in my death. I have manifested here the appearance of sickness. At Chuwar I am going to manifest the appearance of death. There is no need for a palanquin. Some of you go ahead to Chuwar.'

Then some of the young Repas went ahead, but the Master was the first to arrive at Driche Cave. At the same time another Milarepa left, accompanied by the older monks. Another appeared at Poisonous-to-Touch Rock and manifested the symptoms of illness. Another was served by the disciples who had come to meet him at Chuwar. Another preached to benefactors on an outcrop at Rock Cave. Inside different houses, one Milarepa appeared to each occupant who presented him with offerings.

Then those who had left in advance for Chuwar said, 'The Master has arrived in Chuwar before us!'

The old monks said, 'He was accompanied by us on the journey.'

As the others arrived, each one said, 'The Master is here. We have been with him.'

Some said, 'He is in my house.'

Other disciples said, 'He is teaching at Dahkhar (Rock Cave).'

Each of the worshippers said, 'I invited him into my house to receive offerings.'

Everyone told a different story. Then they questioned the Master and he replied, 'All of you are right. I tricked you.'

Then he stayed at Driche Cave, manifesting sickness.

At this time, the rainbow and all the other signs that had appeared during the Master's previous discourse could be seen in the sky over Chuwar and on the mountaintops. Everyone was then certain that the Master was going to depart for another realm.

Calm Light Repa, the Master of Ngandzong, and Repa of Seban asked, 'To which Buddha realm does the Master expect to go? Where shall we direct our invocation? What last instructions will the Master give us? What form of practice should we follow?'

The Master answered:

'Invoke me wherever you wish. Wherever you invoke me with faith I will be with you. Whatever your aims, they will be fulfilled. In an instant I will be in the Pure Land of the Buddha Immutable. Here are the instructions I promised you: After my death, give Retchung the things that you know I have used, my staff, and my robe. They will serve as auspicious symbols for his meditation through the control of breath. Retchung will be here soon. Do not touch my body until he arrives. This hat of the Master Maitrepa, and this staff of black aloe wood, are signs that the teaching of the Buddha will be maintained through profound meditation and perfect seeing. Therefore, give these things without fail to Tonpa of Ü [Gampopa]. Calm Light, take this wooden bowl. Ngandzong Tonpa, take this skull-cap. Repa of Seban, take this tinderbox. Repa Hermit of Di, take this bone spoon. You other initiated disciples, each take a strip of my cotton robe. These are not great riches, but all are equally tokens.

'Now, here are very important instructions concerning something which you disciples have not known about. Hidden under the hearth lies all the gold that I have amassed during my lifetime, and a will that distributes it among you. After my death, read the will and follow its directions.

'As for the manner of practicing the Dharma, there are rich people who consider themselves good devotees. They may give a hundred useful or useless things as alms, but only with the motive of getting back one thousand in return. This is only their way of glorifying worldly life. Human beings indulge covertly in harmful deeds without regard to displeasing their all-seeing guardian deities. Afraid they will not achieve their worldly aims, they try to do good; but since they are unable to renounce the desire for recognition, they are actually consuming poison with their food. Do not drink this poison of the desire for recognition. Abandon everything you call Dharma practice but which actually is directed toward glorifying the worldly life. Devote yourself to true spiritual practice.'

The Repas asked, 'Can we engage in an active life if it proves beneficial to other beings?'

The Master answered:

'If there is no attachment to selfish aims, you can. But that is difficult. Those who are full of worldly desires can do nothing to help others. They do not even profit themselves. It is as if a man, carried away by a torrent, pretended to save others. Nobody can do anything for sentient beings without first attaining transcendent insight into Reality. Like the blind leading the blind, one would risk being carried away by desires. Because space is limitless and sentient beings innumerable, you will always have a chance to help others when you become capable of doing so. Until then, cultivate the aspiration toward Complete Enlightenment by loving others more than yourselves while practicing the Dharma. Dress in rags, and content yourselves with little food, clothing, and recognition. Discipline your body and be mindful of your spiritual goal. This should be done for the sake of all sentient beings. To guide you on this path, remember these words.' And he sang this song:

'I prostrate myself at the feet of Marpa the Translator.
Those who wish to know and practice the Dharma,
Who merely venerate their lama
Without fully entrusting themselves to him,
Will be but slightly benefited.
Without receiving true initiation,
Mere words of Tantra will blind you.
Without being guided by the true meaning of the Tantras,

All your practices will lead you astray.
Without meditation according to the profound instruction,
He who practices asceticism only torments himself.

He who does not subdue desire and illusion
Only speaks sterile and empty words.
He who does not know profound skillful means
Will fail, however great his effort.
He who does not have the key to the profound meaning of the Dharma
Will be long upon the Path, however great his courage.
He who accumulates no merit and seeks only his own liberation, reaps rebirth.

He who does not give up what he has accumulated for the sake of the Dharma
Will not achieve perfection, however much he meditates.
He who is not deeply content with what he has
Sees the wealth he accumulates taken by others.
He who lacks in himself the source of happiness
Finds only pain in outer pleasures.
He who does not subdue his demon of ambition
Finds only ruination and strife in his desire for glory.

Selfish desires stir up the five poisons.
Temporal desires separate the dearest of friends.
Self-glorification evokes resentment in others.
Keeping silent about oneself will prevent conflicts.
By maintaining tranquillity and avoiding distraction,
In solitude you will find your companion.
Humility leads to the highest goal.
He who works with care will quickly achieve results.
Renunciation brings great fulfillment.

The practice of the secret path is the shortest way.
Realization of emptiness engenders compassion.
Compassion abolishes the difference between oneself and others.
If there is no duality between oneself and others,
One fulfills the aim of all sentient beings.
He who recognizes the need of others will discover me.
He who finds me will achieve Enlightenment.

To me, to the Buddha, and to the disciples
You should pray as one, considering them as one.'

Thus he sang. Then he added these words: 'I do not know if I have much longer to live. Now that you have heard me, do as I have done.'

He spoke and entered into a deep state of meditation.

And so, at the age of eighty-four, at sunrise on the fourteenth day of the twelfth month in the year of the Wood Hare,[14] under the ninth lunar constellation,[15] the Master passed into nirvana.

At that time, over this region there appeared widespread and wonderful signs indicating that the dakas and dakinis had assembled. The clear sky was adorned with a design of interlacing squares in all the colors of the rainbow. At the center of every square was a lotus with eight multicolored petals, four of which, in sacred colors, pointed to the four cardinal directions. Upon each lotus were mandalas which in their geometry and architecture were far more marvelously designed than the works of skilled artists and builders.

There appeared in the firmament above them an inconceivable variety of offerings from the gods, such as rainbows and five-colored clouds, forming themselves into parasols, banners, canopies, bunting, and billowing silk.

There was a great shower of blossoms in different shapes and colors. Over the mountaintops clouds in five colors formed themselves into stupas with their pinnacles pointing toward Chuwar. The melody of the celestial orchestra was sung in praise of Jetsun,* while the most fragrant incense permeated the whole place. Everyone witnessed these signs, and many human disciples saw dakas and dakinis welcoming Jetsun with many offerings. Human beings did not look upon the naked bodies of celestial beings as indecent, nor did the gods sense the unpleasant odor of human beings. Moreover, gods and men communicated with each other, engaging in conversation and jokes. These marvelous signs lasted until the completion of the Master's funeral.

During this time the benefactors in Nyanang came to know about the death of the Master. They went to Chuwar and spoke to the chief disciples and to the benefactors of Drin about bringing

* Honorific religious title used for both men and women.

the Master's body to Nyanang. The people from Drin refused and made preparations for the cremation. The followers from Nyanang said that the cremation should be delayed until all the benefactors from Nyanang arrived in Chuwar to look at the body. Then they went away and came back with a large band of men to claim the body.

Thereupon the chief disciples attempted to settle the dispute, speaking in this manner: 'The followers from Nyanang and Drin are equally faithful disciples of the Master. Since Jetsun passed away at Chuwar it is not proper to take his body to Nyanang, but the people from Nyanang should remain here to observe the cremation. The relics should be distributed equally to all.'

Even after the intervention of the disciples, the men from Nyanang, proud on account of their stronger force, were preparing to fight. At that moment, a celestial youth appeared in the sky at the center of the light and rainbow and sang this song in a voice resembling that of the Master:

'O great disciples and lay followers gathered here,
Contending over the corpse!
Hear this verdict:
I, a celestial disciple of Jetsun, will settle this dispute.
The mind of Milarepa, supreme among men, has merged into the non-arising Dharmakaya.
Without mind, no physical vehicle exists.
The Master's body will soon dissolve into the Dharmakaya.
No substance or relics will remain.
Therefore, it is foolish to quarrel over the corpse.
All you who do so are acting foolishly.
Since you will not get it by fighting,
Invoke Jetsun with deep veneration.
If you call upon him from the depths of your heart,
His will and compassion will manifest without hindrance,
Even though his Dharmakaya is Non-arising Emptiness.
Then you will receive the relics of his Nirmanakaya (Earthly Body).'

With this, the youth vanished like a rainbow.

The lay followers were overjoyed at the thought of seeing Jetsun. Ignoring their quarrel, they invoked the Master. Great disciples and lay followers from Drin no longer feared that the body would be taken away by force.

At the same time, it so happened that the people from Nyanang found they had another body of Jetsun which they carried away to Lachi and cremated at the Eagle's Egg in the Great Cave of the Conquered Demon. All the signs, such as the arch of rainbow and light, the shower of blossoms, the fragrance of perfume, and the sound of music, appeared there just as at Chuwar.

Meanwhile, at Chuwar, the chief disciples and lay followers worshipped the Master's body. After six days they examined it and found it transformed into a radiant celestial body, as youthful as a child eight years old.

The great disciples discussed the matter and came to the conclusion that the Venerable Retchung would not arrive in time. They agreed that if the body were kept any longer, there would be a risk of not having any remains as objects for worship and devotion. The best course would be to cremate the body immediately.

The face of the body was shown to all. Then the body was moved to a cremation cell erected upon the rock which had served as the Dharma throne for Jetsun's discourses. At the base of the rock a mandala was created out of colored powders. Around it were placed the finest offerings that human beings could produce, although these were surpassed by the celestial offerings which appeared in the heavens. At dawn the cremation ceremony began and the funeral pyre was lighted. But the body would not receive the fire.

At that moment five dakinis, one from each of the five orders,[16] appeared before them and sang this song:

'Rām,[17] all-perceiving Tummo is the Supreme Fire.
Since the Great Sage meditated throughout his life,
What need is there for a man-made fire?

Having unceasingly perceived the earthly body in the form of a yidam,
How can there be a dead body today?

Since the mandala of the yidam in its exquisite beauty is inherent in the body of this yogin,
What need is there for an earthly mandala?

Since the lamp of his inseparable mind-energy is ceaselessly burning,
What need is there for a paltry butter lamp?

Since he partakes increasingly of the five elixirs,
For whom is this sacrificial cake?

Through adorning himself with the purity of morality
He removed the stain of the two defilements.
For whom is the purifying vase to be held?

The sky is filled with clouds of fragrant perfume
And the whole mandala of offerings.
Today, there is no need to burn your incense.

Four orders of dakinis are singing chants of praise
While the chief dakinis are offering worship.
Today, in what manner do you perform the ritual?

Since a host of awakened Masters encircle him
And a multitude of great yogins pay their homage,
What need is there now to touch his body?

Since the Master has realized ultimate reality,
What need is there to beautify his dead body?

Since it is an object of both celestial and human veneration,
There is no need for you to own it!
Devote yourself instead to the universal veneration.

Observing the precepts of the lama and yidam
There is no need for other instruction.
Continue to follow the precepts.

Since the Master's body is a heap of priceless gems,
Give up the dispute over ownership and be calm.

Since the instructions of the enlightened lama are secret,
Abandon the desire to talk about them. Keep silent!

The secret instructions are the living breath of the dakinis,
Practice them in complete retreat, or risk pollution in its many forms.

In a concentrated striving toward liberation,
Many obstacles arise, so meditate in complete secrecy.

Through the rebukes of your wonderful father
Realization will emerge,
So cast away your doubts.

As for the story of the Master's liberation,
There is no need to proclaim its fame.

Blessings will flow from the song of the supreme dakinis,
So increase your faith.

O fortunate disciples, there are many realized saints
Among the spiritual descendants of Milarepa.

O gods and men,
No epidemic shall ravage the people and animals of this land.
All you people gathered here tonight
Will never again be born in lower realms.

In the mandala of the Suchness of Sunyata[18]
Perception and awareness are one.
So break your clinging to dualities.

There is special significance in the final instruction of
the dying Master,
So strive to fulfill his words.

May all of you live forever in the supreme Dharma,
The Source of peace and joy!'

As the song ended, the Master of Ngandzong said, 'Even though the Master's instruction to delay the cremation until after the arrival of Retchung agrees with the content of the dakinis' song, we do not know when Retchung will arrive. The body might soon dissolve itself into Emptiness.' Calm Light Repa said he was sure that Retchung would come soon, as indicated by the Master and the dakinis, and also because of the way the Master's body defied the fire. 'Until then, let us devote ourselves to the worship and veneration of the Master.'

At that time Retchung was residing at the monastery of Loro Döl in Southern Tibet. One morning, in the early dawn, while he was in a mixed state of contemplation and sleep, he perceived a host of dakinis who were about to carry away to another realm a crystal stupa radiating light throughout the heavens. He saw the crystal stupa being praised in song and worshipped with offerings beyond imagination by the community of the Vajrayana tradition and lay benefactors who filled the earth, and by the celestial beings and dakinis who permeated the sky.

Retchung prostrated himself on seeing Jetsun leaning from the stupa and heard the Master say, 'Retchung, my son, even though you did not arrive in time as I asked you, my mind is full of joy that we, father and son, are together at last. It is uncertain when we shall meet again, so let us treasure this rare occasion.' Radiating a joyful smile, the Master repeatedly touched Retchung's head. Retchung realized the uniqueness of this meeting and a faith arose in him such as he had never known.

Retchung awoke. He recalled the Master's previous words. Hoping that his lama had not yet died, he felt he must go quickly to see him even though he might not reach Chuwar in time. As he was invoking Jetsun with a faith of unbearable intensity, two women appeared before him in the sky and said, 'Retchung, your lama has passed into the Pure Land of the dakinis. If you do not go quickly you may never see him again in this life. Go now, without delay.' The warning in the dream and seeing the sky filled with rainbows and lights aroused in him a memory of the lama and a yearning to go to him.

He left Loro Döl at early dawn as the cocks were crowing. Maintaining harmonious unity with the purest awareness of the lama, Retchung, in an act of devotion, drew air into his body and, retaining it, with the force of a well-shot arrow covered in one morning a distance that for ordinary travelers would take two months. At sunrise, arriving at the pass on the ridge of Mount Podzi between Dingri and Drin, he rested a moment. He saw signs of inconceivable wonders which filled the entire space of the heavens, the mountains, and the surface of the earth. He was overjoyed. Over the summit of Mount Jowo Razang he saw innumerable celestial sons and daughters amid the domes of lights and rainbows, bearing innumerable offerings of the five sensory ecstasies, worshipping fervently and prostrating themselves toward Chuwar.

Seeing these signs, Retchung was filled with apprehension. He asked the celestial beings the significance of these spectacular signs, and particularly who was being worshipped. Some goddesses said, 'Have you been cut off from the world, seeing nothing and hearing nothing? These offerings are being made by celestial beings of higher realms to the holiest Master on this earth, Mila Laughing

Vajra, who is being worshipped by both gods and men at Chuwar as he enters into the Pure Land of the dakinis.'

Hearing this, Retchung felt as if his heart were being torn out. He hurried on his way. When he was very near Chuwar he saw Jetsun sitting on a big rock shaped like the square base of a stupa. Just as in the dream, the Master showed his joy and greeted him, saying, 'My son, now you are here.'

Thinking that the Master had not really died, Retchung felt an inconceivable joy arising in him. He bowed at the Master's feet and spoke with veneration. The Master answered all his questions.

'Retchung, my son, I will lead the way, follow me.' So saying, the Master went ahead and instantly disappeared!

Retchung continued his journey and arrived at Chuwar. At the Master's cave he saw the great disciples, monks, and lay followers mournfully worshipping the Master's body. Not knowing who this man was, some new monks stopped Retchung and prevented him from going toward the body. Saddened by this, Retchung sang in an aggrieved tone this Song of Sevenfold Devotion:

'O Master, protector of sentient beings,
O Master, Buddha of the Three Ages,
While in the realm of your Dharmakaya wisdom and compassion,
Hear this song of lamentation
From your unfortunate disciple Retchung.

O Venerable Lama! Miserable and tormented, I cry out through this song.
Longing to be near your body I went forward
But this unfortunate son could not see your face.
Look at me with compassion, O Gracious Father.

To you, the Buddha of the Three Ages
Who possesses Wisdom, Compassion, and Power,
I, a mendicant, prostrate myself through the three entrances of body, speech, and mind,
And make the offering of meditation according to your teaching.
I purify the harmful deeds arising from imperfect and distorted perceptions
And take a great delight in all your perfect actions.
May you continue to turn the Wheel of the Sacred Law,
May you be ever-present and not dissolve into nirvana.

May I dedicate the virtues of my meditation and realization
to the fulfillment of your intention.

May I realize the result of this dedication, and
May I see your face.
I, whom you first treated with compassion,
Am now being prevented from seeing your body.
Unfortunate am I, not to see the living Master;
Yet may I behold your face in death,
And after seeing your face
May I receive directly or through visions your most valuable instruction for overcoming obstacles in the two higher stages of meditation.
This is the content of my invocation.

Master, if you do not act out of compassion for your son,
Whom else will you protect with your fatherly wisdom and love?
O Father, do not take away from me the hook of your compassion.
Look at me from the expanse of the invisible realm.
May the Master, Seer of the three modes of time, look at Retchung, your servant who is ignorant of wisdom.
Your son, Retchung, is tormented by the five poisons.
Look down on me, O Father, possessor of the Five Supreme Awarenesses.
Look with compassion on all sentient beings.
Look at Retchung out of your love.'

So Retchung sang in sorrow. At the sound of Retchung's voice, the radiance in the face of the Master's corpse faded out, and at the same time a fire emerged from the body.

Upon hearing the voice of Retchung, Calm Light Repa, Master Repa of Ngandzong, Seban Repa, and several others of the Vajra brethren with the lay devotees came to welcome Retchung. Resenting the action of the young Repas who had prevented him from seeing Jetsun's body, Retchung would not move forward until his song was finished.

At that time, though the Great Master had passed into the crystal clarity of the Dharmakaya, he came back and said to the young Repas, 'Do not behave like that toward Retchung. "One live lion is better than a hundred masks!" Let him come to me.'

To Retchung, he said, 'My son, do not feel frustration. Do not be overcome by resentment. Come before your father!'

Everyone was astounded and filled with immense joy. Retchung embraced Jetsun's body, weeping with such joy that he fainted. When he came to himself, he found the great disciples, monks, and lay devotees all seated in front of the cremation cell. The Master was completely free from any illness. Appearing as an indestructible manifestation which united form and emptiness into one, and enthroned upon an eight-petaled lotus, the Master radiated like the anthers of a flower. Sitting in the asana of royal ease, his right hand extended in the preaching mudra, pressing down the flame, the left hand in a supporting mudra at the left cheek, he said to all disciples and devotees, 'Listen to this answer to Retchung's song and to the final words of this old man.'

The Master sang from the cremation cell this indestructible song called Six Essential Principles:

'Listen, Retchung, dearest to my heart,
  to this Song of My Last Will of Instructions.
In the ocean of three samsaric levels
The illusory body is the great culprit,
Striving toward fufillment of material aims,
With little time to renounce worldly efforts.
O Retchung, renounce worldly endeavor.

In the city of the illusory body,
The illusory mind is the great culprit,
Enslaved by the flesh and blood of the body,
With little time to realize the Ultimate Reality.
O Retchung, discern the true nature of mind.

On the border between mind and matter,
  inner consciousness is the great culprit,
Drawn into the realm of conditioned perceptions,
With little time to realize the uncreated nature of reality.
O Retchung, capture the fortress of unborn emptiness.

On the border between this world and the next,
  consciousness in the intermediate state of the Bardo[19]
  is the great culprit,
Seeking a body even though deprived of body,

With little time to realize Ultimate Reality.
O Retchung, work your way toward that realization.

In the deceptive city of the six classes of beings,
There is a great accumulation of defilements and evil karma
following impulses of desire and hatred,
With little time to perceive the All-Encompassing Emptiness.
O Retchung, abandon desire and hatred.

In the invisible realm of the heavens,
There is a Buddha who skillfully uses falsehoods,[20]
Guiding sentient beings toward relative truth.
Little time have they to realize ultimate truth.
O Retchung, abandon concepts.

Lama, yidam, and dakinis, three united in one –
Invoke them!
Perfect seeing, contemplation, and practice, three united
in one –
Master them!
This life, the next, and the intermediate, three united in
one –
Unify them!

This is my final instruction and my very last will.
O Retchung, there is nothing more to say.
My son, devote yourself to this instruction.'

Having thus spoken, Jetsun dissolved himself into the All-Embracing Emptiness. The funeral pyre was instantly transformed into a celestial mansion, square in shape, having four entrances with ornate porticos. Above it gleamed a rainbow and a canopy of light. The parapet of the roof was surmounted by parasols, banners, and other ornamental offerings.

The flame at the base took the form of an eight-petaled lotus blossom, and the curling tips of the fire unfolded into the eight auspicious emblems[21] and the seven royal insignia.[22] Even the sparks took the form of goddesses bearing many offerings. The chants of worship and the crackling of the dazzling fire sounded like the melodious tones of various musical instruments, such as violins, flutes, and tambourines. The smoke permeated everything with the fragrance of perfume and, in the sky above the funeral pyre, young gods and goddesses poured a stream of nectar from the vases they held, and offered abundant delights for the five senses.

The lamas and the venerable lay people were filled with joy. All the disciples, monks, and lay devotees saw the funeral pyre in the form of a resplendent celestial mansion, while the corpse itself was seen variously as Hevajra, Chakrasamvara, Guhyasamaja, or Vajravarahi. Then the dakinis sang with one voice:

'After the passing away of the Master – the Wish-fulfilling Gem –
Some weep and others lament.
At this time of their grief and mourning
There springs up by itself a dazzling fire,
The flame in the form of an eight-petaled lotus blossom,
Eight auspicious emblems, seven royal insignia, and many other delightful offerings.
The roar of the flames is orchestrated into melodious tones
Resembling the music of conch shells, cymbals, violins, flutes, miniature cymbals, tambourines, and hand drums.
Out of the glittering sparks emerge dakinis of three levels – outer, inner, and inmost,
Worshipping and bearing offerings of a myriad kind.
Amidst the smoke, rainbows, and light, there are clouds of offerings,
Such as parasols, banners, glorious knots, and swastikas.[23]
Innumerable dakinis of enchanting beauty carry away the relics of bone from the funeral pyre,
Astonished that the Master's body is being cremated even though it has been rendered formless, leaving no residuum.
In the expanse of the Lama's Dharmakaya, there gathers the cloud of Sambhogakaya through his resolute will and compassion,
Producing actions of Nirmanakaya like an unceasing rain of flowers.
He thereby brings the crop of seekers to their fruition.
The Dharmadhatu, the ultimate nature of all things, is empty, unconditioned, and devoid of becoming.
The emptiness is without coming to be and passing away.
Even the conditioned arising and dissolution are empty in their innate nature.
So cast away your doubts and misgivings.

After this song, day passed into evening. The form of a dazzling flame disappeared. Everyone saw the creamtion cell as completely transparent. Disciples, and lay people, looked at the relics of the corpse. Some saw a huge stupa of light standing in the cremation cell, while others saw such forms as Hevajra, Chakrasamvara, Guhyasamaja, or Vajravarahi. Some others saw sacred implements, such as a vajra, bell, vase, and seed syllables[24] of mantras representing enlightened body, speech, and mind. Others saw in the cremation cell a white light with its golden rays, a placid pool of water, a burning flame, a swirling wind, and invisible offerings delightful to the senses and beyond imagining. Yet others saw the expanse of empty space.

The disciples opened the entrance of the cremation cell, and then all slept beside it in the joyful expectation that a great quantity of sacred relics and evolved crystals[25] would appear in many wonderful forms.

In the early dawn Retchung dreamed of five dakinis in colors of blue, yellow, green, red, and white, draped in silken robes and adorned with ornaments, some made of bone and others of jewels. They were surrounded by their female retinues in similar colors. All were carrying innumerable offerings of the five sensory ecstasies and were worshipping the cremation cell. The chief dakinis were carrying away a sphere of white light from the cell, draped in a curtain of white silk.

Retchung was fascinated by the spectacular scene. Then he moved toward the cell wondering if the dakinis were taking away the relics and the evolved crystals. The dakinis flew upward into the sky. He awakened all his Vajra brethren. As they began examining the cell, they saw that the dakinis had carried away all the sacred relics, leaving nothing, not even the ashes. Saddened by this, Retchung demanded from the dakinis a portion of the relics as the due share of human beings. The dakinis replied, saying, 'If you, great son of Jetsun, are not content with the direct awakening of your consciousness in its Dharmakaya state, this being the most sacred of all relics, you should invoke the Master so that out of his compassion he might grant your wish! As for those human beings without veneration for the Master – who shone like the sun and moon – no relics or evolved crystals will be left for them either. They never valued him, not even at the level of a glow-worm. These relics therefore belong to us.'

After saying this the dakinis remained motionless in the sky. Then Retchung, recognizing the truth of what the dakinis had said, sang this invocation:

'O Master, when you were with your Lama Marpa
You strove faithfully to fulfill all his commands.
Because of that you were given teachings bearing the profound truth.
Then you awakened and liberated all fortunate seekers.
Embrace us and all sentient beings with your compassion, and
Grant us your relics for our devotion.

O Master, when you lived in mountain solitude,
Through your persevering meditation
You achieved the power to cause miraculous manifestations
As the sign of your realization,
And your fame spread throughout the land.
Embrace us who have seen you or heard you, and
Grant us your relics for our devotion.

O Master, when you were amidst your disciples
You were compassionate for all without partiality.
In you we beheld the complete flowering of insight and foreknowledge.
You were filled with loving kindness for sentient beings.
Embrace us, the fortunate seekers, with your compassion, and
Grant us your relics for our devotion.

O Master, when you were among the multitudes you mercifully evoked in them the unfolding of an enlightened attitude.
You led all who sought you to the path of liberation.
To those in misery you were particularly compassionate.
Embrace us, the fortunate seekers, with your compassion, and
Grant us your relics for our devotion.

O Master, when you abandoned your illusory body you were fully awakened to inmost truth.
Inwardly you perceived all phenomena as the Dharmakaya and became supreme among all dakinis.
Embrace us, the fortunate seekers, with your compassion, and
Grant us your relics for our devotion.
Embrace us, your children, who are assembled here.'

Retchung thus invoked his Master by singing tearfully in a mournful tone. Thereupon the chief dakini cast from her hand a sacred object, as large as a hen's egg, which projected a stream of light in five colors and descended toward the cremation cell. All the chief disciples stretched out their hands, each claiming it for himself. Then the object ascended again and was absorbed into the light which the chief dakini was holding. The light then split in two, one part becoming a lion throne with a lotus cushion surmounted by moon and sun. A crystal stupa took shape from the other part of the light and came to rest upon the throne. Lights in five colors began to shine forth from the stupa. The stupa was one foot high and was surrounded by the Thousand and Two Buddhas.[26] Its four terraces were occupied by resplendent yidams of the four classes of the Tantra in their natural order. Seated inside its spherical chamber was the form of Milarepa, about six inches in height.

The dakinis who were prostrating themselves and worshipping him sang this song, supported by two others who were guarding the stupa:

'Oh sons! Dewa Kyong (Sustainer of Joyful Peace), Shiwa Ö (Calm Light), Master of Ngandzong, and other blessed disciples clad in cotton.
With the intensity of your veneration and yearning you call upon the name of your spiritual father, that he may grant you, and all human beings, the relics and the evolved crystals as objects of your devotion.

By the force of your invocations coming from the depths of your hearts, and by the power of Milarepa's compassion, you have seen the emanation of his Trikaya and thus you need not return to the cycle of birth and death.
If you devote yourselves faithfully you will attain full Enlightenment.

From the unique sphere of the Dharmakaya emerged the sacred relic as big as a hen's egg.
It is an object of devotion for all human beings.
Yet you cannot get it by seizing it.
Why should it remain amidst profanity?
But if you earnestly invoke Jetsun again, his compassion for you will never diminish, for there is a solemn

commitment of all Buddhas for your sake.
Through their ever-unfolding actions arising out of the Dharmakaya, earthly manifestations emerge in their diverse forms.

Your Yidam Chakrasamvara appeared together with his consort in the posture of union, adorning themselves magnificently with ornaments of sepulchral bones.
The sky was filled with a mandala of deities.[27]
The offerings of the dakas and dakinis spread like a cloud.
The supremely manifested Sambhogakaya gave the initiation which enables you rapidly to achieve realization.
If you are capable of invoking them, their spiritual influences will never diminish, for there is a solemn commitment of all dakinis for your sake.

By the ever-unfolding actions of the Buddhas in the Dharmakaya their reincarnations take on diverse forms.
Therefore, there appeared a crystal stupa one foot in height, surrounded by the Thousand and Two Buddhas, as depicted in the Sutras, and ornamented with the yidam described in the four classes of the Tantra.
What a wonderful vision before our eyes!
If you are capable of invoking them without being distracted, their unfolding actions will never diminish, for there is a solemn commitment of all guardian deities for your sake.

The lama who has unified all three aspects of Enlightenment acts by appearing in many miraculous forms.
It is indeed wonderful that he manifests himself in this small but visible form as an object for our devotion.
If you are capable of invoking him from the recesses of your heart with an intense veneration and yearning,
His influence on your direct realization will never diminish, for there is a solemn commitment of all awakened Masters for your sake.

If you sincerely abide by your own spiritual vows, all guardian deities will support you.
If you can live in mountain solitude, the upholders of wisdom, dakas and dakinis, will naturally gather around you.

Applying yourself sincerely to the Dharma is the advance sign of your rapid realization.
If you are free from desire for pleasure, you have removed the root of your mental defilements.
If you do not cling to the notion of personal self and universal substance as true reality, obstacles and disruptive forces will be banished.

If you no longer cling to duality, your insight has reached its perfection.
If you can perceive samsara and nirvana as empty, your meditation has reached its perfection.
If self-denial springs forth from the depths of your consciousness your practice has reached its perfection.
If your lama foretells your destined task, your commitment has reached its perfection.
If you seek to serve all sentient beings, your aim has reached its perfection.

If Master and disciples achieve a spiritual harmony, their relationship has reached its perfection.
If you recognize the signs and state of your realization, your perceptive visions have reached their perfection.
The quality of your communal harmony, your awakened experience with its inner warmth and all its signs, let these, my children, serve as your share of the relics.'

After this song, the dakinis showed the stupa to all disciples. When the dakinis were about to depart to other realms, they placed the stupa upon a throne of precious jewels. Wishing to beg of the dakinis, who were holding the stupa, that they leave it as an object for human devotion, Shiwa Ö (Calm Light) Repa invoked them with this song:

'O Father, you assumed the Nirmanakaya form in order to serve others.
You are the awakened seer as the Sambhogakaya.
As the invisible Dharmakaya you embrace the expanse of the cosmic universe.
I invoke you, the ultimate state of reality.
The stupa the dakinis are holding in their hands,
Give it to us, your children.

O Venerable One, when encountering other enlightened saints,
You were like a casket filled with precious jewels,
You are the priceless seer, O Venerable One.
I offer my devotion to you, who achieved the perfect knowledge.
The stupa the dakinis are holding in their hands,
Give it to us, your children.

O Venerable One, when you were serving your lama,
You were like the wool of white sheep,
You, the awakened seer, bestowed benefits on all beings.
I offer my devotion to you, the Compassionate One.
The stupa the dakinis are holding in their hands,
Give it to us, your children.

O Venerable One, when you were renouncing worldly pursuits,
You, immutable seer, were like the king of all ascetics.
I offer my devotion to you, the Indomitable One.
The stupa the dakinis are holding in their hands,
Give it to us, your children.

O Venerable One, when you were meditating upon your lama's instructions,
You were like a tigress feeding upon the flesh of a corpse.
An awakened seer, you were free from all doubts.
I offer my devotion to you, the Persevering One.
The stupa the dakinis are holding in their hands,
Give it to us, your children.

O Venerable One, when you were in complete solitude,
You were like a block of flawless iron,
Never wavering, the awakened seer.
I offer my devotion to you who are free from falsity.
The stupa the dakinis are holding in their hands,
Give it to us, your children.

O Venerable One, when you were producing signs of your inner power,
You, the awakened seer, were like the elephant and snow-lion,
Free from all frailty.
I offer my devotion to you, the Fearless One.
The stupa the dakinis are holding in their hands,
Give it to us, your children.

When you were gaining illumination with joyful warmth,
You, the awakened seer, were like the full moon permeating
the whole earth.
I offer my devotion to you, the Selfless One.
The stupa the dakinis are holding in their hands,
Give it to us, your children.

O Venerable One, when you were guiding your foremost disciples,
The encounter was like a fire-glass under sunlight,
You, the great seer, brought them to the awakened state.
I offer my devotion to you, the Gracious One.
The stupa the dakinis are holding in their hands,
Give it to us, your children.

O Venerable One, when you encountered material wealth,
You, the awakened seer, were like mercury fallen on the ground,
You, the awakened seer, were never stained.
I offer my devotion to you, the Perfect One.
The stupa the dakinis are holding in their hands,
Give it to us, your children.

O Venerable One, when you were guiding a multitude of people,
You, the awakened seer, were like the sun rising over the earth,
dispelling darkness.
I offer my devotion to you, the Wise and Merciful One.
The stupa the dakinis are holding in their hands,
Give it to us, your children.

O Venerable One, when you encountered a vast multitude,
You, the awakened seer, were like a mother meeting her only son,
Seeking to do your utmost for their good.
I offer my devotion to you, the Most Loving One.
The stupa the dakinis are holding in their hands,
Give it to us, your children.

O Venerable One, when proceeding toward the realm of the
dakinis,
You, the awakened seer, are like a wish-fulfilling vase,
satisfying the wishes of all.
I offer my devotion to you, the Marvelous One.
The stupa the dakinis are holding in their hands,
Give it to us, your children.

O Venerable One, when giving prophetic directions,
You, the awakened seer, were like a finger pointing,
never erring.
I offer my devotion to you, Knower of the Three Modes of Time.
The stupa the dakinis are holding in their hands,
Give it to us, your children.

O Venerable One, when you were giving instructions to hasten
our realization,
You, the awakened seer, were like a father giving away riches
to his son, free from attachment.
I offer my devotion to you, the Compassionate One.
The stupa the dakinis are holding in their hands,
Give it to us, your children.'

To this invocation of Calm Light Repa came the answer in a song from the form of Jetsun in the stupa, dispelling errors of judgment about things that appear to be alike.

'O you who are faithful and well-destined,
Who invoke me in resounding tones of distress,
Listen, excellent disciples, clad in cotton,
I am Milarepa.

In the emptiness of my all-pervading Dharmakaya,
There is neither gain nor loss.
My earthly body was dissolved into All-Embracing Emptiness.
All its ordinary relics and the evolved crystals became
a single stupa emitting lights.
For all sentient beings who seek to earn merit this is
the sacred object.
Its seat of dwelling will be the Buddha realms and its
guardians the five classes of dakinis.
Celestial beings and dakinis will revere and worship it.
It will vanish if left behind in the realm of human beings.

As for your share, my disciples,
I awakened your inmost awareness, identical with the
Dharmakaya.
For this is the holiest of all sacred relics and evolved crystals.
In your striving toward illumination, you will face errors of
judgment regarding similarities and differences.
Absorb them without forgetting, and discriminate accordingly.

Associating yourself with a spiritual father who is a
perfect lama, and
Associating with a person of good quality resulting from
his past karma,
Even though the two appear alike, beware of misjudgment.

Perceiving the innate emptiness of your awareness, and
Dwelling in a non-conceptual state induced by mind,
Even though the two appear alike, beware of misjudgment.

Reaching an original state of naturalness in meditation, and
Clinging to a mere shell of quietude which mind has enforced,
Even though the two appear alike, beware of misjudgment.

The inward dawning of a spontaneous self-release, and
Being mentally aware of concepts that seem right,
Even though the two appear alike, beware of misjudgment.

Perceiving the stainless nature of mind in its nakedness, and
Serving others out of kindness for their benefit,
Even though the two appear alike, beware of misjudgment.

Signs of attainment emerging from one's efforts in inward
realization, and
Gaining material wealth in abundance owing to one's past karma,
Even though the two appear alike, beware of misjudgment.

Prophecies of the dakinis, upholders of supreme wisdom, and
The resounding call of supernatural forces,
Even though the two appear alike, beware of misjudgment.

Unfailing support of the guardian dakinis, and
Tempting obstacles schemed by the forces of Mara,
Even though the two appear alike, beware of misjudgment.

The stainless sphere of the Dharmakaya, and
The relics of earthly substance,
Even though the two appear equally worthy of veneration,
beware of misjudgment.

The blossom of the Nirmanakaya arising out of All-Encompassing
Emptiness, and
The celestial flower from the heavenly realm of sensory ecstasy,
Even though the two appear alike, beware of misjudgment.

A stupa contrived by obstructive forces, and
Another created through the miraculous acts of the yidam,
Even though the two appear to be alike, beware of misjudgment.

The cosmic mansion with its dome of light and rainbow arch, and
The rainbow and light of natural phenomena,
Even though the two appear alike, beware of misjudgment.

Faith originating from past karmic links, and
Faith induced by circumstances,
Even though the two appear alike, beware of misjudgment.

Veneration arising from the depths of the heart, and
Veneration produced out of modesty and concern for conformity,
Even though the two appear alike, beware of misjudgment.

Striving most earnestly toward Enlightenment, and
Hypocritically pleasing one's lama for the material pursuit
  of this life,
Even though the two appear alike, beware of misjudgment.

Seeking to realize one's aim through perseverance, and
Throwing verbal resolutions to the wind,
Even though the two appear alike, beware of misjudgment.

This stupa in the custody of dakinis, keepers of wisdom,
Being in the realm of Enlightened Ones, past, present, and future,
Is the celestial mansion for awakened dakas and dakinis
And is the meditation cell of your Lama Jetsun.

There is in the east a Buddha realm where a mandala of dakinis
  is gathered.
In this supremely joyful realm dwell the glorious Chakrasamvara,
  Avaloketsvara,[28] and Tara.
In this absolutely peaceful realm awaits the multitude of
  dakinis to welcome this stupa.

If you make invocations from the recesses of your heart,
Then do so with spontaneous tears of joy.
This object of veneration is so wonderful, shower it with wisdom,
Sprinkle it with water of enlightened attitude and
Let your excellent and unwavering faith be your protection.
If you wish to receive initiation into the non-dual illumination,
Place your head directly beneath the stupa.'

When the song was over, the dakinis moved the stupa through the space above the foremost disciples. Projecting downward a stream of light that touched each head, the stupa thereby endowed each one with power. Most people saw a form of Milarepa emerge from the stupa and ascend to the space above. Each group saw him differently. Some saw him as Hevajra, others as Chakrasamvara, Guhyasamaja, or Vajravarahi. Each yidam was surrounded by a mandala of emanations, male and female, which were then absorbed into the chest of the principal yidam. The mandala itself was transformed into a mass of light in the sky, and moved toward the east. Everyone present saw the dakinis adorn the stupa with silken attire of various kinds, put it in a jeweled casket, and then carry it away to the east.

Some of the disciples saw Milarepa in the form of a Sambhogakaya Buddha adorned with jeweled ornaments and seated upon a lion, whose four feet were being supported by four dakinis while Vajravarahi was leading the lion on a halter. They were proceeding toward the east, attended by innumerable dakas and dakinis carrying an assortment of celestial offerings such as parasols and banners, and giving forth a great sound of music. Others saw the stupa being carried away by a white dakini in a palanquin lined with white silk. And there were other wonderful visions of many kinds.

The disciples, monks, nuns, and lay people were heartbroken at having no share of the sacred relics. Mournfully they cried out in heart-stirring prayer. Though his form was invisible, out of space came a voice resembling that of Jetsun, saying, 'O sons, do not allow yourselves to be overcome with so much grief and despair. As for your share of the sacred objects, there is a marble slab on which have appeared four sacred syllables carved in relief. Go and search for it below the rock base of the cremation cell.'

The disciples accordingly searched the rock and found exactly what had been foretold. All were relieved of their grievance about the lack of sacred relics. This wonderful stone slab is enshrined for the devotion of human beings at the solitary temple of Chuwar.

The chief disciples were certain that they would be born among the foremost future disciples of Jetsun wherever he attained his Supreme Enlightenment, even though for the time being they were aggrieved at his departure to another realm. They were also certain that all aspects of Jetsun's life would fulfill the great purpose of the Dharma and satisfy the need of sentient beings. The foremost disciples were even confident of achieving their goals for themselves and for others through their dedication to the path of liberation.

The disciples reached a unanimous agreement that they should search for gold beneath the hearth as directed by Jetsun in his will, even though, judging from his way of living, the gold as such might not exist. On digging up the hearth they found a square piece of white cloth. Wrapped in this was a knife with a cutting blade, the point being an awl, and the back arranged as a steel for striking fire. There was also a piece of raw sugar, together with a note which read as follows: 'When cut with this knife, the cloth and sugar will never be exhausted. Cut as many strips from the cloth and as many bits from the sugar as you can, and distribute them among all the people. Everyone who tastes the sugar and touches the cloth will gain liberation from the lower realms, because these things, being the food and clothing of Milarepa throughout his meditative awakening, were blessed by the Buddhas who appeared in the past. Any sentient being who has heard the name Milarepa even once, and in whom it produced veneration, will not go through the cycle of rebirth in the lower realms for seven lifetimes. These things were prophesied by the Buddhas of the past. Whoever says that Milarepa had possessed gold, "stuff his mouth with shit."' This particular expression of Milarepa's caused laughter among the foremost disciples, even though they were aggrieved by his death. At the bottom of the note the disciples saw this message:

'This was my yogin's food throughout my meditation,
It has sustained me all my life.
It is the food of compassion which produces yogic power
and Enlightenment.
Sentient beings who eat this food will close the door of rebirth
Into the realm of hungry ghosts.

The white cotton cloth is the robe of Tummo-Wisdom.
All those who wear it on their body or around the neck
Will close the door of rebirth
Into the burning and freezing realms.

Those who receive my blessing through my relics
Will gain liberation from the three lower realms.

All those who already have a spiritual bond with me
Will henceforth never be reborn into the lower realms,
And will gradually attain to Complete Enlightenment.

Those who are capable of responding with trust
Even when they only hear the name of Milarepa
Will remember their past names and family lineage through
seven past lives.

To Milarepa, your undaunted father, the whole universe is gold.
What need have I for a packet of gold dust?
My children, strive to live according to my instructions and
You will fully realize your immediate and ultimate goals.'

The piece of raw sugar was then sliced with the knife into countless pieces. Each part was as big as the original piece. Similarly, as the white cloth was cut into many pieces, each square became the same size as the original. They were then distributed to all who partook of the sugar and touched the cloth. The sick and miserable were relieved of their sufferings; those who were full of evil intent, of passions and prejudices, found themselves possessing the qualities of faith, striving, wisdom, and compassion, and finally even achieved their liberation from the realms of misery. The sugar and the cloth each person received lasted his lifetime without being exhausted.

On the occasion of the funeral, when the disciples were worshipping the corpse of Milarepa, there fell a shower of four-colored and five-colored blossoms. The blossoms, descending nearly within the reach of man, re-ascended toward the sky and disappeared. A few that landed vanished when touched by human hands, but the blossoms that lasted were of exquisite beauty. Those in three colors, being as delicate as the wings of bees, lay ankle deep at Chuwar, and in other places the ground was covered by them, giving a different hue to the earth. After the cremation the spectacular signs, such as lights and rainbows, slowly grew dimmer and dimmer until they all disappeared.

On every anniversary of Milarepa's death all the phenomenal signs such as rainbows and lights, the smell of celestial fragrances, and the sound of music appeared in the clear sky in the same way as on the day of Jetsun's passing. The wonderful signs appearing on each occasion were so fantastic that they could not be identified in terms of our concepts or be expressed through our speech. For example, even in freezing winter, flowers bloomed, the region enjoyed abundant harvests and prosperity, and no violence or epidemics ravaged the earth. These signs were not recorded for fear of appearing exaggerated.

In summary, after the final departure for the Buddha realm of Milarepa, the greatest of saints, the story of his life became a clear example of supreme liberation, and the result of his infinite compassion and universal concern was seen in the emergence of his spiritual descendants. Those disciples who achieved Complete Enlightenment were as numerous as the stars in the night; those who achieved non-return to samsara were also many, as particles of dust on the face of the earth. Those men and women who had entered the path of liberation were too numerous to be counted. He caused the teachings of Buddha to blaze forth like bright sunshine and guided these sentient beings away from temporary and permanent miseries toward happiness and the root of happiness.

This is the ninth chapter of the life of the great saint Milarepa, dealing with the dissolution of his earthly body into All-Encompassing Emptiness on his having completed his enlightened tasks, in order to arouse a spiritual urge and awakening in sentient beings. Furthermore, it deals with how, through his unceasing and ever-unfolding actions, he will serve sentient beings till the end of samsara throughout cosmic space!

Supplementary Note

Among the disciples predicted to Jetsun by his yidam and dakinis, and also by the dream he had at the time he met Calm Light Repa, were the eight foremost sons. Of these, the sunlike disciple was the matchless Dakpo Rimpoche (widely known as Gampopa); the moonlike being was Retchung Dorje Drakpa (Renowned Vajra); and the planetlike ones were Master Jangchup Gyalpo of Ngandzong, Calm Light Repa of Gyetrommey, Repa Seban of Dotra, Khira (Hunter) Repa of Nyishang, Digom Repa of Mu, and Sangye Kyab Repa. The thirteen nearest sons were Shengom Repa, Lengom Repa, Meygom Repa, Tsapūh Repa, Kharchung Repa, Rongchung Repa, Dorje Ouangchuk Repa of Takgom, Jogon Repa Darma Ouangchuk, Dampa Gyakpūhwa, Charuwa of Likor, Master Gedun of Lo, Kyoton Shakyaguna, and Master Tashibar of Drey. The foremost disciple, Gampopa, and five of the thirteen sons were fully ordained monks.

The four highly advanced women disciples were Retchungma of Tsonga, Sallay Ö of Nyanang, Paldar Būm of Chung, and Peta Gonkyi, who was Jetsun's sister. Then there were twenty-five awakened seers who had reached the final stages of their path and a hundred others described as starlike who had perceived the ultimate nature of reality and would not return to samsara.

Besides that, there were a hundred and eight great meditators who had had a sublime experience in meditation and achieved the state of joyful warmth on the path. Then there were a thousand and one great meditators, men and women, who had renounced worldly pursuits and had reached the primary stage of realization. Countless ordinary people who became Jetsun's disciples, having been spiritually destined, had cut forever the stream of movement toward the lower realms by virtue of their spiritual bond with Milarepa. Apart from all these human disciples there were other disciples among the supracelestial beings, such as the five sister dakinis.[1] Among subcelestial beings there was the Demon of Lingpa Cave.

Having completed Milarepa's cremation, all human disciples who were present at the time of his death left for their mountain solitudes, where they spent their whole lives in meditation in accordance with Jetsun's instructions. But Retchung set out toward Ü province to meet Gampopa in order to give him his share of the sacred objects. Following Jetsun's prophetic guidance, Gampopa, although late, was proceeding toward Chuwar when he met Retchung at Yarlung Pūhshar. After handing over to him the sacred treasures, such as the hat of Acharya[2] Maitrepa and an aloe-wood staff, Retchung told him the news of Milarepa's death. Thereupon Gampopa fainted. When he revived, Gampopa, grief-stricken, prayed fervently. This was recorded in his own biography.

Gampopa invited Retchung to his own residence and received from him the complete instructions for higher esoteric meditation on Chakrasamvara. Retchung gave him the Dharma teachings and also Gampopa's share of the sacred robe, and then left for the monastery of Loro Döl. Having transformed his earthly body into Sambhogakaya, Retchung finally merged into the All-Embracing Emptiness.

Calm Light Repa, Khira Repa, Retchungma Paldar Būm, and Sallay Ö also passed away in a similar manner by dissolving their bodies into the emptiness of the Dharmakaya. The others who died leaving behind their mortal remains had also attained the Dharmakaya. The foremost disciples who in this life achieved Enlightenment, and also all those who passed away leaving behind their mortal remains, have served the good cause of the Dharma and given benefits to sentient beings throughout the cosmic universe through the wonderful qualities, attainments, and good examples of their lives, as well as by leaving behind the relics of their bodies and the evolved crystals.

The life of the Master, Mila Zhepa Dorje (Vajra Laughter), the greatest of saints, supreme among men, is comprised of twelve major events, three of them being his pursuit of a worldly life and the other nine depicting his striving toward achievement of the supreme peace of nirvana.

Thus, Milarepa attained in one life and in one body the Enlightenment known as the Buddha Vajradhara with its unique characteristics such as the Four Supreme Manifestations[3] and Five

Aspects of Wisdom.[4] During this life the Master sowed seeds of awakening in the consciousness of sentient beings and brought these seeds to full blossom. In his illumination and purity the Master traversed all Buddha realms.

This story of liberation, the life of Milarepa, leads to the path of emancipation and supreme knowledge. This great gift, bringing joy and inward excellence, bestows glorious wealth, in an unending stream, upon all sentient beings who pervade the cosmic universe. May they all be blessed with ever-unfolding virtue, prosperity, happiness, and illumination!

Colophon

This story of the liberation of Milarepa,
Like the wish-fulfilling gem, radiating the light of action,
Brightened the teaching of all Buddhas
And fulfilled the hopes and aspirations of sentient beings.
May this noble offering be pleasing to the Buddhas of the past.

Poetry adorns the beginning of this story and the end.
May this be a pleasing feast for learned men fond of
figurative speech.

The words of this story arouse faith, stirring even the hairs
of the body.
May this be a pleasing feast for those noble monks yearning to
escape samsara.

The true meaning of this story reveals the inherent unity of
apparent and ultimate realities.
May this be a pleasing feast for those compassionate and
awakened ones.

By reading this story, fetters of the Eight Worldly Reactions will
be broken.
May this be a pleasing feast for ascetics who have renounced
mind-clinging.

By hearing this story, faith will arise spontaneously in readers.
May this be a pleasing feast for those destined to practice the
Dharma.

By being mindful of this story, one will instantly cease
mind-clinging.
May this be a pleasing feast for those seeking Enlightenment
in this life.

By linking oneself with this story,
One will fulfill the noble aims for himself and for others.
May this be a pleasing feast for those teachers of the Dharma working for the benefit of sentient beings.

By performing acts of liberation one will fulfill the intent of the lineage.
May this be a pleasing feast for devotees seeking to fulfill the Master's words.

The compassion of Jetsun through this story of liberation will protect sentient beings from suffering.
May this be a pleasing feast for all beings of the three planes of samsara!

The source of this pleasing feast is the story of liberation of Mila Laughing Vajra.
It is the wish-fulfilling gem in all its glory and splendor, endowed with the Four Boundless Attributes,
Standing at the top of the Banner of the Buddha's Teaching.
This celestial gem of lapis lazuli pours forth wonderful gifts to those in samsara and nirvana,
Fulfilling the wishes of sentient beings deprived of the wealth of true awareness.
Through veneration of this story, with offerings,
And by invoking it to grant gifts of fulfillment,
There rains down the medicine of the Five Awarenesses,
Which heals diseases of the five poisons
In those lying in the sickbed of samsara.

I express my solemn wish to share through its sublime quality
The gift of the Seven Jewels of the Awakened Ones[1]
With all sentient beings driven into unceasing suffering,
Thereby satisfying the need of those in samsara and nirvana.

I express my wish that all those who hear the name of Milarepa
May achieve Enlightenment in its four aspects in this life.
May they achieve power and energy to guide sentient beings in the cosmic realm through innumerable incarnations.
May these wishes be fully realized through this dedication of merits to all sentient beings.

This manuscript on the life of Milarepa, the greatest of yogins, with the songs revealing the path of liberation and Complete Enlightenment, was written down fully and accurately by Durto Rolpai Naljorpa (Peripatetic Yogin of Wilderness and Cemetery). It was transmitted to me by my lama according to the secret oral tradition, although I have seen many other accounts of Jetsun's story. It was completed on the eighth day of the twelfth lunar month, in the year Puhrbu* in Dhok Lachi Gangra (Snowy Region of Mount Everest), the great sacred abode of the dakinis. May it serve the cause of the Dharma and bring peace and happiness to all sentient beings until all the cycles of life have ceased to exist!

May blessings be with all.

* Earth Monkey year (1484).

Translators' Notes

PROLOGUE

1. *Dharmakaya.* See page xxii *ff.* of Introduction.
2. *Rahu* is the eighth planet with its crown, 'Ketu,' considered to be the ninth planet, according to traditional astrology. Ancient Indian mythology depicts Rahu as a demonic celestial force, terrifying in appearance, with nine heads. Moving through space, Rahu periodically devours the sun and the moon, causing eclipses. The sun and the moon then make their way out through an opening in his throat.
3. *The five Skandas* (or *aggregates*) are the five causally conditioned components of all existence, especially human existence. The apparent ego-entity is actually no more than a process of phenomena, a congeries of psychophysical events constantly in flux. These constituent processes are classically grouped under five headings: (1) form (*rupa*), (2) feeling (*vedana*), (3) perception (*samjna*), (4) mental phenomena (*samskaras*), and (5) mental consciousness (*vijnana*).
4. *The eight perfect attributes.* The Tibetan text has '*ouangchuk ludan*,' meaning literally 'the supremely powerful possessor of serpent-gods.' These are eight in number in the cult of the serpent-gods. The reference to serpent-gods is metaphorical. For the sake of clarity this passage has been rendered, following the more common term, *ouangchuk yontanye*, as 'the eight attributes of the supremely powerful one,' or simply 'eight perfect attributes.'

In Buddhism the Eight Perfect Attributes listed below are said to belong exclusively to the realm of Sambhogakaya Buddha:

1. Attribute of formal manifestation in infinite varieties.
2. Attribute of intentional communication with others.
3. Attribute of total awareness.
4. Attribute of the power to transform into any intended form.
5. Attribute of all-encompassing mind which embraces all universes.
6. Attribute of perceiving and partaking in the sensations of the body caused by spiritual enlightenment.
7. Attribute of bringing about the fulfillment of the wishes and aspirations of all sentient beings.
8. Attribute of the power to maintain any intended form for a great length of time.

These eight perfect attributes differ from the similarly named 'eight attributes' of the Brahmanic tradition in India.

5. *The ten transcendent powers.* These are:

1. The power of Buddha-mind, encompassing the entire realm of knowledge and directly perceiving the intrinsic nature of the laws of the universe, particularly as they apply to the life of sentient beings. The Buddha-mind sees with absolute certainty that happiness is produced only by thoughts and deeds that are virtuous and never by those that are evil, whereas suffering is produced only by thoughts and deeds that are evil and never by those that are virtuous.
2. The power of cognizing distinctly all the future results of the various kinds of karma. Also, the power to see the effect of interacting forces at the cosmic level.
3. The power of cognizing the potential for liberation in every human being which forms the inherent nature of the eighteen psychophysical elements (the six senses, the six sensory objects, and the six aggregates of consciousness). See *The Eye of Wisdom* by the XIVth Dalai Lama.
4. The power of cognizing the nature and degree of the inner aspiration in individuals.
5. The power of cognizing the intellectual sensitivity of individuals.
6. The power of knowing and perceiving all the diverse paths which lead to the higher realms of existence, liberation, and Complete Enlightenment.
7. The power of understanding all the innumerable forms of the contemplation on the various stages of enlightenment.
8. The power of cognizing all the past karma of every individual.
9. The power of cognizing the exact moment of death for every sentient being, and the power to transfer its stream of consciousness to many successive lives.
10. The power of perception that sees all the different methods of terminating or transforming mental defilements and that sees the various kinds of results these methods produce.

6. *Dakinis.* See page xxvi ff. of Introduction.

7. *Yidam.* See page xxv ff. of Introduction.

8. '*Awakened supporters*' are the dakinis.

9. *Vajrayana.* See page xv ff. of Introduction.

10. *Consort dakinis.* This refers to Milarepa's practice of transformation through sexual union with the consort dakini Tseringma ('the long-lived one').

11. *The four divisions of the Tantra.* A reference to the whole collection of texts containing the teachings of Vajrayana, which are divided into four categories according to the nature of the meditation practice and psychological approach commensurate with the level of the individual's potentiality. The four are:

1. *Jagyu,* the stream of action (Kiryat Tantra).
2. *Chogyu,* the stream of action and meditation (Charya Tantra).
3. *Naljorgyu,* the stream of inward purity (Yoga Tantra).
4. *Naljor Lamagkigyu,* the stream of unsurpassable inward purity (Anuttrayoga Tantra).

12. *The Eight Worldly Reactions* are the emotional reactions that arise from the mind's clinging to self. The eight reactions are grouped into two parts,

positive and negative. The four positive reactions are: to be pleased by pleasure, praise, gain, and delightful words; the four negative reactions: to be disturbed by displeasure, criticism, loss, and dreadful words.

13. *Bodhisattva.* This refers to Bodhichitta. The term Bodhisattva is used in two major ways, corresponding to two levels: the path of the Bodhisattva and the Ultimate Realization itself. A Bodhisattva is one who strives to engender within himself a great compassion for sentient beings and who strives to attain transcendent wisdom so that he may both work for the liberation of all sentient beings and achieve full enlightenment himself. A Bodhisattva is thus either one who has achieved virtual enlightenment but has chosen to work for sentient beings through unending chains of reincarnation, or an ordinary individual who has received the Bodhisattva ordination and has thereby resolved to seek his own enlightenment for the sake of sentient beings.

14. *Dakas and dakinis and the twenty-four energy centers of his vajra-like body.* There are three orders of dakinis in the Vajrayana tradition. *Dakinis of the first order,* otherwise described as 'spontaneously enlightened dakinis' (Lhenkye Khadroma), are usually depicted as yidams such as Vajrayogini, Tara, etc., arising from Sambhogakaya's power of unfoldment. *The second order* are invisible dakinis known as 'those who are born in the Heavenly Realms' (Schingkye Khadroma). Among them are emanations of dakinis of the first order and also others who have reached this level through their attainment. According to the apparent meaning given by the tradition, they function from the invisible heavenly realms that encompass twenty-four sacred places located in various parts of India and Tibet. According to the actual meaning, however, the dakinis represent the ultimate nature of all psychophysical forces within every human being who has within himself the corresponding 'twenty-four realms'.

The third order is comprised of those 'born of realization of mantra' (Ngakkye Khadroma). They are to be found among human beings who are either potential dakinis or who have reached various levels of inner realization through their own inborn understanding or through the stages of the Vajrayana path.

Incidentally, the diverse forms of yidams in both sexes depicted in esoteric iconography are only indications of Sambhogakaya's transformative power. The bewildering diversity of forms and their sex distinction cannot and must not be viewed as objective realities, for they are only a psychological expedient for communicating the great truth of interdependent relativity together with its inherent character of non-duality and ultimate emptiness.

Vajra-like body refers to the Vajrayana teaching that hidden in the human body and mind are great potentialities of purity and intrinsic reality. Vajrayana considers man's five aggregates as five orders of Buddhas and considers the five elements – earth, water, fire, air-energy, and space – as five female Buddhas. The five defilements are to be transformed into the Five Transcendent Awarenesses through the meditation process. A yogin such as Milarepa can and does achieve enlightenment by exploiting the hidden potentialities of the human body and mind.

15. *Heruka.* Etymologically, *he* signifies the intrinsic emptiness of all causes,

ru stands for the intrinsic emptiness of all effects, and *ka* signifies the emptiness that lies in the very nature of all things. Thus, Heruka is identifiable with the ultimate nature of reality. Heruka is also used as the name for yidams in their terrifying aspect.

There is yet another designation of the wrathful yidam – 'he who drinks blood' – which originates from the Sanskrit term 'Rudhika'. Therefore, Heruka is he who kills the four kinds of maras by drinking their blood.

In esoteric discipline one's personal lama is looked upon as a living embodiment of Heruka.

16. *Eight armies of gods and demons.* The term generally refers to eight assemblies of supernatural forces. Specifically, it refers to the eight chiefs presiding over the eight armies of gods, goddesses, yama, yaksa, raksa, tsan, nagas, and gyalpo.

17. *Trikaya aspect of mind* refers to the character of human consciousness as an integral system. The intrinsic emptiness of the mind or the stream of consciousness represents Dharmakaya; the intrinsic lucidity of inmost awareness represents Sambhogakaya; and perceptions and thoughts unfolding without obstruction are Nirmanakaya.

18. *Buddha Vajradhara.* Vajradhara is the highest manifestation of enlightenment, the visual representation of Dharmakaya. The literal meaning of 'Vajra' is diamond, especially in its aspect of unbreakable hardness or solidity. In its higher meaning, Vajra connotes the intrinsic nature of enlightenment – the indestructible and inseparable union of transcendent wisdom and boundless compassion, as well as the supreme bliss and the ultimate emptiness.

Being the highest cosmic force arising from Dharmakaya's expanse, Vajradhara represents the supreme integrating force and the source of unfolding compassion. In Vajradhara all Sambhogakaya forms, their qualities and functions are unified. Hence Vajradhara is described as the all-pervasive sovereign of the attributes of enlightenment.

19. *Four Aspects of Enlightenment.* This analytical term refers to the Three Aspects of Enlightenment (Trikaya) with the addition of the Essence Aspect (Svabhavekakaya). This Essence Aspect is the inherent character or foundation of Dharmakaya. It is defined simply as the pure realm of enlightenment. Being non-substantive it is also unstainable and is that which makes possible the elimination of all intellectual and emotional defilements. The pure inner space of enlightenment and ultimate awareness is normally brought under the term Dharmakaya. The two other aspects are the highest manifestation (Sambhogakaya) and the earthly manifestation (Nirmanakaya).

20. *Five Transcendent Awarenesses.* See Note 14 above and Note 5, First Part, Chapter 3.

FIRST PART, CHAPTER 1

1. *Yogin* is Sanskrit and *yogi* is Hindi.

2. *Tilopa, Naropa and Marpa.* The two main lineages of the Kagyüpa Order are Ringyu (Ring-bryud), the 'long line' of teachers in the exoteric tradition, and Nyegyu (Nye-bryud), the 'short line' of teachers (otherwise described as the direct lineage). This latter lineage descends from the great teacher Tilopa,

who received the secret oral transmission concerning the esoteric teachings, particularly those that later came to be known as the Six Doctrines of Naropa. (See Note 10, Second Part, Chapter 4.)

3. *Ngonga and Ogmin:* names for the Pure Land of Buddha. Ngonga: Perfect Joy, the Buddha realm of Akshobhaya (The Unshakable One). When an initiate visualizes the Five Buddha Realms in his meditation, Ngonga is thought of as situated in the east. The term Ogmin means literally 'not being under,' hence the highest Buddha realm of Sambhogakaya. Sometimes Ogmin as an adjective qualifies the noun Ngon-ga so as to present a descriptive term, Ogmin Ngonga – the Highest Joyful Realm.

4. *Nyingmapa.* The 'ancient Order', known also as the school of the Old Translations, originated in the eighth century under Guru Padmasambhava and Vimalamitra, both of whom came to Tibet from India. It is one of the four main schools of Tibetan Buddhism still existing today outside Tibet.

5. *Mantra.* A mantra is either a single syllable or set of syllables looked upon as sacred. In Buddhist tantric meditation, mantras are visualized in radiant forms or sung at varying voice levels. Sometimes, however, the practice takes the form of a silent transmutation of the mantric sound into union with the dynamic energy of the breathing.

The tantric texts define mantra as the direct means which man can employ to protect himself from mind's delusive imagery of duality and all the unhappy consequences arising from it. The various methods of meditating on the mantra lead to quieting the mind, so that the initiate can work his way toward rekindling a spontaneous inner awakening, a glimpse of which he may have already perceived at the time of the initiatory ritual.

Buddhist mantras together with the principles and practices of self-transformation were originally given by the great enlightened masters. Mantras have many levels of meaning which can be learned only from an experienced teacher, and only by following his prescribed procedure.

The Hindu tradition considers the basic mantra 'OM' as the supreme voice of God and attributes objective power to it. Buddhism, on the other hand, recognizes no such absolute objective power.

6. *'Papa Mila!'* 'Father, what a man! Father, what a man!' In Tibetan, 'mi' means man and 'la' is a necessary reinforcing exclamation. Thus the expression, Father (papa), what a man! (JB)

7. *Sacrificial effigies.* The use of sacrificial effigies originates in the ancient customs of Tibet's native religion called Bön, a form of nature worship. Effigies of men, women, and even domestic animals formed from wood-blocks or made out of soft dough glazed with colored butter are offered to gods and spirits as ransom to secure release of the victims from their evil influence. Rites are performed at homes either by lay spiritualists or sometimes by Buddhist tantric monks. See Note 4, Second Part, Chapter 8.

8. *Tsa.* Abbreviation for Kya Ngatsa.

9. *The year of the Water Dragon.* The year is 1052 of the Christian era.

FIRST PART, CHAPTER 2

1. *Dzo*. Cross-breed of the yak and the common cow. (JB)
2. *Chuba*. The sleeves of the Tibetan chuba, when they are folded back, go from the elbow beyond the hands and can serve as a whip. (JB)
3. *We will run at the sound of the drum, and run when the smoke rises*. This expression refers to the condition of destitutes and beggars looking for alms, especially from homes where religious rites are taking place with sounds of music, such as drums, and where smoke is rising from the kitchen chimney. On such occasions patrons distribute cooked food.
4. *Cult of the Eight Nagas*. The Eight Nagas as the eight Serpent-Gods. (See Note 4, Prologue.)

FIRST PART, CHAPTER 3

1. *Tsampa*, the principal food of Tibetans, is made by roasting grains of barley as we roast coffee. It is roasted a little at a time in iron basins with rounded bottoms. To prevent the grain from burning it is stirred constantly with a whisk, twig, or spatula. When ground, this roasted barley is tsampa. (JB)
2. *Gungthang*. Evans-Wentz erroneously translates this name as 'Central Plain.' Actually, there are several meanings for the Tibetan term '*Gung*' – 'high' or 'systematic order' are two; it is also a term meaning a kind of Himalayan leopard. Perhaps the best rendering of Gungthang is 'High Ground.'
3. *The monk quickly returned*. This journey from Yarlung to Mangyul and back would represent, for a good Tibetan courier, a minimum of forty days. (JB)
4. *Maroon-faced Dza* refers to one of the three principal guardian deities of the Nyingmapa Order. Known as Dza, he is also considered to be a celestial force identified with the eighth planet, Rahu, and the ninth planet, Ketu. Dza is the king of demonic forces that are part of the eight armies of gods and demons. (See Note 16, Prologue.)
5. *Hūm*. This is part of a particular kind of mantra known as *drak-ngak*, a terrifying spell. The sacred syllable 'Hūm' in general symbolizes the nature, attributes, and power of Buddha-mind. Broken into five parts, this syllable in Sanskrit or Tibetan represents the Five Transcendent Awarenesses of Buddha-mind, namely: (1) awareness of all-pervasive emptiness, (2) mirror-like awareness, (3) awareness of spontaneously arisen compassion, (4) awareness of discrimination, and (5) awareness of equanimity.
6. *Paht* is the last syllable of this terrifying mantra. A sorcerer utters this syllable along with others in casting a spell upon his enemy. A yogin, on the other hand, utters this spell as part of a meditative process to dissolve adverse inner forces that stand in the way of his enlightenment. In esoteric meditation this syllable is uttered in full force to bring the mind back to attention.
7. *Mandala*. The Tibetan text mentions only the general term 'mandala'. In the light of the earlier reference to the name of the principal guardian deity 'Dzadong Marnak,' the Maroon-faced Dza, one can conclude that the association or identification of the mandala was with the guardian deity. Evi-

dently, the mandala here is to be understood in the literal sense as being the symbol representing the conclave of the Maroon-faced Dza and his emanations. Thus a mandala either painted or constructed with colored powders is placed at the center of an altar with the appropriate ritual objects and the offerings of various kinds set in the front in rows on the lower level. A detailed description would require consulting the actual text on this form of sorcery.
8. *Triple Refuge.* The Triple Refuge common to all Buddhists is comprised of the Buddha, the supreme guide to liberation and full enlightenment; Dharma, the path leading to cessation of samsaric conditions and causes, and thereby to realization of the truth; Sangha, the assembly of arhats and Bodhisattvas who support devotees of the Dharma. (See also Introduction.)
9. *Throw a pinch of food into the air.* A habitual gesture among pious Tibetans who throw bits of food into the air as an offering to the gods. (JB)
10. *Ninth course of bricks.* Tibetan houses are built of earth stamped into molds or wooden forms. The marks of these stacked molds remain visible on the walls. Tibetans use these marks to measure the height of the snow. One gyang-rim measures about two feet. (JB)

SECOND PART, CHAPTER 1

1. *The Teaching of the Great Perfection.* This phrase refers to the Atiyoga doctrine, which is the highest form of esoteric teaching in the Tibetan tradition.

The first phrase *to triumph at the root* refers to the innermost character of man, his primordial awareness. This awareness is said to be unstainable by the power of egoistic delusion and unalterable even by the Buddhas. The ultimate essence is said to consist of an inseparable unity of supra-normal cognition and its inherent emptiness so that it transcends the duality of samsara and nirvana, which exists as long as man is ruled by his delusion of self and its phenomenal conditions.

This leads to the phrase *to triumph at the summit*, which implies a higher insight in the path through a spontaneous awakening. This state is brought about first through the empowerment of initiation and is then rekindled through meditation in all modes of self-transformation. The phrase *to triumph in the fruit of enlightenment* refers to the non-existence of enlightenment as an object apart from man's original awareness. *To meditate on it by day is to be a Buddha in one day*, etc., implies that enlightenment is inherent in one's awareness at every moment of man's stream of being and that initiates simply open themselves to this truth.
2. *The banner-of-victory* is one of the eight auspicious emblems. This traditional standard is raised on the rooftops of Buddhist temples, monasteries, and private dwellings that possess the complete set of the Buddhist Canon, about 329 volumes, known as Kagyur (the translated scriptures) and Tengyur (the translated elucidating treatises).
3. *Six classes of beings.* This refers to all sentient beings, traditionally divided into six classes: celestial beings, demi-gods, human beings, hungry ghosts, animals, and beings of hell.
4. *Stupa.* A reliquary in which sacred relics or the embalmed body of a lama

are preserved. There are also numerous temples built in the form of a stupa, for in the Buddhist tradition a stupa stands for the Enlightened Mind of Buddhas or lamas. Like an architectured mandala, the various structural forms represent the noble principles of the path, the attributes of excellence, and the stages of spiritual perfection. Eight great stupas were built both during and after the life of the Buddha, marking the major events of his life: birth, renunciation, the conquest of the forces of Mara, enlightenment, the first sermon, his visit to a celestial realm where his mother was reborn, his victory over opponents in public debate and mind power, and his final passing away.
5. *Rimpoche* is a term of reverence, meaning literally 'the Precious One,' used in addressing lamas. The term is also associated with the ancient traditional symbol of the Wish-fulfilling Gem. In invoking his personal lama, a devotee may address him as 'my lama who is the Wish-fulfilling Gem.'
6. *Nyima Latö.* Western Tibet.

SECOND PART, CHAPTER 2

1. *Yidam Chakrasamvara.* Yidam is the generic term. Chakrasamvara is a particular yidam belonging to the order of Mother tantra. The theory and practice of self-transformation associated with this yidam deal mainly with the development of transcendent wisdom and with the realization of primal awareness, described as the emptiness of luminous clarity. However, it does not exclude the discipline for attaining to the Sambhogakaya form, which is the main practice according to Guhyasamaja as described in Note 2, below.
2. *Guhyasamaja.* One of the yidams, according to Anuttara Tantra. Guhyasamaja is Dharmakaya's manifestation unifying in himself the attributes of all Buddhas. The theory and practice of self-transformation associated with this yidam deal primarily with the development of boundless compassion as a motive force and with skillful transmutations of the psychophysical aggregates, and particularly their hidden energies, into the Sambhogakaya form. This yidam belongs to the order of Father tantra. There exist different forms of Guhyasamaja.
3. *The Dharma.* Dharma refers to two sets of principles for spiritual perfection. First: the teachings embodied in the Three Containers (Tripitaka) and the practice of self-transformation by means of perfect ethics, perfect contemplation, and perfect wisdom. In Mahayana Buddhism all these are condensed into one single principle, namely Bodhichitta – Enlightened Mind – the joint development of boundless compassion and transcendent wisdom. Second: the term 'Dharma' refers to the metaphysical standpoint of Buddhism regarding the relative and absolute nature of reality.
4. *Twenty-four mortifications.* This refers to the ordeals Naropa underwent during his spiritual quest under the Lama Tilopa. These are described in *The Life and Teachings of Naropa,* trans. by Herbert V. Guenther, Oxford, 1975.
5. *Dorje Pahgmo.* Vajravarahi in Sanskrit. The name of a dakini and a form of meditation practice.
6. *Hevajra.* One of the yidams according to Anuttara Tantra. The teaching of this order belongs to the Non-dual tradition (meaning neither exclusively Father nor Mother tantras). It combines the elements of both the Father and

Mother tantras. This in a practical sense means combining the two essential practices, namely, the transformation of the earthly body into the Sambhogakaya level and the realization of the inborn emptiness of awareness.

7. *Eight Thousand Stanzas.* Astasahasrika Prajnaparamita.

8. *Taktugnu.* This refers to a Bodhisattva who went through inconceivably numerous ordeals in search of the Dharma. There is a life of Taktugnu in Tibetan.

9. *Kagyü* refers to the teachings from which the Kagyüpa Order derived its name.

10. *The Two Divisions* refers to the main divisions of Hevajra Tantra.

11. *Good omen.* In all Tibetan literature, when an unexpected arrival interrupts a reading or a recitation, the last words pronounced are considered significant in relation to the destiny of the newcomer. (JB)

12. *Udumbara.* According to Tibetan literature, a very rare lotus of fabulous color, immense size, and unmatched fragrance.

13. *Mudra.* Mudras are symbolic gestures of the hand or postures of the body which form part of the esoteric practice.

14. *Maitrepa.* Maitrepa was an Indian Buddhist teacher from whom Marpa, in the course of his journey to India, received the esoteric teaching of Mahamudra. Marpa transmitted this teaching to Milarepa, who passed it down to Gampopa, Retchungpa, and so on, until it reached the teachers of the present time.

15. Religious structures are crowned with a brown frieze of tamarisk twigs set on edge and cut close to the wall like a brush.

16. *The four Tantras.* See Note 11, Prologue.

17. *Lotsava* is a general term meaning translator of the Texts of the Dharma.

SECOND PART, CHAPTER 3

1. *Skull-cup of libation.* Kapala in Sanskrit. The libation cup made from the dome of a skull. (JB)

2. *Chakrasamvara mandala.* Refers to the mandala representing the 'temple-palace' housing the conclave of sixty-two deities presided over by Chakrasamvara and the consort-dakini Vajravarahi. The temple-palace and its dwellers are equally symbolic of the highest reality, which the Buddha's Dharmakaya is capable of projecting outward and which Lama Marpa also displayed through the action of Enlightened Mind when empowering Milarepa.

3. *The thirty-two holy places and the eight great places of cremation.* The eight great wilderness crematoria or cemeteries, mentioned in many important tantric treatises, were believed to be located in various parts of the Indian subcontinent. They were chosen and hallowed by many practicing tantrics or yogins as places to exercise the perceptual transformations of abhorrent conditions and circumstances such as take place at the site of a crematorium. In Tibet, too, cemeteries were located in mountains where yogins would go at a certain stage of their practice. In the Tibetan tradition 'the twenty-four holy lands' and 'the eight great wilderness cemeteries' are sometimes referred to as 'the thirty-two holy places.' They are said to have

been hallowed by Buddha with his emanations in the form of Chakrasamvara and the conclave of deities. Today these places are considered to be the realms of invisible dakas and dakinis who support the practice of initiates. Buddhist Tantra considers the various sensitive parts of the human body as a microcosmic counterpart of the thirty-two holy places.

4. *I went to meet you in the guise of a laborer.* Marpa has performed an act of respect without appearing to do so. Thus all the strange actions of this story have a hidden but very simple meaning. The farther one goes to meet a visitor, the greater the honor. Marpa could not have shown a greater deference.

5. *Fire of Tummo.* The term 'Tummo' means 'she who terrifies egoistic forces.' The syllable 'tum' implies heroic action as a skillful means, whereas 'mo' stands for supreme wisdom. The hidden fire of Tummo is aroused in Tsa-u-ma (the median nervous center) and in the various plexi in the spinal column by rechanneling the active energies of the two arteries of the central nervous system. This 'fire' is then used for harnessing the creative energy. This process ensures that purification of physical and psychical elements is achieved simultaneously so that the sensation of supreme bliss is produced. Though this by itself is not the true object of seekers, it is nevertheless used as a means for achieving a complete self-transformation in a most effective way. The practitioner is to bring to bear upon this extraordinary experience his meditative perception of reality. Such perception born of wisdom sees in this supreme bliss the emptiness of substance or self and indeed of all things and therewith is understood the unity of bliss and emptiness.

SECOND PART, CHAPTER 4

1. *Sixty tones of celestial Brahma* refers metaphorically to the sixty supramundane qualities, aspects, and tonal ranges of the Buddha's voice. Among them is the unique power of the Buddha's voice or speech which is believed to be capable of communicating with each individual in the way he understands best.

2. *Eighty-four thousand aspects.* Buddhist scriptures refer to eighty-four thousand aspects of mind's delusion and defilements and, therefore, the parallel existence of eighty-four thousand remedies of Dharma. The numeral designation seems to be an emphatic indication of the magnitude and diversity of the human mind. The eighty-four thousand aspects are divided into four categories, with twenty-one thousand in each category. All defilements of mind are therefore summed up in four groupings: (1) delusion, (2) desire, (3) hatred, and (4) the mixture of these three emotions. Similarly, there are four kinds of Dharma remedies represented by the teachings. The first deals with the manner of perceiving reality as shown in abi dharma and prajnaparamita; the second, with the self-discipline in Viraya; the third, with quieting the mind's duality and awakening higher consciousness in Sutra; and the fourth deals with rapidly gaining self-transformation in Tantra.

3. *Buddhas of the Three Ages.* There are two aspects to this concept. It refers to the Buddhas of the past in this cosmic aeon, such as Khorwajik, Serthub, and O-sung, and Sakyamuni Buddha of the present five millennia and the

remainder of the Thousand Buddhas from Jampa to the last Buddha, Möpa. The concept also refers generally to all those who achieved Buddha-hood in the past and who may achieve it in the present or in the future.

4. *The Three Jewels.* Refers to the Triple Refuge – Buddha, Dharma, Sangha. (See Note 8, First Part, Chapter 3.)

5. *The Lesser Vehicle:* Hinayana Buddhism. (See Introduction.)

6. *Bodhichitta.* This refers to Mahayana's central principle – Enlightened Mind, a complete and unconditional concern for the liberation of sentient beings from the bondage of samsara. Every follower of the Dharma is required to develop not only great compassion for all sentient beings, but also to achieve a complete awakening to the ultimate level of Bodhichitta. Only then can one achieve enlightenment through the selfless action of compassion and supreme wisdom.

7. *The Greater Vehicle:* Mahayana Buddhism. (See Introduction.)

8. *The four aspects of initiation.* This refers to initiation according to the highest order of Vajrayana. The four stages of initiation are as follows:

1. The initiation of the vase is the empowerment through manifestation of the yidam, which prepares the initiate for the inward transformation of perceptive forms.
2. The initiation of concealed union is the empowerment through the speech of the yidam, which prepares the initiate for the transformation of the energies of body, speech, and sound.
3. The initiation of supreme wisdom is the empowerment through the enlightened mind of the yidam, which prepares the initiate for the transformation of consciousness.
4. The initiation of indefinable identification is the empowerment through the ultimate nature of the yidam, which prepares the initiate for Complete Enlightenment. For clarification of the term *hidden meaning*, see Note 16, below.

9. *Great Symbol* (*Mahamudra*). This refers to an awakened state (described as 'primal awareness') which embraces the unfolding unity of highest bliss and its inborn emptiness, signifying enlightened experience and achievement. The meditation of Mahamudra is a means to realize this directly. The great seal is so designated because every initiate who has glimpsed such a state of awareness during the initiation continues to 'affix the great seal' of his insight upon all his perceptions of reality. The Kagyüpa Order speaks of two traditions of Mahamudra, one according to the Sutras and the other according to Tantra.

The various schools of Tibetan Buddhism offer somewhat differing viewpoints on the doctrine and meditative approach associated with the Mahamudra.

10. *The Six Esoteric Doctrines.* This refers to some vital aspects of Buddhist tantric yoga. Sometimes known as the six doctrines of Naropa, they are:

1. The yoga dealing with the supreme Fire of Tummo.
2. The yoga of the subtle body.
3. The yoga of dreams.
4. The yoga of luminous awareness.

5. The yoga of the transference of the stream of consciousness.

6. The yoga of the intermediate state of Bardo.

11. *Transference of Consciousness to Dead Bodies.* This practice of transferring the consciousness-stream into a recently dead man or animal is to be distinguished from transference into a chosen realm at the time of death. Marpa brought the former teaching to Tibet and handed it down to Milarepa, and to his own son, Darma Doday. The latter transferred his stream of consciousness into the body of a bird at the moment of his death in a fatal accident. Following Marpa's instructions, the bird flew to India, where he entered the dead body of a young Brahmin, who subsequently became a teacher known as the Pigeon of the Mysterious Tree.

12. *Garuda.* According to ancient mythology, Garuda was a celestial being that had its abode in the wish-fulfilling tree in the thirty-third heaven. It is considered to be a counterforce against the serpent-gods of the undersea world. In Buddhist tantric tradition there are Garuda-yidams corresponding to the five kinds of Buddha-families.

13. *The Four Infinite Attributes.* Love, compassion, goodwill, and equanimity.

14. *Initiation of Anatmata.* This refers to Anatama, the consort dakini of Chakrasamvara.

15. *Purity of Awareness.* One of the six esoteric doctrines, synonymous with the Luminous Clarity of Awareness. See Note 10, above.

16. *Six modes and the four methods.* This refers to the four methods of explanation and the six modes of elucidating the Buddhist tantric doctrine. The four are: (1) the literal meaning, including that of symbolism and mantra; (2) the general meaning; (3) the hidden meaning (allusions to certain omitted crucial explanations); and (4) the ultimate meaning. The six modes are: (1) and (2) teachings given with or without concealed intention or insight; (3) and (4) those that have apparent or ultimate meanings; (5) and (6) those that have literal etymological meanings and those that have a meaning different from the literal.

17. *Pills of nectar.* The origin of these pills were the enlightened masters of ancient India and Tibet who had the personal power of esoteric alchemy so that they were able to transform five kinds of flesh and five liquids into ambrosia for the benefit of initiates. At the present time, pills are made out of various herbs and extracts from the remaining ancient pills. They are then consecrated through meditation by the lamas. A human skull, real or artificial, is used as a container. The skull is the symbol of highest awareness encompassing bliss and its emptiness. A yogin practices the complete transformation of the senses into the five aspects of illuminating awareness, this being the complete integration of wisdom's insight and the sensation of highest bliss.

18. *The Five Classes of Buddha.* This refers to Sambhogakaya's five manifestations: Vajrasattva, Ratnasambra, Amitaba, Amoghasiddhi, and Vairochana. Each of these embodies specific aspects of enlightened awareness: mirror-like awareness, awareness of equanimity, discriminating awareness, spontaneously fulfilling action, and all-encompassing emptiness.

19. *Damaru and kapala.* The damaru is a double drum made from two skull crowns back to back. The kapala is a libation skull, sometimes natural, sometimes fabricated in precious material.

SECOND PART, CHAPTER 5

1. *Castle of Jewels* refers to the Maharatnakuta Sutra, a Mahayana sutra. The Maharatnakuta comprises six of the 104 volumes of the collected sutras in Tibetan known as Kagyur.
2. *Mara.* Mara exists in four different aspects: (1) as inner delusion, (2) as the five aggregates of psychophysical existence which imprison man in the turning wheel of birth and death, (3) as the unfailing force of death, (4) as a demon in both an external and internal sense – as King Garab Ouangchuk of the Deceiving Heaven of Domination (Shentrul Aungjey), and as the power of inner egoistic attachment; both of these seek to seduce man into harmful action and distract him from beneficial pursuits.
3. *Om, Ah, and Hūm. Om* symbolizes the manifestation of enlightenment. *Ah* symbolizes the speech of enlightenment. *Hūm* symbolizes the supreme knowledge.
4. *Mount Tisi.* Mount Kailas. For Tibetans this is the sacred abode of Yidam Chakrasamvara and many immortal arhats, while for Hindus it is the realm of Shiva and his consort Uma.
5. *The Realm of the Dakinis.* Besides the apparent meaning, the real meaning is the supreme state of Dharmakaya.
6. *The dakinis of the three stages of the Path.* Those that dwell in three realms, viz., space, earth, and the subterranean realm. These dakas and dakinis, as invisible beings or as humans, have achieved the primary, higher, transformation or enlightenment.
7. *Eight armies of gods and demons.* See Note 16, Prologue.
8. *The twelve goddesses.* Twelve invisible dakinis who were said to have been subdued by Guru Padmasambhava at Palmo Palthang in Porong, West Tibet, and who were assigned by him to protect practicing initiates and yogins of the Vajrayana Order.
9. *Dusolma.* A goddess in wrathful aspect whom Marpa recognized as the guardian of the Kagyü tradition.
10. *I arrived in three days.* In three days Milarepa made a journey which by natural means would have required several months.

SECOND PART, CHAPTER 6

1. *Bones of my mother.* The bones are crushed and mixed with clay from which figurines or small stupas are made.
2. *Jaw of a lion.* This image designates the portion of wall that overhangs.

SECOND PART, CHAPTER 7

1. *Tsayi Koron.* Another name for Milarepa's birthplace, Kya Ngatsa.
2. *The Maras.* The plural of Mara. (See Note 2, Second Part, Chapter 5.)

3. *Cord of meditation.* Called gom-thak in Tibetan, this is a meditational belt made from cotton or woolen cloth. The meditator may wear it from the left shoulder around his chest and back as well as over one or both knees.
4. *Figurines.* Sacred images of clay, cast in copper or wooden molds.
5. *Source consciousness.* This refers to what is known as the source of all consciousness (*Alaya-vijnana* in Sanskrit). The Indian Buddhist school of idealism (Yogacara) propounds the theory that all thought processes originate from or dissolve themselves into the source consciousness. The whole phenomenal world is but a mental product, 'objective reality' an illusion of mind. It is the same mind that creates a 'real' self out of mere imagination. While denying such a duality, this school confirms the subjective reality of source consciousness – defined as transparency and awareness only. It is considered to be completely neutral, in the sense of being a foundation or base. In esoteric tradition the source consciousness is the mirror-like awareness which is realized when the mind's delusions are dispelled. Ordinary mind is overcome with defiled thought (nyonyi or nonyid) which may be compared to impurity that stains the source consciousness. Through the transformative process, the defilement of thoughts is cleared away and the nature of pure awareness then realized as enlightenment.
6. *Single green piece which had the form of the pot.* This relic still exists and is kept at Tashilhunpo.
7. *What shall I mix with his water?* Adding barley flour to water is a Tibetan custom.
8. *The four boundless attitudes* are the same as the Four Infinite Attributes mentioned in Note 13, Second Part, Chapter 4.
9. *The Kali Yuga* (the Dark Age) refers to the fourth and last cycle of time of our universe. The first three were known as Satya Yuga (complete happiness), Treta Yuga (threefold happiness), and Dwapara Yuga (twofold happiness). The Kali Yuga era is marked by (1) intellectual sophistication at the expense of spiritual attainment, (2) decline in the quality of life, (3) increasing menace to an already shortened life-span, (4) misguided concepts and mental impurity, and (5) widespread violence and conflicts.

SECOND PART, CHAPTER 8

1. *The goddess Tseringma.* One of the five sister goddesses who became disciples of Milarepa and who were later the guardians of his religious order.
2. *The Six Ways of Being Aware of One's Lama.* Refers to Milarepa's song in which he lists the sixfold remembrance of his lama. (This song is recorded in 'The Hundred Thousand Songs.' See the English translation by Garma Chang.)
3. *The goddess Tara* is one of the yidams. Depicted in many different forms, she is considered to be the embodiment of the unfolding compassion of all Buddhas.
4. *Bön* was the ancient religion of Tibet before Buddhism. The original Bön religion was a form of nature worship. It teaches faith in supernatural forces, including the supreme creator, fellowship among the human community, and harmonious living with surrounding nature. Present-day Bön religion is a

highly developed system of metaphysical theories and meditational techniques.

5. *Chidrö Thigtsakma.* Milarepa's song with this title deals with the practice of Dharma in order that one may face one's inevitable death with great joy. The term Chidrö means joy at death; Thigtsakma, that which is like the timely repair of a leaking roof.

SECOND PART, CHAPTER 9

1. *Geshe.* A monastic title conferred upon lamas or monks who have successfully passed a series of examinations in the form of public debates in subjects ranging from the Buddhist canon to metaphysics and logic.

2. *Bodhisattva precepts.* See Note 13, Prologue.

3. *Five objects of sensory joy.* Form, sound, smell, taste, and touch.

4. *The five levels of vision.* The physical eye, the heavenly eye, the wisdom eye, the Dharma eye, and the Buddha eye.

5. *The eight orders of gods and nagas.* The same as the eight armies of gods and demons. (See Note 16, Prologue.)

6. *Fourfold Power of Action.* A 'powerful guardian deity,' a Bodhisattva who has achieved extraordinary power, sets upon himself the task of bringing about the fulfillment of various aims for himself and others through the Fourfold Actions, namely:

   1. The Action of Pacification: refers to the purification of mind, elimination of suffering, and healing of diseases;
   2. The Action of Progressive Achievement: refers to practices for expanding the faculties of the intellect, increasing happiness, achieving longevity, and so on;
   3. The Action of Inspiring Potential Seekers: refers to the drawing in of all universes and beings toward oneself so as to place them under one's spiritual influence, or in order to enhance one's spiritual service for their benefit;
   4. Wrathful Action: refers to the wielding of negative power in order to eliminate all adverse influences and to protect humanity from the tyranny of counter-spirituality.

7. *Six medicinal herbs.* This refers to (1) saffron (gurkum), (2) cardamom (kakola), (3) nutmeg (dzati), (4) bamboomana, similar to sandalwood (chugang), (5) clove (lishi), (6) dried ruta (sugmail).

8. *The five poisons.* A reference to five basic mental deficiencies or emotive tendencies: delusion, desire, hatred, jealousy, and conceit.

9. *Five Aspects of Transcendental Awareness.* Same as the Five Transcendent Awarenesses. (See Note 5, First Part, Chapter 3.)

10. *Shonnu (Kumara).* This refers to a simile Milarepa used to drive home the point that the hour of death is inevitable and irreversible. Even the Buddha was overcome with a fatal disease and allowed his physician Shonnu to feel his pulse in order to diagnose the disease.

11. *The four divisions of the day.* Dawn, morning, afternoon, and dusk. These periods are chosen for meditation every day, especially when an initiate goes into retreat for a fixed period of time.

12. *The Great Seal of Emptiness.* Emptiness is identified with Mahamudra as being the ultimate nature of reality, so that an awakened mind perceives the indelible imprint of emptiness on all things, conditioned and unconditioned. (See also Note 9, Second Part, Chapter 4.)
13. *The five inexpiable sins.* Willfully murdering or causing the death of (a) one's father, (b) mother, (c) an arhat, or (d) injuring the Buddha, and (e) communal dissension among the members of the spiritual community which interrupts the struggle for liberation. In the post-Buddha era, (d) and (e) were understood to mean the killing of one's spiritual master and the instigation of civil war within the sacred community of Dharma.
14. *The year of the Wood Hare.* The year 1136.
15. *The ninth lunar constellation.* A constellation whose characteristics are firmness and fulfillment. The day thus marks Milarepa's great fulfillment, his passing into the emptiness of Dharmakaya.
16. *The five orders of dakinis.* The assembly of dakinis who represent five spiritual characteristics or psychological attributes both in their transcendent nature and their physical manifestation. The five forms of dakinis are like the five families of Buddha and the five aspects of transcendent awareness.
17. *Rām.* This sacred syllable represents the Source of the Fire Element in its ultimate nature of Emptiness inherent in the fire.
18. *Sunyata.* A term meaning emptiness as distinct from nothingness. Buddhist schools perceive sunyata as being either the inherent emptiness of self or substance, or the emptiness of both self and substance. The latter represents Madhyamika's concept of reality as being total emptiness, without any real identity even down to an infinitesimal atom. Yet such emptiness is also understood as the source of all possible causes and effects in the material or mental world. The interdependence of phenomenal causes and conditions is synonymous with the inherent emptiness of all things.
19. *Bardo.* The intermediate state of the life-cycle between the present and future lives. The events of the Bardo state are said to begin at the final phase of death when disintegration of the elements and forces within man's psycho-physical aggregate takes place. Tibetan tradition considers the understanding of death and Bardo as an equally indispensable element in the transformation of one's living experiences.
20. *A Buddha who skillfully uses falsehoods.* Here is a case, one of many in this text, where a translator even with the best intention can easily make a serious mistake through a literal or arbitrary interpretation. An enigmatic stanza such as this has to be examined thoroughly on the basis of both a sound knowledge of exoteric Mahayana teachings and the intricate Buddhist system of elucidating texts in terms of either apparent or actual meaning – just as the esoteric teaching of Vajrayana needs to be elucidated in terms of the six modes and four methods (see Note 16, Second Part, Chapter 4). The reference in the song to 'Fully Enlightened in the Invisible Heaven' is an allusion to Maitreya – who in reality is a Buddha, considered to be the Buddha of the coming age. According to the Sutras, he presides over the Joyous Heaven (Gadan Lhainey). Milarepa is here gauging the level of the audience, the celestial beings who can understand only the teaching concerning relative truth. His reference to 'Buddha who speaks falsehood' is no

doubt an allusion to the skillful means enlightened teachers are capable of employing in order to effect the fullest benefit for their disciples.
21. *The eight auspicious emblems.* They are (1) a parasol, (2) a pair of goldfish, (3) a conch shell with a rightward spiral, (4) the knot that has no end, (5) the banner of supreme excellence, (6) the Wheel of the Law, (7) the vase of great treasure, (8) the lotus.
22. *The seven royal insignia.* The precious queen, the minister, the warrior, the wish-fulfilling gem, the wheel, the elephant, and the horse. They symbolize the Seven Jewels of the Awakened Ones. (See Note 1, Colophon, below.)
23. *Swastikas* are an ancient Buddhist symbol of truth and eternity. The term means, literally 'that which is eternal.'
24. *Seed syllables of mantra.* This refers to what is called 'the root mantra' (Tsa-ngak). It is the basic mantra associated with every yidam. The root mantra is so called because a few simple syllables can unfold a vast and varied teaching concerning the complete transformation of man's inbred conditions.
25. *Evolved crystals.* The evolved crystals are generally called 'bodily relics' – kudoong ringsel. They are of tiny pill size, pearl colored, and are found in the ashes of the corpses of highly attained men and women. It is widely held that the original evolved crystals multiply if preserved in a proper manner. Hence the name 'multiplying bodily relics' – phel doong. Among the types of crystals is that called 'Sharirum,' which is said to shine in five hues.
26. *The Thousand and Two Buddhas.* This refers to the thousand Buddhas of this aeon.
27. *A mandala of deities.* Meaning here a conclave of deities.
28. *Avaloketsvara* refers to the yidam who embodies the infinite compassion of Buddhas. Chief among the present-day incarnations of Avaloketsvara are the Dalai Lama and Gyalwa Karmapa.

SUPPLEMENTARY NOTE

1. *The five sister dakinis.* The same as the five sister goddesses: Dorje Tseringma, Dorje Yudonma, Miyolosangma, Chopen Drinzangma, and Tekar Drozangma.
2. *Acharya Maitrepa.* The teacher of Marpa who gave him the esoteric Mahamudra. (See Note 14, Second Part, Chapter 2.)
3. *Four Supreme Manifestations.* They are the elaboration of the three aspects of Buddha, namely, Svabhavekakaya, Dharmakaya, Sambhogakaya, and Nirmanakaya.
4. *Five Aspects of Wisdom.* The same as the Five Transcendent Awarenesses. (See Note 14, Prologue, and Note 5, First Part, Chapter 3.)

COLOPHON

1. *The Seven Jewels of the Awakened Ones.* Seven Jewels of the Arhats are so called because they are indispensable for achieving the liberation: (1) full trust in the Triple Refuge, (2) purity of morality, (3) generosity, (4) acquisition of right knowledge, (5) industriousness, (6) self-restraint in the light of social and environmental considerations, and (7) conscientious conduct (deeds).